WHERE MY AI

GET ON YOUR BIKE KEN

WHERE MY ANGELS LED

GET ON YOUR BIKE KEN

by

Ken Pidcock

Published by Ken Pidcock
2019

ISBN 978-1-5272-3560-1

© Ken Pidcock

Printed by JASPRINT, Washington, NE37 2SH

To Barbie, beautiful, loving and brave
and my two wonderful daughters

CONTENTS

LIST OF ILLUSTRATIONS

PROLOGUE

Bert Tomlinson and his wife Joyce went to bed wondering if they would ever have another child. It had been over nine long years since Gwen was born, and they desperately wanted their second. They would not know until several months later that their coupling had been successful, but Joyce had little time to celebrate because Bert died in the back seat of the car, driven by his mate. They both suffered the same fate, as the car burst into flames after the crash. Bert never did see his second daughter, but they had already decided on names, and Barbara was his chosen one, Nancy as well added Joyce.

Barbie

Fred Pidcock retired wearily into bed in the next county of Yorkshire, after a hard day's work at the colliery. Effie was soon to join him, also weary from a long hard day in the fields singling sugar beet. They had undressed in darkness, as it was not the done thing to see each other naked. This may be hard to believe, because she had already given birth to ten children. Effie must have been thinking that she surely would have no more babies as they overcame their weariness and made love. Nearly ten months after Barbara had been born in Derbyshire however, Kenneth, their seventh son and eleventh child, was born. It had been a very difficult delivery, and, delighted with another son, there was a feeling of relief too that she would be unable to have any more. Searching for a second name, after using up seventeen of the most popular ones already, they hit on Maltby, his Grandmother's maiden name.

What odds would you get against these two offspring, born in poor circumstances fifty miles apart, meeting and spending half their lives overseas and travelling around the world together?

Ken

PART ONE

Early years

IN THE PEA FIELD

THEY WERE STANDING IN A SMALL GROUP by our gate as the lorry pulled to a stop. Ted got out of the driver's cab and walked round to open the tailgate, and the half-dozen women picked up their stools and buckets and went round to the back to clamber onto the lorry. They used a stool, or for the older ones, a little leg up from Ted, the farmer Frank Lodge's son, who was a big strong lad and well able to lift them on bodily if that had been necessary. Lastly, Ted lifted me on. I was in a pram and barely a year old and my mum, well into her 43rd year, was one of the ladies in the group.

Ted then fixed the tailgate, the ladies sat on their stools or an upturned bucket, and we set off to the next stop to repeat the process until the lorry was full, with some standing and some sitting on the sides (after being warned by Ted!) and eventually we got to the designated pea field. Health and Safety hold your breath!

The first sight of the pea field would produce either a groan if the field was small and would be finished before lunch, or, if it was a large field, a satisfied gleam would appear, because this was going to be a full day!

The longer the day of course, the more money was made, because this was piece work. The pay was per 40lb bag, and I don't know what the rate was on that day, but I can remember working for 1 shilling and 3 pence per bag (just over 6 pence in modern currency!) in 1942 when I was eleven, and each bag would take the better pullers about an hour to fill.

The hundred or so pea pullers would line up along one hedge, get a bag from the farmer and start pulling, that is to grab a few stalks near the base and pull them out of the ground. Then pick off the peas individually and put them into a bucket or straight into the bag. I always favoured the bucket because I could judge pretty accurately that so many bucketfuls equalled 40+ lbs.

The farmer had two men going behind with pitchforks turning the straws over to see if any peas had been left, or straws left not pulled! 'No straws or stones in the bags ladies, and keep in a straight line' they would keep repeating. The straws would then be ploughed in for fertiliser, an excellent source of Nitrogen, or collected like hay for use as animal fodder.

When the bag was full it was taken to be weighed at the scales, but one had to make sure that there were plenty in, so that no time would be wasted going back for a few more. One would then bring back a new bag containing the overflow to start the process all over again. On a good day the experts could fill about ten bags. You will be able to work that out (12 shillings and 6 pence, or 62½ new pence per day for those who can't!)

The younger half
from left: Sarah (Jenny), Sylvia and Daisy. Ken and Jack

I don't know if I was a good baby or not. I guess they would take it in turns to replenish my bottle if I wasn't! That is, mum's group of 4 who used to pull together. They had to share, because some of them couldn't carry the bags back to the scales. That was Elma's job, as she was considerably younger than the others. She was a wiry little lady who would take two together to save time if there was a queue at the scales. I suppose I offered some consolation for my nuisance value as Frank (farmer) Lodge always used to let the pullers take a boiling home in their buckets, and that was where the bottom of the pram came in useful.

IVY HOUSE

I was the eleventh child of Fred and Effie Pidcock. I was born in a little farming village of Norton, about eight miles north east of Doncaster. Mum had five boys: Walter, Arthur, Les, Edwin and Lawrence; then she had twins, a boy, Jack, and a girl, Hilda. The pleasure of at last having a daughter must have been immense, but tragically it was short lived. Although she was the stronger of the twins, it was she who contracted pneumonia when she was a year old and died. Poor mum must have been heartbroken.

God was kind though because after the regular two years interval, Daisy was born, then Sarah, Sylvia and last of all, me, Ken, on 15 April 1931. No, we weren't triplets, the statutory two-year period was observed between each of us too. Apparently it was the custom to breast feed and to let baby sleep in with the parents as long as possible. This was supposed to lengthen the period between babies, but whether that really influenced the outcome I can't say. It seemed to have worked in our family.

The house in which I was born was condemned and pulled down before I began to recognise my surroundings, but the house I do remember was the one the family moved into, Ivy House, which apparently used to be occupied by the vicar. It was an imposing building in the village at that time, with five bedrooms upstairs and a drawing room, dining room and two kitchens downstairs. The first two were 'posh' rooms that we hardly ever used except on very special occasions!

We lived in what we called the 'big kitchen'. It had originally been two rooms and the adjoining wall had been removed. It had a large, old-fashioned open fireplace with a boiler at one side, from which we got our hot water, and the oven at the other. There was a perforated plate on a swivel where the kettle rested and could be moved over or away from the hot coals. It even had a hook, to hang the kettle on I think, but that was hardly ever used.

The 'little kitchen' was down two steps on the right, opposite the pantry under the stairs. This little passage also led to the front rooms, which we called the dining room and the drawing room, but they were really our 'posh' rooms and only used on special occasions. Here in the little kitchen there was also an open fire with a back boiler, a recent addition and the main source of our hot water supply, and an oven. This little kitchen was where we washed ourselves as it had a large stone sink in one corner. Yes, everyone washed in there because there was no such thing as a bathroom! All the washing up was done in there too. We must have had to carry water to the big kitchen which had no water supply, to wash clothes etc. because there was too little room for that in the little kitchen.

I suppose that originally the big kitchen was the servant's quarters. The clue to that was found above the adjoining steps where there was a row of bells, worked on wires and pulleys from the rest of the house. At least the bells were still there, but the wires had been removed, I suppose to facilitate the decorating. There was also a scullery leading from the big kitchen out onto the back yard. The scullery had a large copper built over another fire grate. This must originally have been in which to do the laundry during the times when there were servants but I only remember it to be used to boil pig potatoes. These were bought cheaply because they were too small in those days to be used for commercial purposes. We children used to sneak in when they were ready, to peel and eat them. They always tasted delicious.

We did bath though, no, we didn't say 'bathe'. We had the tin bath in front of the fire in the little kitchen. That was all the privacy the older ones got! Don't ask me how regular this was, but it was at least once a week! The rest of the time it was 'top and tail.'

The house was set in one third of an acre of land with a high wall around. We had numerous apple trees, both eating and cooking varieties; and several pear and plum trees. The apple trees on the front lawn were very special. We never knew which variety they were but they grew very large, were lovely sweet eaters and 'fell' beautifully when cooked. I cannot recollect ever climbing the plum trees but each of us had found our own ways to the tops of the other trees, especially when there was ripe fruit in difficult to get at places. We also had black currants, red currants, gooseberry bushes and a strawberry bed.

Opposite the back door, leading into the big kitchen, was a two-storey garage building, but the second floor became increasingly hazardous as it gradually decayed. There were three sections to it, two of which had mangers at one end, obviously used as stables at some time. I remember brother Les used to slaughter pigs in there to supplement our rations during the war.

We had outhouses too where we kept pigs and hens, and because dad worked at the pit, one was converted to a coalhouse, to store the 1 ton of coal per month allocated to each collier. We used to use it up too because we had so many fires burning daily from early until late. Oh, and last but not least, we had the outside loo. No, they weren't WCs, there were just two holes in a broad shelf of wood side by side, with a bucket underneath each, hidden from view. These buckets were collected and emptied every Thursday morning from an opening round the back! It seems that in the past it was custom to go to the loo in pairs! We children did when it was dark because we would be too scared to go on our own. I never envied the men who had the job of going round the village emptying the buckets. I remember that sometimes they had to be very careful to stop them spilling over, because ours was a particularly long stony yard! Before WCs were introduced however, someone had to do it.

LIFE DURING THE WAR

I have mentioned that dad worked at the local colliery at Askern, a village two miles away. He had come here from East Leake in 1911 with my mum and a small baby, looking for work, I suppose, at the newly opened pit. Even as I write, I can't comprehend that this was over a hundred years ago and I'm talking about my father! Mum had been a nurse, but that ended when she was married. I suspect that the same rule applied to nurses as did for teachers. Once married you were disqualified from teaching. That was the reason there were so many elderly spinsters in the teaching profession at that time. They had to make the choice between teaching and marriage.

At one time Askern was a beautiful little spa village with Roman Baths and a delightful boating and paddling lake. That was before they sank the pit! The unfortunate consequence was that almost immediately the spa waters drained away, and Askern became just another sprawling mining village. Askern was unique in one way. It was the only place in the world called Askern. Theoretically, one needn't put the town, county or country on a letter when addressing it. I am not sure if anyone has ever tried out that theory though.

Askern did keep the lake but had lost its attraction and, most importantly, its spa status. It is both regrettable and incredible that a later village council actually pulled down the pristine Roman Baths in order to build the Hydro, a large village hall which could have been located elsewhere, but at least they retained the name! The Roman Baths had probably been the best preserved examples in the country. Without the colliery, who knows, Askern could have become another spa town like Bath or Buxton.

Dad then had an accident down the pit. Apparently a runaway tub trapped him and broke his ribs. This meant that he could no longer work underground but was relegated to work 'On t' top'. This was a big blow. Surface workers were only paid a pittance compared with the men underground, and with a young family to keep, I guess that was why mum joined the band of ladies who worked when they could for the farmer for most of the year. Work ranged from stone picking (stone picking was collecting stones exposed after ploughing), singling and pulling sugar beet, pea pulling and potato planting, picking and sorting etc. Later he would experiment with carrots and other vegetable crops.

By the time I was born, Walter must have been over twenty and since school leaving age was at fourteen, there were probably four of my brothers working. Though they were only paid as apprentices, this would help enormously to our status. We started off being extremely poor – and I mean POOR! Not by today's standards, where you are supposedly poor if you don't own the latest mobile phone or designer clothes! Our shoes invariably had holes through, socks were darned (mended) until they fell apart and trousers, if they hadn't rips in them, must have been mended at some time.

We didn't have carpets as they had to be bought. We pegged our own rugs from hessian (old sacks) and cut up old clothes. Cloth was cut into strips about 4 inches by 1 inch. The peg was a wooden clothes peg with one leg removed and the other whittled to a point. A hole was made in the sack and one end of the strip of cloth was pushed through with the peg. Another hole was made nearby and the strip pushed through from the other end to form a U so that two ends of 2" each were both at the same side. This was repeated with the strips being 'pegged' as close together as possible until the whole piece of hessian was covered. Woe betides any of us children if we left too big a gap between the strips! A sack from the farm which had been used to carry chaff made a really big rug! I remember as many as four of us pegging on one rug at the same time, and we could even peg patterns into the rugs using different coloured cloth. The downside of the rugs was that they had to be taken outside to shake the dust from them. The larger the rug, the harder it was to shake. They were great dirt collectors but were warm to walk on in the winter.

I remember the cold winter nights. We sat in a semicircle round the fire, as close as the arc would allow. The more of us there were the deeper the arc, hence the less warmth we would glean from the fire. This was probably where we learned to share and share alike. If it was supper time we would often take turns to toast bread on toasting forks in front of the upright grills. The one thing that one couldn't escape from in a large family was the realisation that there were other people as important as you. We had no chance to acquire the present day attitude of me, me, me.

Another thing I remember was that we were all kept scrupulously clean, as was the house. I remember well, one day in primary school when there was a hand inspection and I was singled out as having the cleanest hands, and also the neatest moon-shaped cuticles! Even now, I remember how proud I was to go home and tell mum.

Being economical in everything we did was instilled into us from an early age. I can remember riddling the ashes onto a pile in the garden, so that all ashes over a quarter of an inch were reused on the fire. The fine pile of ash was then spread over the garden. I thought at first that was to get rid of an unsightly pile but was later to learn that it was also to fertilise the soil.

I mentioned apprenticeships. Mum vowed that 'None of her children would ever 'ride t'rope' (a colloquialism for getting in the cage and being dropped to the coal face suspended by ropes.) and each son was put into a trade. Walter became a Master Baker and Confectioner; Arthur went into the Police, Les became a Butcher, and Edwin a Carpenter and Joiner. Only Walter actually remained in his profession for the whole of his life, while my other brothers chased more lucrative jobs after the war.

We gradually emerged from being poor to being reasonably 'comfortable'. I remember even getting a toy pedalcar for Christmas when I was five, instead of the usual apple, orange and nuts and a new shiny penny in our stockings, hung for that purpose at the bottom of the bed.

You won't realise why we were gradually better off though, and I bet you can't guess! Sons always handed their full wage over to mum! For that they were given pocket money depending on age and the amount handed over. It must have been during this period that the house was converted from gas to electricity, and most importantly, luxury of all luxuries, we had one of the bedrooms converted into a bathroom and toilet. This also included a large, hot-water cistern, enabling us to have constant hot water while ever there was a fire lit in the little kitchen.

Mum still went out to work though, and I don't know how old I was but I must have been very young when I heard mum relating how she had told Frank Lodge that 'You'll have us pulling our B.... rops (mum's yorkshireisms for intestines) out!' They had been working in a soggy field of sugar beet. That statement turned out to be rather prophetic as she was taken out of the field later that week with a prolapsed womb! It must have been the turning point in the harmony inside the house between mum and dad but that was something I didn't understand until I too became an adult. Mum often related though that she had been 'stitched up', literally!

1939 changed all that! Walter and Arthur had both married and I remember each time there were twenty-two of the family seated (Sylvia and I had to stand!) round the large extending table in the drawing room for the wedding feasts. Within months after the outbreak of the Second World War, Les and Edwin had been conscripted into the Army and Lawrence was called up into the R.A.F., soon to be followed by Jack because he had reached the call-up age of eighteen. There were just mum and dad, the three girls and me left at home. The result on the family was devastating. Suddenly there was only dad's pittance of a wage to pay for everything, his last take-home wage before he retired was just over £6 per week and that was years later. Once again we had joined the ranks of the really poor.

This is the period of my childhood that I remember most. We had all been well behaved and regimented before because mum was a real Victorian mother! She had to be. Now we were even more regimented. We each took turns on a strict rota basis to wash up, dry the pots, put them away, lay the table, chop the sticks, get the coal in, peel the potatoes, dust etc.; and we all learned how to use the poncher, dolly pegs, rubbing board and, later on, turn the handle backwards and forwards for fifteen minutes on the newly acquired 'Darling' washer. Cleanliness also extended to the house and though mum always took responsibility for black leading the fireplaces, we had to learn how to polish the hearth with Red Cardinal and scour the doorsteps and stone flags with a rubbing stone to make them a creamy yellow colour.

We still went to school of course, and dad went to work on his bike. The pit was two miles away and there were hardly any cars seen in the village in those days. We washed, ironed and cleaned the house, somehow, in between times.

Daisy became very ill in her teens and was away in hospital for a while. I was too young to comprehend much but when she came home we took it in turns to sit beside her bed with ice packs to keep her temperature down. Looking back, it must have been miraculous for those days. She had recovered from tuberculosis which left her with only part of a lung at each side. She was simply wonderful though. She never went to school after that, never could have employment, and in those days there was no such thing as unemployment or sickness benefits! She was in no way mobility impaired and seemed to do most of the housework when everyone else was out and apart from shopping, she hardly ever went out herself! She was a lovely sister, for I can never recall her complaining once and I never recall her getting upset or angry and she always had a smile on her face. I am quite certain that she never met another male person outside our family group. She was as intelligent as everyone else and in spite of all predictions, she did live to be a companion for mum until well into her sixties.

How did mum discipline us? I say mum because I cannot ever remember dad touching any of us. She literally gave us a good hiding and on severe occasions it would be called a thrashing! Did I ever resent it or think ill of my mum? Most certainly not! When we were punished we always knew that we had done something wrong and therefore deserved it. No real harm was done and we knew that she loved us really. The worst happened when it was connected to the family name. 'What will people think of us?' was instilled into us. When we were in Africa later in life, we observed lions in the wild and occasionally, if the cubs became too boisterous, they got a sharp cuff about the ears, so it is quite natural to punish offspring. I wonder what has happened to the maxim, 'spare the rod and spoil the child.' How true that has been demonstrated in today's society. When we were young, one very rarely saw children being a nuisance or 'creating' in public, but it is commonplace nowadays, in fact it is unusual now to see a well-behaved child unless it has a dummy or food stuffed in its mouth. Mum never had to shout at us, but it is not unusual now to hear verbal abuse of children. Does that make sense? I believe strongly that verbal or emotional punishment can be far more devastating than corporal punishment. Isn't that the origin of the phrase 'the pen (or word) is mightier than the sword'?

I do not remember much about primary school. We had to walk the half mile there and back, which was almost halfway to Campsall where we used to go to church. I remember it being interesting and somewhere that we had to attend. I had no recollection of being better or worse than anyone else and I certainly can't remember it entering into life at home. It must have been somewhat of a surprise, therefore, when, in 1942, I was one of only four pupils in Norton to pass the 11+ examination during that year. Remember, I was from one of the poorest families in the village. That, although it did not seem significant at the time, was to change my life completely and, to some extent, I suppose, that of the whole family.

GRAMMAR SCHOOL

At eleven years old, one doesn't realise the implications when certain events happen. This must have registered with mum and dad though, for it meant I had qualified to go to grammar school. This may not seem important but they must have realised that it meant that if we accepted the place, it would mean that I could not contribute to the family income when I was fourteen, the normal school leaving age, and most probably for longer!

It also meant more expenditure on uniform and the other expenses connected with higher education. No, silly, there was no such thing then as child allowances or benefits, and, if there were such things, mum would not dream of suffering the social disgrace of having to apply for them! I remember well her once saying that if we did apply for benefit, they would come round to assess us and then tell us to sell the very nice furniture we had in the front rooms, albeit that it had been bought from auctions and sales for next to nothing, and would realise only a tenth of its true value if we had to sell it.

This could not possibly have escaped the attention of mum and dad, especially mum who was the one who made all the decisions. It is to my lifelong gratitude (though maybe I did not realise it at the time) that they not only let me go, but insisted that I should go. I came to understand later how proud mum must have been. None of my siblings had passed their 11+. In fact it was a joke with all of them that their reports always said 'if he was as good in the classroom as at sports, he would do well!' Secretly it was mum's dream that her youngest son would go to university!

It was also somewhat of a surprise to a young boy that people I hardly knew in the village stopped to congratulate me. Personally, as I have said, I never felt better than anyone else. I just knew how to work things out. I don't know where my proficiency in Maths came from but it may be that I never had time off from school, so never missed any of the important stages, which I later understood were most crucial in understanding Maths. Maths consists of a series of building blocks to learn. If you take one of the blocks away, the building collapses, because each block depends for support upon the last one.

I had started working in the fields for Frank Lodge during the holiday periods and sometimes at the weekends, and at this time I was allowed to keep some of my earnings to pay for the expenses attached to school like uniform and gym kit and football boots etc. I never received pocket money, nor expected it, and was scrupulously honest with my savings – which were hardly going to be enough anyway.

We were not streamed at all in the first year. I was put in 1P, which was the first letter of our teacher called Miss Price.

I guess I was lucky. We had good teachers and I was particularly interested in Sciences and Maths, so did not need to do much work in them. I then began a period of misinformation about which I am not particularly proud but nor am I too ashamed.

We had plenty of room in the house but money was scarce and electricity was expensive, and I still had to do my share of jobs at home. Homework couldn't very well be done in the middle of the family and I would need a light on and heating in the other rooms, which were decidedly cold, so I started pretending that we either didn't get homework or that I did it at school in spare periods. At least I now like to think that I was that thoughtful as a child and not that I was just naughty! I certainly did try to complete my homework when I could, either on the school bus or at dinner times.

School was both enjoyable and demanding. I managed to do reasonably well and always used to vie for the top spot in Maths with one of the girls. I was always near the top in the Sciences too and that is probably because of my years of groundwork in the SJAB (St John's Ambulance Brigade).

I must mention the St John's Ambulance Brigade as it proved to be important in my life. Mum, an ex nurse, was in the ladies section and she used to take me along to the meetings from being about eight years old. I was used as a patient for them to practise on, bandaging my pretend wounds or fractures. I had to be quiet during talks and lectures etc. so I had to listen, and quickly picked up the subject matter. I remember well being a favourite 'patient' because if they didn't know something or did something wrong when they were practicing on me, I could usually put them right. I was too young to realise what a precocious little prig I might have seemed to be. I had, however, learned the different types of wounds and fractures, the names of all the bones in the body and the circulation of the blood before I ever took Sciences at school.

I naturally joined the SJAB Cadets and attended the meetings regularly. Being wartime we had many opportunities to have parades and I learned to blow a bugle in the band. When it came to the Remembrance Day Service I was selected to play *The Last Post* at church, which I felt was quite an honour.

I remember too that there was a period when our front rooms were commissioned by the Army to use as the Sergeants' Mess. It must have happened just before D-Day, the day we invaded France. There had to be a mass migration of troops southward to the south coast and this was one of the coordinated stopovers on the way. I have forgotten whether mum used to cook for them but I do know that our food was well augmented by extra rations as a consequence. The Army soon had to move on from our village, so unfortunately the extra rations didn't last for more than a month or two.

Thinking back to how we used to spend our evenings after dark. There were too many jobs to do in daylight with such a big garden! We either listened to the radio or played cards. That was when we had no rugs on the go of course. We listened to the serials like *Dick Barton, Special Agent* and *ITMA* (Tommy Handley in 'It's that man again'). Electricity had recently been introduced but radios still ran on batteries. I say batteries, but ours ran on what we called an accumulator, which was a square glass container 4in x 4in x 8in filled with acid, covering plates of what looked like zinc or lead. I remember that they only lasted a week or two and we had to take them down to the cycle shop to be recharged, so we had to have spares to fill in for the days that it took to recharge them.

I suppose that is where I got my affinity for playing cards. Dad taught me how to play knock out whist, rummy and, later, cribbage. I used to look forward to my brothers coming on leave from the forces because we then played 'Solo whist', 'Nap' or 'Stop the Bus', oh, and Newmarket was also a favourite if the sisters wanted to play. I was given no quarters for being young, but was expected to play as well as the rest, and so quickly became competitive. I've just realised, the sisters only played in the 'fun' games, or for match sticks. The more serious games, playing for a few coppers, were all male.

The highlight for me was when mum organised Whist Drives in our front rooms in aid of the War Effort. I used to pray for there to be one short so that I could fill in. By the time I was ten I was playing regularly by right. Playing whist was soon to lead to the most significant event of my life.

An evacuee from London used to go to school with me as he lived a bit further away from the Royal (Pub) Corner where we used to catch the School Bus. It gave me an insight to the fact that there were areas suffering from the consequences of the war and that we were quite fortunate living in our sheltered country area. We were invariably kicking a ball about on the way and while we waited for our bus to arrive.

It was about seven miles to PJGS, The Percy Jackson Grammar School, and we had a special bus which collected all us pupils from the outlying villages. If I had to stay after school for sports practices I would have to go home by service bus to Doncaster and change buses there. That was the equivalent of going round two sides of a triangle. Later I was sometimes able to borrow my sister's bicycle. Sarah was working by then and had managed to buy one from her 'allowance'.

It was a good life for me at school because I became involved in organised sports, and following the tradition of the rest of the family, it might have appeared on my school reports too that 'if I was as keen on my lessons as I was at sports I might do better!' There were four classes of thirty in each year up to the 5th year, which was when we took the 'School Certificate', now replaced by GCSEs. We had to pass in at least six subjects, including English, or we failed! If you didn't pass in English, or if you only passed in five subjects, then you failed and had to stay on at school an extra year and sit the whole exam all over again! These had to be academic subjects too. There was no such thing as 'soft options' in those days.

After a lifetime in teaching, I still think that this was a better system. It certainly sorted the wheat from the chaff and it kept up the standard of the English Language, so badly lacking today! I can't understand why red marks went out of fashion. I still wonder what is wrong with knowing something isn't correct. Red marks in your books indicate that some things are wrong and need to be put right. Why pretend they don't exist in order not to make the child feel too upset? Do children know now when they have made a mistake or do they grow up to think that it isn't important! I had plenty of red marks in my books and it never did me any harm. I wonder if it was more for the teacher's benefit than the pupils'. Did they think it was their fault that there were so many red marks? Do they think it is a reflection on their teaching?

I was put in 2S for the second year, meaning 2 Science. Whether they streamed according to intelligence or aptitude I will never know, or care really, but it was our impression that 2L (Language) was considered to be the top class. I wouldn't have wanted to be in the language class anyway. No one had taught me the importance of languages at that stage but I was to find plenty of time in later life to regret not taking History and the Languages more seriously!

It had already been established that ours was the 'sporting' class as we provided 75% of all the teams in all the sports. This carried on even to the senior teams when we had progressed to 5S, for then, few of the sixth formers even got a look in.

BARBIE AND I MEET

I was only thirteen and a few weeks from my fourteenth birthday when the life-changing event happened. Even though I went to a mixed school, I was among boys who thought more of sports than of the other sex. Of course we had fantasies, but after all, I lived miles from any of my school-mates, so could not easily socialise with any of them, boys or girls. I felt very low on the pecking order in any case, as I knew some of my mates were seeing girls outside school and it never occurred to me that it was because they were neighbours. I always considered myself as a bit gawky!

Youth hostelling -
I said I looked gawky!

I went to a 'Whist Drive and Dance' in the Hydro in Askern. It was organised by the St John's Ambulance Brigade, hence I was allowed to go along with my dad. I had been a member of the SJAB as a junior since I was nine. Looking back, I reckon I must have been one of the youngest ever to get a medallion, for I had six junior certificates by the age of sixteen. Three junior certificates were the equivalent of one senior certificate, so at sixteen when I took my next examination I qualified for the third senior certificate, which was a medallion.

But I digress. There were children of my age messing about while we were playing whist because they had come with their parents and they couldn't play. I didn't win anything at whist, but I was allowed to stay a while at the Dance because one of my brothers was on leave and would be there to take me home. I had learned to dance a little, but could only do a waltz and a quickstep, and, because my brother was always dancing and I was bored, I plucked up courage to go across the room and ask one of the girls, whom I had seen running around earlier, for a dance. I saw from her identity bracelet that she was called Barbara Tomlinson. Things went well until the music stopped and changed to a Slow Foxtrot! Well, I was so embarrassed I just said 'Sorry I can't do this' and walked off! I didn't realise that I had left her in the middle of the dance floor!

I walked home with my brother after the Dance. It was too late for buses and walking the two miles saved us the taxi fare. I mention this because half way home, while passing a grass field, from over the hedge I heard what I thought was someone crying out in pain. I looked at my brother and was puzzled for ages afterwards because he just said 'Come on, leave them alone! '

Apparently Barbara and I had talked enough during the dance (I don't remember a thing!) to let her know that I was in Campsall Church Choir, and guess what! On Sunday night, there she was in the Congregation. After church it was about half a mile to Campsall corner where the road divided, one branch to Askern and one to Norton. We walked along with the crowd which included my mum and we were obviously afraid to make it obvious that we knew each other. When we arrived at Campsall corner, we had to go our separate ways.

I knew she was called Barbara from a silver identity bracelet that she wore. She said I had pulled her plaits, but would I do a thing like that? Seeing her at church became a regular occurrence to look forward to, and the crowd walking back home soon became a crowd of two.

I remember one of the first questions she asked me was 'When are you fifteen?' How embarrassing that was. I was old enough to know that girls of that age preferred older boys, so I was dumbstruck. It was a week short of my fourteenth birthday. I didn't lie, but my fears were unfounded. She was there the next Sunday, sitting in the same place in the congregation where she could see me in the choir stalls, frilly ruffle, cassock and surplice and all. She made sure that she was shielded by a pillar from my mum at the other side of the aisle.

Barbara went to Pontefract & District Girls High School and her bus passed ours every morning at the Royal Corner or thereabouts, where I was invariably kicking a ball about with two of the other boys who went on the same bus as me, so we got to waving as we passed and occasionally passed letters through her mates who knew my mates. I was puzzled for ages when a friend at school from Askern referred to her as Barbara Maycock! I was convinced that he had the wrong girl, but then I learned that her father had been killed in a car accident before she was born and her mother had married Harry Maycock when she was a baby. She was known locally, therefore, as Barbara Maycock, but never had her name changed legally.

Our courtship wasn't easy. In those days respectable people didn't let children out at night unchaperoned, so our meetings were at church and the occasional Whist Drive & Dance. My family were never hostile but never in full agreement as I think my mother had me earmarked for one of the farmer's daughters in the village, which I suppose in her eyes would have been a 'step up'. Certainly Barbara's mother said to her 'I hear you are seeing that lad from Norton! He comes from a great big family and his dad is always winning at Whist! Make what you will of that one, and how history repeats itself!'

It was certainly years before we were 'invited' to our respective homes, but then, until one was earning a wage, it was not the custom to be thinking of courting. This period in our lives was dominated by our urge to see each other as often as possible, which was never as often as we would have wished, what with going to different schools and our home commitments.

The war ended in 1945 and we had all celebrated as we had supposedly 'won'. At least we were not overrun by Fascism but rationing and austerity lingered on for years. It wasn't made easy because our empire at that time was as powerful collectively as the U.S.A. and so although we have always been close allies of the Unites States, we were made to pay dearly by them for what we had borrowed from them during the War. It was something called 'Lease Lend' and the UK was nearly bankrupted by it, some say deliberately so! I guess that was the start of the diminishing of our Empire, but I am not a politician and I guess that there were other factors involved. I was destined to learn more of those at first-hand later in life.

Just as dad had survived the trenches in the First World War, it was a blessing and a miracle for our family that all four brothers came home safely. Les, Edwin and Lawrence had all served overseas, and Jack was deployed constructing decoy aerodromes for the Nazis to bomb by mistaking them for the real thing. Edwin was directly involved in the fighting from El Alamein, through North Africa and all of Italy. He was left for dead on the beaches at Salerno when the first wave was repulsed, having collapsed from a stomach problem, but was fortunately picked up and hospitalised when the second wave established a permanent beachhead. He returned to the fighting and was awarded the Military Medal, but like dad, he never talked about his experiences. He was promoted to Sergeant and was offered a commission but turned it down. He wanted to stay with his squad.

Unfortunately we were to have a tragedy unrelated to the war. Walter, our eldest brother, ruptured his liver while carrying a two hundredweight sack of flour. In those days there was little they could do when abscesses formed, especially on the liver, and after a short while he died. It is always sad looking back. Had that happened today, modern medicine, I'm sure, would have cured him, but as it was, he left Vera and their two little girls, Christina and Barbara, who were actually to become two of our bridesmaids.

One other family in the village was not so lucky, and it was Barbara's sister's fiancé who was one of the casualties. Otherwise the village had escaped from the atrocities of the war. The nearest action we saw was when a Jerry plane jettisoned a bomb on its way home from raiding either Sheffield or Manchester, and it landed in a field two miles away. We all went to the field as soon as we could to look for shrapnel as a keepsake. We had often seen the glow of the fires raging at night in those cities, however, reflecting off the clouds.

I was sixteen and examinations were approaching. I realised that I had to justify the sacrifices made by the whole family to send me to grammar school. I hoped that it would not be too late as I had not studied as diligently as I should have. I hadn't had the ideal learning environment at home but I knew that I was fairly safe except for a doubt about the dreaded English Language examination.

I was pulling peas one day near home. Most of the time we would be miles away in fields rented from other farmers, but this day we were fairly close to home. I heard a voice say 'I've brought your dinner Ken' and turned round to see dad approaching with a basket. He'd brought egg, sausage and chips, still steaming hot. It was still nicely plated up in a flat-bottomed basket and then after a while he said 'Oh and I've also brought you a letter.' I wondered what it was at first, but it looked official. Then I realised what it might be and opened it with more than a little fear. I need not have worried though because I had PASSED with a Distinction in Maths.

There were big celebrations to be made now, of course, but we were still poor, and by now all my brothers had married and left home, so there were still only the three girls and me remaining at home.

Daisy could never work, but Jenny was a shop assistant at a milliners and Sylvia went into nursing, as a student at first, so neither earned anything significant. I reiterate that I cannot be more grateful to mum and dad. There was never any question that I would not carry on at school, and I shall for ever wonder in retrospect whether I ever repaid them enough for their sacrifices, I only know that I tried. I therefore joined the Sixth Form with a view to taking my H.S.C. and going to University.

THE SIXTH FORM

Life went on just as before. Sixth form work left more free time in school to do homework, so again I hardly ever did any school work at home. Life was very hectic though because I felt more than ever that I still had to share the jobs at home, in fact I tried to do more than my share to make up for my lack of earnings. I virtually took over the large gardens and all that it involved.

Weekends were now often taken up working for Frank lodge. I think they took a bit of pity on me because of my situation, and as I was only a couple of years younger than his sons I was some sort of company for them.

Ted, the older of the two, often went down to the markets in London to take lorry loads of bags of peas or other market garden produce he had experimented with. He needed to keep awake as he drove down overnight and so it was worth his while to pay me to accompany him. I remember well that we had to try to constantly keep talking so that he wouldn't nod off at the wheel, and this was proved to be necessary when his wheels touched the curb on more than one occasion. There were two or three regular stops for lorry drivers on the way. This was before the motorways were built with their service stations and I remember Kate's Cabin on the A1 in particular, for its pint pots of steaming tea and great wedges of sandwiches.

I did occasionally go to play with a couple of the neighbours, but on reflection we had not a lot in common and all my sport was school orientated. I was now a prefect and captain of 'Lane' House. The school teams were made up of 90% from the same year as me, now mostly coming from the Lower Sixth. I did not excel in anything in particular but was good enough to be an automatic selection for the Football, Cricket and Cross Country teams.

Lane House was named after Alderman Lane, who I remember well because he was the first to introduce the possibility of it becoming a 'Comprehensive' school during his presentation on Speech Day. I'm afraid his captain wasn't, and was never to be, an ardent follower of his philosophy. In fact I was later to blame it for most of the ills in education in England today.

Politics were often debated at home by my brothers, home from the forces. They had left the forces filled with the Labour promises of building a better future and the blatant propaganda instigated by the BBC. Nothing changes does it? I heard it said that in the times before digitalisation, when the television was run on film strips, that they inserted Labour propaganda frames among the normal programmes. The eye could not detect them, but the subconscious did and was influenced by it. It was the brother who had gone to work at the colliery, in fact, who became most anti Union and pro Blue. He was disgusted with the wastage at the colliery and what went on in the name of Union rights. He even talked about someone taking a mattress down the pit to sleep on during the night shift.

The two years that followed were more of the same. I can never say that I am proud of my work rate, but my plea is that the way of life at Ivy House was not conducive to a life of study. Maybe I could have done more, and I don't suppose that I will ever have complete peace of mind. However hard I had tried though, I doubt that I would have had sufficient intelligence to get a County Major Scholarship, ensuring free University tuition, so I tell myself now that it made no difference in the final analysis. I don't think that I could have bettered the career I eventually followed by getting a few extra marks. To my descendants reading this, I do not recommend that you follow this philosophy. You won't have the same excuse to offer!

It was in similar circumstances that I found out that I had passed my Higher School Certificate. Again one had to pass all subjects. Well, passes in three main subjects or in two main subjects and two subsidiary subjects would be sufficient. All had to be academic subjects of course.

The normal combinations for the science students were Maths, Physics, Biology and Chemistry, but my choice was different. Firstly I knew we had no Chemistry teacher because he was away on War service. I was good at Mathematics, so I opted for Pure Maths, Applied Maths, Physics and Biology. This was a strategic choice because in Maths one either understands or one doesn't understand. If one understands, then one can usually work out the answers from first principles, hence not much swatting is necessary. Biology was my passion anyway – a legacy from my days in the SJAB – and one can pass Physics at the subsidiary level almost solely on one's knowledge of Maths.

That is exactly how it worked out, and that was why only one other girl and I from our school passed the H.S.C. during that year! I had passed in the three main subjects, and passed Physics at the subsidiary level. The students who had opted to take Chemistry had all failed! We were all overjoyed at home, though I sometimes said that my joy was mixed with relief, but I don't think that was really true. I never really doubted my Maths and Biology which would have been sufficient. It was only the sort of relief which I am sure was experienced by even the best students.

Again it must have occurred to mum and dad that I would not contribute to the family coffers for a number of years, but it was now established that I would go on to study further, and I must admit that it was somehow pleasing to see the pride in mum's eyes. Dad hardly ever showed any emotion, but I know that he was secretly pleased too.

There was now, however, an added complication looming. All young men had to do National Service. That meant eighteen months in the forces learning how to defend the country in the event of another war!

My schoolmates who had not passed had to choose between staying on at school to retake the H.S.C., or leaving education and finding employment. Living seven miles from school meant I virtually lost touch with them, which didn't seem significant at the time, but as it transpires I cannot remember seeing any of them ever again. How many people can say that? For me there was no choice. I had to complete my N.S. first, because I had been admitted for the 1951 intake at Durham University.

The day after leaving school I went pea pulling. I didn't think about it, it was the thing to do since our lives revolved around money. It was always a disappointment when the weather made it impossible for the farmer to work in the fields, but it was not long before I started working for the farmer regularly as a farmhand. They must have realised my predicament and they knew that I worked hard for them. I say they, because Ted and David had a big say in the running of the farm by now. I was paid 2 shillings (10 new pence) per hour, and at last I was contributing to the family income – albeit for a short time.

I do not recall exactly when, but I know at some stage I was told to 'put some away' for the expenses to be incurred later, and I had already been well grounded in this anyway. I was eighteen and nothing changed at home. I worked all hours, saw Barbara every Sunday at church and the occasional evening at the Picture House, but then in those days one wasn't an adult, or treated as an adult until one was in proper employment.

By now, as I have already explained, all my brothers were married, leaving just the three girls and me at home. Mum started taking in lodgers to supplement the family income. There were always two, but for a short time I remember as many as four men staying at one time, all manual workers working on nearby building sites.

One lodger we cannot forget, and that was Walter, an ex German Prisoner of War, who had decided to stay in England. He had a 'Norton Dominator' motorbike, remembered by its distinctive throaty roar as it drove up the drive. He came to us as one of the lodgers and over the course of time we noticed that there was an attraction between him and Sylvia, and it was no surprise when they came out into the open and announced their engagement.

Mum had three girls, but each one had a sad tale to tell. One week before the wedding day, with wedding gifts piled on the table in the front room, a policeman called to say that there had been an accident at work. Walter had fallen from the scaffolding and impaled himself on some railings, killing him instantly. It was not only his tragic death that was devastating, but all his personal possessions were collected by the police, leaving Sylvia without a single memento except for the wedding presents. His possessions, even his watch and his ring, were sent to his next of kin in Germany. I don't think Sylvia ever got over that, and remained a spinster until her death. Jenny, she later preferred to be called Sarah, went to work in the U.S.A. but must have had a traumatic experience there because she came back home but I never was told why. She was then badly let down by a boyfriend in London and remains a spinster to this day.

NATIONAL SERVICE

Every day I looked for the post and the inevitability of my call-up papers. When November came and went, I began to get worried. Eighteen months in the forces took me very close to when I should be starting University. I should not have worried though. I was requested to present myself at Blandford Barracks on 8 December 1949. Discharge would therefore be due in June, 1951, or so we all thought.

Life in the Army was a blur for the most part, yet I could write a separate book on it. I remember well the first day we were marched to the Quarter Master store to be kitted out. Then the mad panic to get it all pressed and stacked away and the hours of 'Spit and polish' began – yes literally! – to get the boots shining we used to spit on a boot, then apply polish on the plastic handle of a toothbrush, bought specially for that purpose, and then rub it in with the plastic handle using small circles.

After hours of this and finishing off with a buffer they shone like glass!

The following day was the most dramatic. We were all marched as a squad to the barbers' shop! I had a right mop of curly hair but it wasn't the longest by any means. It couldn't have taken the barber much more than an hour to cut all thirty six of us! In the chair, six or seven strokes from the nape of the neck upwards with the shaver, then a quick scissor cut of an inch all over the top. 'Next please'. I honestly saw some lads, who were to become my best mates, come out crying! We had no time to get over it though because I cannot remember ever walking anywhere – it was all double-quick time – left right, left right, left right, leeeeft!

What a shock it was to us all, but guess what? We were soon vying with each other as to who had the shiniest boots, the best 'squared off' bedding, etc. Yes as soon as we got up we had to fold the three blankets and two sheets into a perfect rectangle. Blanket, sheet, sheet, blanket with the third blanket wrapped neatly round them!

Our platoon had a Corporal in charge whereas the other four platoons all had Sergeant Instructors. I am sure he had to try all the harder to impress. We always knew that we were the smartest platoon, but of course we could not be seen to be the smartest on the passing out parade and be awarded the cup, because that would have caused the sergeants to 'lose face!'

From a motley crew of raw beginners, we had been moulded into a smart, regimented unit. We were quite proud of it too, and not many of us would say that we hadn't enjoyed the discipline. Why, oh why don't they have National Service now? It would solve the unemployment problem, instil some discipline into them, and could even teach them a trade. Sorry, children now are not brought up tough as we were, and mustn't be shouted or swore at!

We were then apportioned out to our trade courses. I had missed the intake from which Intelligence or Education Officers were recruited, much to Barbie's displeasure, because her college friends' boyfriends were all either in the Education or Intelligence Corps, so started army life as sergeants. It would not have been sensible to send me on a trade course as I was earmarked to be a teacher, so I was sent to Arborfield, to embark on a Clerk's course. This was a period when we were able to slightly relax. We learned how to type, use a 'Gestetner' copying machine – this was before the age of word processors and computers – and make out company orders etc. Of course, if we had paid attention more and tried harder, I wouldn't be taking as long to type this book! It is too easy to get into bad habits, because as soon as it was over we reverted to looking at the keyboard – which I am doing at the moment! Actually the time dragged on a bit and we couldn't wait for the course to end and find out to where we were going to be posted.

When the time came to be posted on to a unit, we all rushed to the notice board to find out to where we had been posted. Guess what? Mine came up and I was going to go to R.E.M.E. (The Royal Electrical and Mechanical Engineers) Workshops, St Andrew's bay, MALTA! I don't think that Barbie's first reaction was as excited as mine, but I have to admit that there was a certain amount of thrill attached to the thought of travelling abroad. I had then three weeks embarkation leave, so more work on the farm and then preparations to go.

Honestly, one would have thought that I was going to War! I was only going to be away for about fourteen months! It was a good time to be at home for a while though, even though disharmony was becoming more evident between mum and dad. It was obvious that something had gone wrong with their sexual relationship. I now know that it must have been related to mum's operation, but I have also found out that this could have been overcome, except that they probably had too puritanical minds. I guess mum had very 'straight laced' ideas on sex.

Whoever was at fault I do not know, but I knew it had become irreparable. Once when mum called dad a fornicating old bugger, I told mum what that meant, thinking that she didn't understand the meaning, but of course I now think that she knew perfectly well what it meant. There was an incident after a particularly bad row with dad when mum threatened to go and drown herself in the river Went and disappeared through the gate. Our Les happened to be at home at the time and we went over the back wall to cut her off. We caught up with her and Les told her not to be a silly bugger and we brought her home.

One night when I was younger and my brothers were away during the war, I was sleeping on my own in the middle bedroom. This was above the dining room and a passage behind it led to mum and dad's bedroom above the drawing room. There were two beds in my room, a double and a single, and I slept in the double by choice because it was further away from the 'bogey' hole, a walk-in wardrobe in the corner and so christened by us children to frighten each other.

I was awakened by feet padding along the passage behind me. My door opened and mum came in and lay down in bed beside me. A short while afterwards there was further padding of feet down the passage, and dad came in and said 'Come on Effie, come back to bed with me'. Mum didn't move, so dad lay down on the floor by the side of the bed. It must have been freezing because we didn't have carpets upstairs and he was on cold linoleum. He obviously couldn't bare that for long and kicked the bed, got up, and went back to his own bed.

It was an emotional time when I had to say goodbye to the family, and most of all for me when I had to say goodbye to Barbie for a while. We promised to write every day, and whenever possible we both kept our promise.

I embarked from Liverpool on the Empress of India, a troop ship, to the Mediterranean. It had three funnels and was the biggest thing I had ever seen at the time. We were kept busy in true army style, but also had a little time off to relax. We had to experience the feel of sleeping in hammocks, which was quite pleasant when one got used to it. Most of us suffered from seasickness for a couple of days, but then we got our sea legs and could really enjoy the rest of the cruise. Going from Liverpool and down the Irish Sea wasn't particularly interesting because there wasn't a lot to see until we were approaching Gibraltar. That was quite spectacular to view for the first time, going through the straights, seeing the famous 'Rock of Gibraltar' which formed the European half of 'The Pillars of Hercules'. We looked for the corresponding 'Pillar' on the African side but didn't see anything. We didn't know then that there was a dispute over two African candidates for the title. The spectacular sight of the rock though was to impress us every time we went through in the future.

Quite a number of our troops disembarked to join the garrison in Gibraltar and then off we steamed to Malta. Again there was nothing much to see until we reached Valletta Harbour. Valletta is the capital of Malta, and the harbour is spectacular in its own way. We were to appreciate it even more later on in our tour of duty. The overriding impression of the Mediterranean Sea, however, was its blue colour. When I wrote home I described it as 'like steaming through Royal Blue ink', partly due, I believe, to the reflection from the vivid blue skies.

We were then whisked off the ship into lorries and driven through Valletta, along the coast through Sliema and round St Georges bay and St Andrews Bay to the R.E.M.E. workshops which overlooked it. This was to be our home for a while and, compared with UK barracks, it looked beautiful.

We were housed in attractively built, two-storey, stone buildings. The stone was a creamy colour and was mined locally. It was soft and could be cut into blocks quite easily, which hardened as they were exposed to the air and thus became very solid and strong.

Barracks in Malta – Better than a Nissan hut!

We entered the barracks through the middle archway which faced the stone stairs. At each level there was a dormitory off to the right and left, each for a full platoon of twenty-two men. They were spacious and airy, having huge window openings, and they never seemed to get too hot even in midsummer.

Of course we were still in the army. This wasn't done in any way haphazardly. We were formed up in lines. Marched everywhere, single file up the stairs, stand by your beds at attention, told how to 'barrack' the beds every morning, three blankets and two sheets each folded in perfect rectangles, as in training: blanket, sheet, sheet, blanket, with the third blanket folded round and squared off. That is how it had to be every morning with the sergeant inspecting daily. After he had run his finger under the bed and behind the locker, heaven help you if he found any dust, but compared with England? – heaven.

The Cookhouse was halfway down to the bay and the food was plentiful and very tasty. We must have had some very good cooks. After lunch every day we had an hour to spare, so we continued down to the bay. Here there were two rafts at 20 and 40 yards from the two diving boards, one spring board and one high diving board, built into the rocks at the side. The rafts were quite cleverly constructed, four 40-gallon drums, anchored to the seabed, with a wooden square on top covered in cocoa matting. It was perfect on which to sunbathe, lark about, or dive from.

Now, I couldn't swim! Mum had always said, rather illogically, that I couldn't go to the Baths until I could swim. I solved that by finding two projecting rocks in the water. I started by pushing off from one to glide to the other, then trying to go further and further out in a semicircle. I then tried to introduce what I thought I had seen as a breast stroke, and guess what? It worked, and within a week I could make it all the way to the first raft.

We had all been taught a trade but now we had to get experience and use it. Motor Mechanics, Radar Mechs, Radio Mechs, Electricians, Fitters etc. all went to their various workshops, and I went with Taffy into the Orderly room to publish the Daily Orders, type all the letters and duplicate all information consistent with running a Unit. We soon became proficient and though it was easy enough, there was plenty to keep us occupied, and more, throughout the working day. Not many NSmen (National Servicemen) enjoyed the experience as much as we did.

It is a maxim in the forces that you never volunteer for anything. Well we certainly bucked the trend. Whenever the Orderly officer came to address us, either on parade or in the Mess, and asked for volunteers, there were many of us who instantly shot up our hands. Why you might ask? Well it was usually sport oriented.

One famous day he wanted eight volunteers. He then picked the biggest and toughest looking among us and took us to one side. 'Can any of you row?' he said. And I think we all said 'No.' 'Well now you are going to learn' he said. We then had weeks of training in a 'Whaler', apparently weighing a ton, because he'd had a challenge from the Navy and the Air force to race against them. We were actually put on special rations, 'to build us up' he said, and we were excused duties to practise. The day of the race came and of course the Navy won, but at least we beat the R.A.F.! We had never expected to beat the Navy lads anyway.

On another occasion we had an inter-service cross country run and I and our Orderly Officer came 2nd and 3rd. We were beaten again by a guy in the Navy, a Petty Officer called Pape I once counted at least eleven different activities in which I had taken part.

Runner up to P.O. Pape

What must have been the highlight of the tour though, was when we were selected to be the leading platoon on the March Past in honour of Princess Elizabeth's visit to the island before she became the Queen. Two things to observe – one, we in the R.E.M.E. must have been considered the smartest squad on the island, and two – I was selected as the Right

It felt good having them apparently saluting me!
The Princess is out of shot to the left.

27

Marker of our platoon. I have a photograph to prove it.

A statement was issued which really devastated me for a while. The National Service had been extended from eighteen months to two years! What on earth was I going to do about college, which was due to begin in September, and my discharge was not scheduled until December?

I had applied for and been accepted into Durham University. After a year in the Army though and not having seen a book during that time, I began to get cold feet. I knew that the fallout rate after the first year at universities was pretty high in those days and after all the sacrifice that mum had made for me, I just dare not risk it. I applied for and was accepted at St John's College in York to become a teacher, which I considered a much safer option. I was destined to study to be a teacher in any case, because I would have had to pay for any other course of study in a university. In those days there were no such things as bank loans. We hadn't bank accounts anyway. I know mum had set her heart on me going to university, but without any means to study or anyone to give me guidance I just dare not risk failing, which would have meant wasting a year. I actually thought that I had forgotten everything in Maths that I had ever learned.

I suffered several weeks of anxiety but then we were given the good news. Anyone in my position could get early release to attend college. What a relief!

What I haven't mentioned during my army days is that apart from when Barbie was touring Europe, we kept our promise and wrote every day to each other. There was a saying in the army that bromide was put in our tea to curb any sexual urges. I certainly was too busy to think about any other girls anyway, and if I remember rightly, the Maltese girls were all chaperoned very carefully by one or other parent. I never heard of any liaison between military personnel and the local ladies. The exception to this, as I was later to find out, was in the 'gut' district of Valletta.

Spare time in the barracks was usually taken up in the NAAFI (Navy, Army and Air Force Institutes) or, more usually, playing cards in the barracks, 4, 7 or 9 card brag being the more popular choices. We played for pennies to make it interesting but no one's pocket was seriously hurt.

One free morning, our Sergeant came into the barracks and asked if anyone was interested in going to Valletta, so a group of us decided to join him. We walked there, which must have been a good few miles. Looking over the harbour, which was, I believe, the largest deep-water harbour in the Mediterranean, was certainly impressive, with many ships of all sorts and sizes, both Naval and Commercial. At times a good proportion of the Royal Navy was found there. We then went off around the shops and I bought presents for mum and Barbie. There were many of the usual tourist stalls, so I bought little silver filigree broaches and embroidered silk mats, and we then went to eat.

After eating, the Sgt said he would take us down the 'Gut', so off we went. Most of us hadn't a clue where we were going but, like sheep, we followed along behind. We turned down a side street and some of us, who were not in the know, began to get a funny feeling. There were ladies dressed up and heavily made up, and making 'come on' gestures towards us. It suddenly dawned upon us that we were in the 'Red-light' district.

The party split up then. We didn't know where the rest went but four of us stuck together and started to make our way out – I think with red faces! The 'Ladies' realised what was happening and began to make fun of us. One darted out suddenly and snatched a beret, not mine thank goodness, and ran off with it. We had to walk back to the barracks minus one beret – the culprit having to somehow acquire another one before the next Kit inspection!

At some time during my stay I was promoted to lance Corporal and later to acting Corporal, which was good, only because it was a rise in Army pay and hence I had more savings. I have no idea why I had been promoted ahead of Taffy, who had joined at the same time, but I must have done something right. Maybe it was because I was always a volunteer, had played in a lot of sports for the company, or just maybe it was because I had been employed as baby-sitter for the Orderly Officer on occasions.

It wasn't all plain sailing however as both Taffy and I had suffered from a bout of athlete's foot and had consequently been excused boots for a while. Even after our feet had cleared up, we retained the habit of wearing shoes to work, until one morning the C.S.M. marched in and marched us both in front of the Orderly Officer and charged us for being improperly dressed! We were both given seven days CB or confined to barracks, which didn't affect us much as we hardly ever went out anyway, except to the NAAFI, and that wasn't out of bounds.

We were later to feel sorry for the C.S.M. as he had a bit of a drink problem and then caused an absolute sensation in the company by blowing his own brains out. There was an enquiry into how he had obtained live rounds from the armoury, but who in the armoury can argue with a C.S.M.? There was an attempt to hush it all up, but of course everyone knew.

At last, August came around and I was posted back to the UK to be demobbed. . This time a few of us were flown home by the R.A.F. from one of the three R.A.F. stations on the island, in an old transport plane. It was only a few days before we were demobbed and on our way home at last.

The train arrived in Doncaster after midnight and there were no buses and no taxis, but the nine miles walk is nothing to an ex-soldier and I was greeted by a banner across the yard saying 'Welcome Home Ken' even though the house was in darkness. Within seconds, everyone was up to greet me and the celebrations began. It was good to be home.

BARBIE'S STORY

I must go back to the beginning now and tell you about Barbie. The following was taken from the notes she contributed before she became too ill to write any more and is almost an exact copy of what she wrote.

I was born by caesarean operation on 27 June 1930. My mother, Joyce Susannah, had married William Herbert Tomlinson (Bert) and they were the Stewards at Cresswell Working Men's Club. Dad was also the chauffeur for the Manager at Cresswell Colliery. Tragically my dad was killed in a car accident a few months before I was born. He was in the back seat of a car driven by his mate and when the car crashed and burst into flames he couldn't get out. I never found out about the other occupants of the car as it was never spoken of, but I believe that they perished too.

Mum, therefore, became a widow before I was born and as a result had to leave the W.M.'s Club. Being mum though, she found a little cottage for my ten-year-old sister and I, and set up a little sweet shop there. She must have found it hard to survive and when Harry Maycock arrived on the scene – a tall handsome miner from nearby – she married again and we all moved to Askern, near Doncaster, so that Harry could work there at the colliery. We lived in a small, rented accommodation behind a shop for a while, but then moved to a new council house at 35, Rushymoor Ave. where mum lived for most of the rest of her life.

I remember little of early life until I went to school. I will always remember the first day there. I had my own peg in the cloakroom, my own little chair at my own little desk, and we were each given our own strong little cardboard box with metal supports at each corner. Inside were ten cowrie shells and a pencil with a sharp point. The name was

Moss Rd. Junior and Infants school. I remember it being a lovely school with wooden floors and lots of flowers and pots of red geraniums along the corridors. The smell stayed with me for years.

No. 35 was on a housing estate and I remember mum planted a lot of bushes along the front to 'get a bit of privacy' she said. I loved every bit of school and continued to do so when I had to transfer to Selby Rd. Junior School. This wasn't just round the corner though and I had to walk well over half a mile to get there. Walking to school was normal in those days and I always remember being top or near the top of the class.

A friend and I were made monitors when we were ten and what Health and Safety would say now I don't know, but every break time we would go early into the staff room to put a pan full of milk on the gas ring to boil for their coffee. I remember well that we could hardly lift it. How we managed never to drop it we will never know!

We had a piano at home which mum played a bit and I was always tinkering about on it in my spare time, so much so that I remember playing 'The Ash Grove' at school to accompany all the schoolchildren singing. I had never had any music lessons at that time and played everything by ear.

It was the biggest shock and disappointment of my life when I got the news that somehow I had failed my 11+ examination. I was heartbroken, and mum also thought it was a disgrace when I had to go to Sutton Rd. Senior School. I was not to be there long, however, because a few places were available at Pontefract and District Girls High School (P.D.H.S.) and I was transferred there. I therefore ended up at the school to which I would have gone had I passed the 11+.

I am sure that mum had a little to pay towards it but I am really grateful that she did. I believe it to be the reason that mum had to continue going out to work. I had to get up early in time to have breakfast and walk up to the Clock Corner, half a mile away, to catch the bus to Pontefract, which left at 8 a.m. It was a ten mile ride, then another long walk to school.

It was good of mum to go out to work, but I hated it. It meant that I was the first home at night except for Thursdays when it was mum's half-day. I had to let myself into an empty house then make the fire, which meant that except in the summer months I was freezing. I had also to prepare the table for tea and I remember being famished until mum came home from work.

It was about now that I started taking music lessons with Mrs Clegg in order that I would be able to read music. Life became very hectic with school taking up nine hours of every day and the empty house to go home to and then music practice and homework in the evenings.

Life changed forever one Saturday in March, 1945. Dad was a member of the Saint John's Ambulance Brigade and mum and dad decided to go to the SJAB whist drive and dance, in the Hydro. Of course they had to take me, but as I couldn't play cards, I just messed about with the other children in the same boat. It appears we were quite a nuisance to some of the serious whist players. After the whist the band struck up and everyone started to dance.

I had noticed this boy across the dance floor with a mop of thick, wavy, blonde hair. I couldn't stop myself from looking at him and he kept glancing across at us and then wow, he came across and asked ME to dance. It was heaven until the music stopped and the waltz changed to a slow foxtrot. He just said 'Sorry, I can't do this', and strode off. After that I simply couldn't get him out of my mind.

I had managed to find out that he was a choirboy at Campsall Church however so I went there on the Sunday evening. Someone pointed out his mother to me so I sat behind a pillar away from her, but where I could see Ken. After the service we walked as a gang to Campsall corner which was about half a mile, then parted company as some of us turned for Askern and Ken and company went on to Norton. This became the routine for the next few years, but the gang quickly reduced to just the two of us.

I saw him the next morning as our bus passed the Royal Corner, but he was kicking a ball about with his mates so didn't see me. It wasn't long before we waved each morning and at times I would write a letter and give to a P.D.H.S. girl from Norton and I would get one back the same way. Later he would save his dinner money and we would go to the cinema in Askern. We queued early to get one of the double seats which were only situated down each side of the upstairs. I think we did more kissing and cuddling than watching the film. I was just mad about him.

I soon started to take exams on the piano and had passed the first six with either honours or 1st Class. In my last year at school I took my final and was heartbroken when the Italian examiner failed me by either two or three points. I would have had ALCM after my name had I passed, and didn't think that I would ever get another chance to take it.

At school I soon got into the sports teams. I loved racing and also won the High Jump. Ken laughed at me later because I described how I ran straight at the rope. Well, the Fosbury Flop hadn't been invented then! I was also quickly selected into the Hockey, Tennis and Rounders teams. I also wore the green sash for hockey as player of the year and captained my beloved Norman House (Blue).

I knew Ken was mad on cricket, and it was the time that Donald Bradman was due to make his last test match appearance at the Headingly ground in Leeds. I can't remember who first suggested it but for the first and only time in my life, and I am sure it was for Ken too, we decided to play wag (It sounds better than truant!) and go to Leeds to watch the test match instead of going to school.

We duly left our homes at the usual times and caught buses to Pontefract and then to Leeds. We managed to get another bus to Headingly Cricket Ground and there we joined a huge queue. Slowly we inched forward and eventually there were only four more people in front of us. Then they closed the gates with a notice saying 'SORRY FULL!' I suppose it was justice on us really.

We got a bus back into town and kept going into Lewis's to find out the score. They had a big score board inside, replicating the one at the ground. Eventually we made our way home, timing it well to arrive home at the normal time. I guess that taught us a lesson we were never to forget.

By now I had been able to buy a bicycle and Ken was able, sometimes, to borrow his sister's. It made meeting much simpler, but didn't happen often enough. Of course it was inevitable that my parents found out. Mum said 'I hear you are going out with that lad from Norton. He comes from a great big family, and his dad is always winning at Whist.'

I was eventually allowed to take him home for tea and mum found out that he was really a nice guy and from then on he just couldn't do anything wrong. He became mum's favourite too! He even broke one of our best china cups while helping to wash up but that didn't matter because it was Ken! Thank goodness I didn't break one though!

It was much later when I was finally asked to Ivy House. I remember we had plums and custard as a starter. Then we had a lovely salmon salad. I remember most that I daren't ask where the toilet was and was just about bursting when I got home.

We would meet whenever we could but once he just never turned up. Apparently he had been up all night with one of their pigs which had an abscess on one of its teats and he had been rubbing it all night with goose grease. He said the abscess eventually burst and the pig got better. He was so caring, always.

This may sound an idyllic childhood but between times it was far from it. In 1940 my sister would be twenty and went along with the common opinion that young men on leave from the forces had to be entertained and sent back to war in a happy state of mind. I guess there were various interpretations of how happy, but I only remember endless rows at home between her and dad and mum. I suppose Gwen wasn't his biological daughter which further complicated the situation.

At some point early in the war she married and her husband was posted to India. This apparently didn't stop her dancing and going out, which didn't help. Then she met John Matthew who worked for the council and he had a car. Owning your own car was very rare in those days. Rows at home became more frequent and Gwen became pregnant. She then went to Sussex where the baby, John, was born. I don't remember anything more about her during that period, but then I remember going to Crowboro in the September holidays and stayed in a boarding house near Gwen. She used to go down to the phone box to ring John every night. It was a great relief when that holiday was over. I remember going home on the train and mum was there at the station to meet me.

For some reason mum thought it was funny to keep me in suspense. I knew my results were due and should have arrived while I was away, but I daren't ask her. Eventually she told me that she had a postcard for me. I was not amused, but immensely relieved at my results.

What bliss to be back and seeing Ken again. More bike rides and visits to church and the cinema occasionally. How romantic, as he produced a bar of McCowan's treacle toffee which had gone soft in his pocket. We had to take it in turn to bite and twist pieces off.

I took my Higher School Certificate and, though I didn't do as well as I had hoped, I was offered and accepted a place at Lincoln Training College to train to be a teacher. In September 1948 I began my college life which was so enjoyable and exciting for me, if only because it was such a huge contrast to life at home.

I was housed at Dial House along the Foss Way just outside the city, and I still keep in touch with the three girls who were housed there with me. I loved going to the cathedral where we had special services for the college. The love of the sound of organ music there was to stay with me all my life.

I am sure that we were no naughtier that normal teenage girls, but I remember that one of the girls had the idea that it would be clever to smoke. Someone produced a packet of cigarettes it certainly wasn't me because they used to tease me that I had the same sixpence in my purse at the end of college that I went with at the start. So we took it in turns to take one or two puffs like the amateurs we were, when suddenly there was a knock on the door.

Someone said 'It's the bishop!' so there was a mad scramble to waft the fumes away, turn off the gas fire, and try not to look guilty.

The best thing to happen at college was when Ken decided to cycle over to see me one Saturday. I had arranged for him to stay overnight with the gardener and his wife, which worked out well except that he said he had forgotten his pyjamas. I later found out that he never possessed any anyway! I lent him a pair of mine, but that provided the joke, relayed on all subsequent meetings with the girls. When he went home the girls told me to make sure I washed them before I wore them, otherwise I might have a baby! Such was the naivety of nineteen-year-old girls in those days! Somehow I can't imagine that happening now.

Ken then got news that his long awaited call-up papers had arrived and he had to go to Arborfield Barracks on 8 December 1949. It was sad not to see him over Christmas, but we started writing every day which was always something to look forward to. Then a brief but pleasant time when he came home on leave, but he also had bad news for me because he had been posted to Malta. I wouldn't see him for fourteen months! We still wrote every day though and apart from us not seeing each other, I know he enjoyed himself because he was always representing his company at one sport or another.

Then I heard the devastating news that National Service had been extended to two years! Heavens, I might not see him until nearly Christmas. I was worried too because he had been admitted into York Teacher Training College in September, so I had no idea what was going to happen. After what seemed ages and ages, we got word that special cases could get premature release, so after all he could come home in August to go to York in the September. Whew. What a relief.

I went with a crowd from college to a dance at the local Airforce Officer Cadet Station at Cranwell. We had good times, and I think that Ken was a bit jealous, but he had nothing to worry about.

Exam time came and I did really well. Not as well as my college mate who copied a text book for her thesis and later found out that the author of that book was one of her examiners. She got a distinction of course!

Then a post was advertised for a teacher at Askern Sutton Road School. I applied for it and was accepted, and so, in September, I would begin my teaching career teaching ten year olds.

During that holiday, a friend and I had a bright idea for us to go hitchhiking through Europe – anything to get away from home. I secretly thought that maybe we could end up in Malta. We did well and had a great time riding on the backs of lorries throughout Europe. We got to the French and Italian Riviera, but realised Malta was out of the question. A matter of a few hundred miles through Italy and then the Mediterranean was in the way.

While coming back on the back of a lorry we met up with a gang of Dutch men. One was in the Dutch Airforce and he took a fancy to me. We all exchanged addresses, but I shouldn't have done really. I had told him all about Ken, so I was a bit surprised when I got a succession of love letters. To a teenager they were quite flattering, but I didn't take them seriously.

I told Ken about everything except the letters and only told him about them years later when we were safely married. In any case, Ken knew all about him, and when Ken and I toured Europe a few years later we actually went to visit him at his home. He then came to tour England and called to see me at home, but Ken just happened, accidentally on purpose, to be with me there as well, so I guess he went away disappointed.

I had just treated it as a friendship but that must have been naivety on my part. When I realised, I felt a bit sorry for him, but I never intended or even thought that I had encouraged him. I had always told him about Ken. That was the reality in those days. Both Ken and I were from a remote village, both had difficult childhoods, and both naive and innocent of the machinations of the outside world.

I had joined the Doncaster Ladies and played both hockey and tennis for them, and while Ken was still away I sometimes went to the dances at the Hydro. I just wanted to be out of the atmosphere at home as much as I could.

I was often asked to dance by a couple of young men and I even went to see one of them box in Doncaster under the name Rocko King. Any excuse to escape from the environment at home. That is all I did though, watch him box. I was never unfaithful to Ken and was really upset when one of his brothers told stories about me that weren't true.

Funnily enough, all the boys or men I knew seemed more than a bit scared of Ken, including the boxer. Little did they know that though he might have looked like a boxer, he was a gentle and kind man and I never knew him to have a fight in his life, and he never used his strength as a weapon, or with which to impose himself, neither on me nor on any other person.

I loved my teaching, even though it was in a rough mining area. Many of the children were very poor and it wasn't uncommon for them to be 'stitched in for the winter'. That meant that their bodies were wrapped in brown paper and their clothes stitched onto it so that it would stay in place. Yes that meant while the cold weather lasted, they never changed their clothes nor could they wash their bodies. Does that make any of you children reading this still feel poor or underprivileged?

Once the headmistress told one little boy, who had a candle running down his nose, to 'Shake yourself' so he literally stood and shook himself. Also, a little girl in my class put her hand up and said 'Please Miss Maycock, Billy Green is playing with his Thomas under his desk' I said 'Billy, just you bring whatever you are playing with and put it on my table'. Such was my naivety, even at twenty-one years old! I loved teaching though and this was to last with me throughout my life and in the many places in which I was destined to travel.

Time seemed to pass so slowly, as it does when you are waiting but eventually August came around and Ken had flown back to Arborfield. At last we were in the same country. Then he came home and came to see me the following day – I was in heaven once again.

We had been thinking of writing our life story for years. We wanted our great grandchildren to know about us; what we had done, and where we had been. In 2011 we were both over eighty years old. We began to write half-heartedly in our spare time, but Barbie had been diagnosed with cancer and it was soon apparent that she was losing her memory. In 2013 I had to take over and write for both of us. Our story now continues from 1951 and I apologise if it might appear to be biased towards me.

ST JOHN'S COLLEGE. (SETTING A TREND)

We were together again, that is we were in the same country now, and life once again revolved around each other. When we saw each other again, after so long apart, we just knew that we had been right to be faithful to each other. Neither of us doubted each other, and the first hug and kiss said it all. As far as we were concerned, everyone else could add up two and two together and make five if they wanted to, but we had that feeling and faith in each other to allay any doubts.

I was to report to St John's College, York in two weeks. In that time I had to equip myself with decent clothes and acquire various course books.

When I had baby-sat for the Orderly Officer in Malta, I remember he wore a very smart pair of deep navy blue corduroys which I thought looked extremely smart, so I was keen to get some for myself. After going round all the shops in Doncaster, the only navy cords I saw were in the Army and Navy Stores. They weren't as dark blue or as smart, but they looked OK in the shop so I got them. Unfortunately they weren't in the same league as the Officer's, but they had to do, even though they never looked smart, and in fact I always felt scruffy in them.

I was lucky to be given a single room, Chapel 3, in the old part of the college overlooking the chapel. It had a nice view over the sweeping drive, but if ever I had wanted to just enjoy looking out of the window, it was much too tiny and not situated where one could sit in comfort from which to view.

All the new first year students assembled in the Junior Common Room to be welcomed by the president, appointed the previous year from the second year students. He gave an impressive speech and then ended by saying that there had been one or two complaints about the toilets and we were to make sure at St John's that we all had a good aim in life.

We then had to choose our specialist subjects, which for me was simple: Maths, with Biology as a 'second' subject. We had general lectures to attend including Education, Psychology and Religious Education. This was a strict Church of England College. Later we were to choose 'short courses', one of which I chose was 'Bookbinding by Hand'. I also did 'Music' and learned how to play the recorder.

After a week I began to realise that I hadn't forgotten any of my maths at all. In fact, what we did failed to stretch me, and I wondered if I had made the wrong decision to turn down the place in Durham. Still, I had made the decision and couldn't change it now. In retrospect, I am rather glad that things had turned out as they did, because I wouldn't have wanted anything to have worked out differently.

It was not long before I noticed that there were students around who were always in green tracksuits. When I enquired about them, I was told that they were the P.E. students. 'Do you mean to say you can train here to teach P.E.?' I asked, and was told in the affirmative. This was news to me.

It didn't take me long to work out what to do. I asked for an interview with the Vice Principal. I told him that I was interested in the possibility of staying on to take the third year diploma in P.E., and that my time table would allow me to take P.E. as an extra 'second' subject along with

Biology. This had never been done before, but after he had seen the Principal, and warned me that my first preferences would not have to be seen to suffer, he allowed me to go ahead on a trial period. That was the first bit of history that I made in my life. I was the first student ever to take two 'second' subjects. Many were to follow my lead afterwards. I had set a precedent!

We were soon inundated with requests from the captains of the various games, asking us to join their clubs. I hadn't played soccer for a while, so eventually I joined the Cross Country club. This was the first time that I had any real training and guidance in actual racing and I revelled in it. I realised that I had not extended myself before. Who knows? Had I done I might even have beaten P. O. Pape. I was not able to beat Mac, the Captain, who had the legs on all of us, but that changed after one race when we had gone to Durham and beaten their T.T.C. After the race he collapsed and was treated for salt deficiency. It was sad that he was never able to race as well after that.

After the first weeks' Maths lessons, I began to pal up with Ernest Draper. He was also taking Maths and was from a mining background like me and so we had a lot in common. We used to meet up in the J.C.R. (Junior Common Room) at night to get the free milk and cakes on offer.

For some reason I had taken a flat electric fire to college. Mum suggested it because we didn't know that it would be centrally heated. We then got the idea of taking the milk and cakes up to Chapel 3 and boil the milk on the fire – quite illegal of course. We began to have supper there, which now included hot cocoa or Horlicks. We soon found that there was a chip shop nearby and often took it in turns to collect some fish and chips, but mostly only chips, and take them up to Chapel 3 with the milk and cakes to feast. The man in the chip shop must have taken pity on us too. He was over generous with the portions, and usually gave us extra scraps free.

It was in the early weeks at John's when the Vice Principal was talking about elocution lessons. He took me on one side and remarked that 'Pidcock, you sound as if you have just come from behind a plough' I have to be honest, because I suppose I did. Several of us were then recruited for elocution lessons! We treated it as a bit of a laugh, but it couldn't have done me any harm.

Ernie was in the Rowing Club, so we could vie with each other about how well we'd done during the previous weekend. We were to stay pals all through college and for the rest of our lives. We were always seen together, and though it never occurred to us at the time, it might have appeared to some that we were more than friends, so much so that one of the lecturers, whom we thought to be gay, went into Ernie's room one night, much to Ernie's embarrassment. I wonder why he never came into Chapel 3?

I bought a bike on the cheap. It was a fixed wheel version, but it enabled me sometimes to cycle home and back over the weekend. When I did, I would always see Barbie as well. She also came on the bus sometimes to see me, and when the Christmas Ball came around she came on her bicycle to stay overnight at the Youth Hostel. We made up a four with Ernie and his latest girl. He was a bit of a Romeo and obviously had acquired far more experience than I had.

I was as bad at names then as I am now, and when another student came to us to introduce his girlfriend, I said 'Didn't you introduce her to me a couple of weeks ago?' She wasn't the same girl of course, and did not even have the same name. Oh dear, I haven't changed!

When the C.C. season was over, I joined the Athletics Club. I used to run both the mile and the three miles in the same afternoon. It sounds crazy now, but I didn't do so badly. Once mum and Sylvia came to see me race but I must have felt the pressure because it was one of the few occasions when I was beaten in the mile. My legs felt like jelly. I was to suffer from that syndrome in most individual sports, because though I could act on the stage, I didn't perform well in some sports when I was put under pressure.

During the summer term the dreaded 'School Practice' came along. We all were allotted to different schools to take over a class to practise the real thing. I must digress again, and explain that all my early life my ambition was to be a doctor, because of my training with the SJAB and my love of Biology, especially in relation to the human body. When I started applying to universities however, I discovered that the only free university courses were in teaching. I would have had to pay to study to be a doctor, which was out of the question. It would have been impossible to get a loan in those days, and none of us even had a bank account, or money to put into a bank.

It is not surprising therefore that I was not comfortable teaching, especially as this School Practice was with primary children and covered all subjects. I think it helped because it was at Norton school and I could live at home. It had the same Headmaster that I had when I was a pupil, so he knew me and my family. I remember he advised me to say 'I' and

'My', rather than 'A' and 'Ma'. It probably helped me more than any of the elocutions lessons had. Later at secondary level I loved teaching Maths and P.E. because I felt comfortable and competent in those subjects. I cannot say that I ever enjoyed teaching any other subject. I did manage to get through the School Practices reasonably well though.

The summer holidays came and went. As with Easter and Christmas it was spent working on the farm for Frank Lodge during all hours of the day, but I still managed to see Barbie regularly.

During the second year at college, life was very much the same. I was disappointed that I wasn't elected as Cross Country Captain, but I was elected as the Athletics Club Captain which was far more demanding. I now qualified for a privileged room on the 'New' wing, although I think that I would have preferred to stay in Chapel 3. The New Wing was good for the boys who wanted to go out at night, because they could use the fire escape, which was a compulsory addition on all new buildings. I can honestly say that I never had cause to use it.

The year eventually reached its climax and exams were due. I was fine until the Maths exam, which to me was the most important, but I woke up with the flu. I found it hard to concentrate, and what normally would have been a doddle suddenly became a blur. The outcome was that I didn't get the distinction which everyone had expected of me, and I only managed a credit. What was hard for me to take was that a colleague, who had spent all year asking me for help, did get a distinction. I was unkind enough to put it down to the fact that one of his relatives was on the board of governors of the college, but that is probably very ungracious of me. I don't think it affected the rest of my life. It was merely my pride that was a bit dented, for I had so wanted to impress mum and the family.

LETTERS AFTER MY NAME

When I had talked about a third year to mum and dad they were all for it, especially when I said that I could put the letters Dip. Phys. Ed. after my name. I never did, but still I was entitled to. I was duly accepted and turned up for the third year in 1953.

The Third Year P.E. students were all boarded out at the home of one of our lecturers. He was on the P.E. Staff, but not one who had much to do with the 3rd Year training, and it worked quite well. I still cycled home occasionally and Barbie still came over to see me, which was nice as she was always invited to have meals with us. The only drawback to that was the teasing and innuendoes directed towards me by the lads.

It was on one visit that I took her to Betty's in York for tea and proposed. There was nothing dramatic like kneeling on one knee etc., but she said yes anyway and that was all that mattered.

If we had thought life was hectic before, then it was nothing compared with what we went through that year. I joined the Rugby Club in order that I could add schools to my list of applications where they played rugby. I managed to play with the third team to gain a little experience, and it came in handy later, but as a player, not as a teacher.

When we weren't in the gym, we were either at the baths, on the playing fields or in the lecture rooms. We began a session of intense learning about the theory and practice of P.E., and what I loved most were the lectures in anatomy and physiology during which I was in my element. For one session each week we went to Leeds University for anatomy and understood it to be the same course which the 1st year student doctors were taking. My experience with the SJAB proved invaluable, and I am pleased to say that I did get my distinction in the end.

The latter half of the year saw us taking examination after examination. We took certificates in coaching and refereeing football, basketball, and rugby. We took them in coaching tennis and all the different events in athletics. We passed certificates in life-saving and personal survival and the ASA Bronze and Silver medals, and even had a twelve-session course in coaching golf, which had us on the golf course for each session with the local Golf Professional.

Of all the places I could have been sent to for School Practice that year, I was placed at the King's School, Pontefract. This was the one that the boys had attended, who travelled on the bus everyday with Barbie when she was at P.D.H.S. I was once again able to stay at Ivy House, and I hardly did any teaching, but was asked to help the groundsman most of the time laying out the athletics track. This suited me down to the ground, and I was able to use that experience at subsequent schools where I taught.

I don't think any of us on the course had much actual gymnastic experience or expertise. None of us were very good by today's standards, but it is said that those who can, do, and those who can't do, teach, and those who can't teach, 'teach how to teach', and that was true of us. Gymnastics had not developed into the sport that it is today. Sessions in the gym were aimed mainly at discipline, and making and keeping the boys stronger and fitter, interspersed with basic gymnastics and games skills. In that respect I believe we did well.

I got credits to add to my distinction in Anatomy and Physiology in my final exams, so I felt that I had done well. As an additional qualification, we had all been given the opportunity to sit for an examination to become Members of the Royal Institute of Public Health and Hygiene. I am pleased to say that I passed with honours, so could also append M.R.I P.H.H. (Hon) after my name. Again, I never bothered to, and I guess one would have to subscribe annually to remain an actual member.

I had already applied to several schools for a specialist post and had chosen those adverts which were closest to home. The chances of a suitable post being available near home were so remote that we never expected one. I was invited for an interview at all the ones for which I had applied, but only attended one, because I was offered and accepted the position at the first interview. That was at Dinnington S. M. School in South Yorkshire. Dinnington was a mining village south of Sheffield, but the key factor was that it had a super gymnasium and acres of playing fields.

Dinnington S.M. School – Gym. Rear centre

PART TWO

Teaching – earning at last

I BEGAN MY TEACHING CAREER AT LAST in September 1954, and at twenty-three years old I was at last earning a regular salary. I can never say often enough how grateful I am to my family, and in particular my mother, who was the driving force behind us all. She would never take money from me, but over the years I bought her a new electric oven, washing machine, refrigerator and even a greenhouse and things the house needed. I tried, but I was never able to repay her for all she had missed because of my education, especially as she was to look after Nikky and Ros through many half-term holidays.

Dinnington was a rough mining village, but it was in need of a P.E. teacher and an ideal place for me to start. The school was a long wooden building which was divided down the middle, one half being a girls school and the other half the boys. The gymnasium was separate and behind the main building and was shared equally between the boys and the girls.

I had to start off in digs, and the metalwork teacher offered to put me up until I could get them arranged. He and his wife lived in a small terraced house, but they were a lovely elderly couple and it was very pleasant staying with them for a short while.

I soon answered an advert and found board and lodgings on a new estate near the school with a lovely middle-aged couple. They had a son, Gerald, who was about my age and hence became a good companion during the week. I began to take clubs after school every day except Friday when I went home, so when Gerald arrived home from work it coincided with me arriving from school and was convenient for us to have the evening meal together.

On one occasion I was walking to my digs and had to pass the girls gate. By accident or design, because no one except me ever seemed to stay for clubs after school, one of the younger lady members of staff was coming out of the gate at the same time. It appeared that she was also in digs which happened to be on the way to mine, so we walked together and chatted. She seemed to hesitate as she reached her gateway, but I just said it was nice talking to her and goodnight.

That was about the only contact anyone ever had between the two schools. It was strange, but at the time that was how it was. What was later said in the girls' staff room I will never know but I guess it was relayed that I was a non-starter.

Barbie had one strict stipulation about the timing of the wedding. It had to be between 15 April and 27 June – that meant during the Whitsuntide holidays. She insisted that we would be the same age in years on the marriage certificate. We decided on Saturday 28 May 1955, but when Barbie told her mother she said we couldn't have that day because she could not have a day off work. She was the Manageress of one of Tyler's shoe shops in Carcroft. We settled therefore on Monday 30 May 1955, which was Whit Monday. We always had a week off from school at Whitsuntide, but it meant two days less to spend on our honeymoon.

Earlier in the term, Gerald, who was mad keen on motorbikes, had asked me if I would like to go to Birmingham with him on his motorcycle to the Motorcycle Show. I needed transport and could not afford a car, so I thought it a good idea to have a look what was on offer. We had chosen a brilliant day for my first experience on the back of a motorbike and we had a very good day out. Gerald was always very careful with his money, so we shared all expenses, and that worked out well for both of us.

I didn't buy one at the show, as I didn't have sufficient funds, but took the knowledge home to Barbie, who offered, bless her, to go halves if I bought one. From that moment we neither of us ever owned any money individually. We had one joint account, and everything we were to own in the future was always shared in both our names.

It was now Easter, which I spent at Ivy House, and the first weekend I went to Sheffield and selected a Matchless 350 cc GLS model. After fifteen minutes tuition from the salesman on one of the back streets behind the shop, I set off back to Norton.

It sounds simple, but it meant going through the centre of Sheffield, bypassing most of Rotherham, and then through the centre of Doncaster before reaching home in Norton. I was obviously a bit tentative, and it all went well until I was leaving Doncaster, when a bus pulled out of a side street on my left, right in front of me. We both stopped in time to avoid a collision, but my bike did slip over onto its side. I was a bit shaken, when a man came up to me and said 'It is OK sir, I am a policeman and was right behind you and you did well to avoid anything worse!' He could see that I was a learner from the L plates, and after taking particulars we went on our way and I never heard any more about it.

Ken and Barbie on our Matchless G3LS

I was still on L plates, but when Barbie said she had a hockey match in Harrogate, I suggested that I should take her up on the bike. Yes, this was quite illegal, but I removed the L plates and we set off. The weather was good and we arrived there and I watched a good game of hockey. It was the first time that I had watched Barbie in action and I was surprised and impressed. She played at C F and scored in a 1-1 draw.

On our way back the skies darkened and it began to drizzle slightly on my goggles and that posed a bit of a problem with the old-fashioned pair that I was wearing. I was obviously apprehensive, especially because I was driving without L plates, and things went well until we were halfway home when I suddenly saw a roundabout ahead. I wasn't going very fast, but too fast I thought to get round a roundabout on a wet road. Anyway there was nothing for it but to try, because I daren't touch the brakes. We heeled over to the left and then over to the right and then to the left again. I could have sworn that my footrests should have touched the ground, but there we were at the far side of the roundabout and we had managed to get round safely. I could only marvel at Barbie, who clung to me and heeled over with me like a true veteran, and that was the first long ride she had ever experienced on the pillion.

Barbie was obviously going to be a frequent passenger, so I applied for and passed my driving test as soon as I could. The wedding was coming up shortly and I didn't want to go on our honeymoon driving illegally.

WE GET MARRIED

Mid morning at Askern Church. Ernest had driven over to be my best man and we both had our new grey suits on with our white carnations. The bells were pealing, but they were a gramophone recording. Campsall Church had a full peal of bells, which would have been preferable, but Barbie was from the parish of Askern, so Askern it had to be, and Askern Church only had one bell.

Wedding group (Mum and Dad are on the left.)

Barbie didn't keep us waiting long before we heard the strains of 'Here comes the Bride.' There she was by my side looking absolutely gorgeous in her Chantilly lace dress and veil, with a bouquet of Sweet Peas and

Lilies of the Valley.

The four bridesmaids had long peacock blue dresses, made by my sister, Sarah, who was one of the bridesmaids with Christina and Barbara, brother Walter's children, and Audrey, a college friend of Barbie's.

After the service, we all went over to the Hydro which Barbie's mum had booked and had a meal which, for those times, was quite a spread. The only speech we remembered was a short one given by the vicar. He finished off by saying that if we ever had an argument we should end it in bed.

We said our goodbyes to everyone at the reception, because we had a taxi waiting to take us to Gwen's house in Doncaster. Here we made a quick change into our motorcycle gear, put the pre-packed cases on the luggage rack (we had bought lovely new box panniers for the occasion) and set off to Bournemouth, where we had booked a room at The Hawthorns Hotel.

That was quite a ride before motorways were built. On long journeys one used to estimate that an average of 30 mph was good, so we expected it to take about eight hours. God was very good to us that day as we never saw one wisp of a cloud in the sky, and we made good time. We had never stayed in an hotel before so we had no idea what to expect.

We were getting rather peckish by the time we were an hour away, and as it was getting late, and, we thought, too late for dinner at the hotel, we decided to stop and get some fish and chips. They were not as good maybe as the ones up north, but we really enjoyed them nevertheless. An hour later we drove into the drive of the Hawthorns and made our way into the far corner of the huge car park. We will disown the bike for the rest of our honeymoon, we thought, as we parked it among all the posh cars.

At reception we were told that, as dinner had ended, they had laid out a special 'Ham and Tongue' salad for us. We were so naive that we daren't tell them that we had just had fish and chips, so we quickly changed and went down to force this huge salad down.

Finally we self-consciously got into bed and then had a giggle because we pulled the cord thinking it was the light switch and it was for room service. No one ever came. I guess it wasn't the first time it had happened and they must have had a laugh at our expense. Then we were in each other's arms.

It was a super hotel and the food was good. We went sightseeing, played tennis, and went to shows. The one we remembered most was the open air synchronised swimming in the open air pool on the promenade. We often referred to it later in life as we were both keen swimmers. I used to tease Barbie about looking like Esther Williams, the swimming film star of that era.

We had a lovely time and enjoyed ourselves, but like all good things it had to end and we soon seemed to be on the bike again and on our way home. Again we were blessed with beautiful weather, and we were too soon back to reality.

Getting married left us with a dilemma. Our schools were miles apart, so we found a room to rent somewhere mid way. The only room available was in the less salubrious part of Bentley, but heck we were newly married and so made the most of it. It was an easy bus ride for Barbie – now very strictly Mrs. Pidcock to the children (she never allowed any of the children to just say 'Miss') – and I had the motorcycle.

We spent half of a term there, Whitsuntide being mid term, and I did try hard to make a go of it. I even dug the lady's garden and planted green vegetables for her, and so we survived for the rest of the term. I am afraid it didn't have the happy ending for which I had hoped. When we later paid a courtesy visit to see the landlady, all she did was complain about the millions of caterpillars with which she had to deal, because most of them decided to crawl up the walls of the house. The motto, it seems, is that before you try to do a good deed, make sure that the recipients are capable of taking care of it once you have gone.

Barbie applied for and was offered a post at the Dinnington Primary School which was conveniently situated almost opposite my school, and we were again fortunate to find temporary digs with an elderly couple in North Anston. We were so lucky. They were a really nice couple and tended to 'mother' us newlyweds, and we stayed with them nearly half a term.

We were naturally on the lookout for a home to rent, when we heard of a cottage becoming vacant in South Anston. 'You haven't a chance' we were told by everyone, because, they said, there were dozens of the local people wanting it. Nevertheless we went to see the farmer who owned it and put in our request.

Much to our surprise we heard from them later that week and we had been successful! Once again God had looked down kindly upon us. We wondered if our luck would ever run out. Actually the farmer had been in a dilemma too. So many of his friends wanted the cottage that he daren't give it to any of them because of the jealousy it would have created. He therefore gave it to us because we were the outsiders.

It was a semicottage which was originally two up and two down, but he converted a bedroom into a bathroom and toilet so that we didn't have to use the one across the yard. Downstairs was a lounge and kitchen. There was access to the yard at the back so that I could keep my bike off the road.

The cottage was built below the road level, so it wasn't long before we were getting ribbed by the rest of the staff. 'I saw you in bed from the top deck of the bus when we were passing' was the usual remark. 'Not with the curtains closed' I usually answered. We remembered always to keep them closed until we were dressed and ready.

We saw more of Ernie now and when he knew that I had played the bugle, he suggested that I join Killamarsh Silver Prize Band. He had been a member a long time and played 2nd cornet. He said if I could play a bugle then a cornet was just a bugle with the addition of valves, and so I joined.

He was quite right because I picked it up very quickly, but it took me some time to play well enough to join him as 2nd cornet. We got into the habit of going over every Sunday. Barbie used to stay with his mum and dad while we went off to band practice.

Mrs. Draper was one of the funniest and happiest people we have known and kept us all entertained by her escapades, or rather tales of things that had gone wrong, like going to watch Ernie at a band competition and getting on the wrong bus and watching the wrong bands in the wrong arena. She also told us how she had once had to shepherd one of his girlfriends out of the back door when another one came to the front door. He had met a new girl called Wendy by now though and the signs were that he was settling down.

School was always hectic and my clubs after school changed with the seasons. I was rewarded after that first year by being given a grade I allowance for my industry, which came in very handy. I had been given a generous allowance of five periods per week with each class, two in the gym, two games and the other I used in the winter for cross country training, and cricket or athletics coaching in the summer.

There was a convenient track about one and three quarters of a mile long which every boy in the school had to run each alternate week, and it had no short cut options. I made it into a race every time, clocking them in on their return. If they beat their previous position they earned a house point, so it remained competitive all the time. No, I didn't sit and wait for the boys to run unaccompanied, I never set a class off unless I went with them. The older boys often tried to beat me but never quite managed it, and it meant I had a run every single day. I have no doubt that the boys admired me for it, but I never had to really extend myself.

I had never been fitter in my life, and I also started evening classes in the gym, initially to boost our income. It immediately attracted most of the local footballers who wanted extra training. I set them on a course of circuit training and football skills, but was careful to do sufficient exercises and apparatus work to satisfy the inspectors when they came around.

By now I had liaised with other schools in the area and we soon had an up and running football league. I can't ever remember losing a game, either at junior – 1st and 2nd years – or at the senior level. My school may have been bigger than most of the others, but if we ever lacked in skill we always made up in enthusiasm. It is hard to say this without sounding as if I am boasting, but we were really successful. Several of my pupils went on to join professional football clubs or train with the county athletics squads.

I had also joined the woodwork evening class and over the years made a large curved tray, a tea trolley/card table, a beautiful bowl turned on the lathe, and, later, when we had a baby, an infant armchair by bending laminated wood into the required shapes, which Barbie upholstered. I found woodwork very therapeutic and took up the hobby again later in life.

You must forgive me for skipping around, as so many things were happening. An important event occurred after the fourth term there, or the second Christmas holidays, because our Headmaster left for a better post in Worksop. We then learned that the Headmistress of the Girls' school was to become the overall Head and that the schools were to be united into one. She was noted for her interest in 'Flower craft' and 'Modern Dance', which hardly inspired our side of the school. Our Art teacher was appointed as Deputy Head, which was another appointment which hardly had us jumping for joy either. He was a lovely man nearing retirement, but very mild and not the disciplinarian we normally would expect the Deputy to be.

This was to manifest itself very soon, for when we returned for their second term of office we were confronted with an eight day timetable. Apparently there wasn't room for the girls 'Flower craft' on a five day timetable. One can imagine the confusion it caused with the pupils. Whenever they needed to remember gym kit, things for woodwork or metalwork, domestic science, or even their English books, they didn't know whether it was day one, three or seven, all being on a different day every week from the previous eight day period. Before my ten year stint at the school was ended we had progressed to a sixteen day timetable and eventually to cap it all, a thirty-two day timetable.

I must tell you about the two occurrences which happened as a consequence. On the first day of the term when the thirty-two day timetable was to be introduced, we all turned up in the morning to find that the timetable had not been completed. As usual, it was left to us on the P.E. staff to look after the whole school, with help from some of the other members of staff. Some pupils were in the gym, but most were on the playing fields. I often wonder what we would have done had it not been fine weather.

The library was taken over by the timetabling squad, who organised a table for each of the days, while subjects, rooms and staff were all colour-coded on strips of paper. Apparently all went well for a while, but it was getting hot and stuffy. The library backed onto the gymnasium side of the building and had a convenient door leading out to the back, so one member of staff decided to let in some fresh air. That would have been fine, but it was extremely windy outside and of course as soon as she opened the door, all the little pieces of colour-coded paper flew in every direction.

Guess what? The P.E. staff were asked to look after the whole school again on the following day.

The T.E.S. (*Times Educational Supplement*) and the *Teachers' World* were delivered to each staff room every week. In the T.W., there was always an article called 'Worry of the week' where one was invited to send in one's particular worry. The chosen entrant got a cheque for £5, which was quite a lot of money in those days. I decided to write in with our worry of the week and the complications of a thirty-two day timetable. I was careful to say 'Pity the P.E. teachers who could hardly reprimand pupils if they forgot their kit.'

When the T.W. was published the following week, there was my article for all to see. Someone, not me, also left it open on the Headmistresses desk. Because it was confidential, no names were mentioned, which prompted a great discussion amongst the staff as to who might have written it, but no one suspected that it was little me. I had obviously thrown them off the scent by my remarks, and anyhow I think a lot of them thought the P.E. department's members were not intellectual enough to write such a letter.

It didn't bother my conscience for long when other members of staff were suspected because the two chief male suspects, still my friends to this day, both left to get good headships at other schools at the end of the term. Maybe my article had helped them to get a good reference.

The nearest tennis clubs were in Sheffield, and Barbie had played against them when playing for Doncaster Ladies. For various reasons we joined the Steel Peech and Tozer Tennis club. It was a works club, and less snooty than some of the others. It was also where Ernie and I had played a few rounds of golf. Of course Barbie got into their first team straight away, and I soon progressed from the third to the second team. We didn't know then that we were to visit her partner in Abu Dhabi later, on our round the world trip.

One of my colleagues on the staff had played for the England Schoolboys at football and was currently playing for the 'Kiveton Wireworks' team in a nearby village. He suggested I should go for a trial, which I did and was soon a regular player with them.

I had told them that I was a centre forward, but had actually never played in that position either at school or in college. I had always played defence, but it was to be an inspired choice. To say it was a successful move was an understatement. This is in no way boasting because I didn't ever regard myself as a skilful ballplayer. I wasn't even a sprinter, but I had two attributes. I was very quick off the mark, and I could shoot. I guess positional sense came into it too and a good squad around me who played to those attributes.

There were not many weeks when the local papers did not say 'Pidcock scores again' or 'Another Hat-trick for Pidcock.' I also scored a double hat-trick once against a weaker team to add to my tally. Barbie relates that once when she was watching me play and as I was running through with the ball, an opposition spectator next to her shouted 'Kill the bugger!' She turned to him and said 'Excuse me sir, but that is my husband that you are shouting about'

There is always a sting in the tail though. We had an active social life, entertaining and going to other friends' dinner parties. We were particularly good friends with one couple, the male partner of whom played for Dinninton Miners Welfare F.C. My night school students of course were the backbone of that team and eventually, having tried for many years, they persuaded me to leave the Wireworks and join their team. This had two downsides. Unbeknown to me, this friend was the one

I replaced – hence the end of a beautiful friendship, because they never spoke to us again. The second downside was that this was a different team with a different philosophy. I just didn't fit into their style of play and I hardly scored any goals at all. I think the pertinent phrase is 'horses for courses' and I now understand all too well when expensive premier league transfers don't work out.

NICKY IS BORN

During the last term of 1956 Barbie told me that she had fainted at school. The Headmaster sent the secretary to the pub next door for a brandy for her. The rest of the staff, who were all more elderly, said that if it had been them he would have got out the bottle of sal volatile. We were aware that Barbie was late with her period, so we went to see the doctor who confirmed that she was pregnant. We were obviously delighted, in spite of the fact that we were using the 'rhythm' method, and had not really planned it. If that does not sound very flattering for Nikky and Ros, it shouldn't upset them. We were casual with sex, and though we were aware of our financial state, we never used contraceptives after a brief spell before rejecting their use, so we took the attitude that if God wished us to have a child then we would welcome it with open arms because it would be heaven sent. It always makes me smile when I hear friends talk of 'trying for a baby'. Trying was never a hardship to us.

With our background we were naturally frugally minded, or careful with our money, so we were not far from where we wanted to be financially, and our respective families were equally delighted. We began to buy whatever we might need when the baby was born. In those days, no one knew the sex of the baby before it was born so we had both boys and girls names lined up, and neither of us minded which sex it would be.

One thing became very obvious. A motorcycle was no good for three. We hadn't sufficient funds to buy a car so I looked for a cheap option which was a sidecar. I answered an advert in the paper and rode down to Birmingham to purchase it. It was from a garage, so the mechanic was able to fit it for me and said driving was far easier than riding solo, so I set off back home, having no experience with a sidecar attached at all.

I hadn't gone very far when I began to veer to the middle of the road going round a left-hand curve. I leaned over as I had been used to doing and nothing happened. 'Oh dear' When I saw traffic coming towards me I said a prayer and more by accident than design pushed the right handlebar. I had just learned a lesson. All one had to do on a combo was touch the correct handlebar with as much as a little finger and the bike responded like a car. One didn't have to lean at all. The sidecar was never to be a success though because Barbie never felt comfortable in it.

Our Headmistress did not particularly like taking morning assemblies and had devised a routine where the staff took it in turn to take three of the five assemblies each week. My turn came around eventually, but I was not destined to take all three. During the last one I was halfway through the assembly when the headmistress came onto the stage. She quietly asked me to go to the secretary's office, and then took over.

I was more than a little anxious. This was highly unusual and I didn't know what to expect. When I got there I was told that Barbie had started to haemorrhage and had been rushed to the Jessop's Maternity Hospital in Sheffield and that I was excused from school and could go to be with her.

Apparently Barbie had been able to get the attention of a neighbour who had called an ambulance. Barbie was tucked up in bed when I arrived at the hospital and the doctor told me that they would keep her stable as long as they could since the baby would be premature, and then they would perform a caesarean if and when necessary.

Barbie also told me that the doctor had said that he estimated the baby would be about five pounds. It is indicative of how my mind worked that I immediately thought that, being the middle of the month, we hadn't got sufficient cash until payday at the end of the month. It was much, much later when I realised that he was talking in lb's and not £'s! Gosh, what a relief.

Travelling home that night was a typical example of the mind driving on automatic. I feel sure that I obeyed the Highway Code, but when I arrived home I could not remember turning one corner, stopping at any lights or indeed being aware of any other traffic on the road at all. I had, however, arrived home safely. I was not going to get away with it without a penalty however when a similar situation occurred later on in life.

When I arrived at the hospital after school on the following day I found Barbie quite distraught. The operation had been performed that morning and she said that she hadn't seen the baby yet, except that she knew it was a girl and that the priest had been to christen her Nicola Barbara and she was in the intensive care nursery. A nurse then asked me if I would like her to take me to see our little girl, and so off we went, leaving an even more worried Barbie.

For reasons of hygiene I couldn't go into the intensive care nursery, but I looked through the windows and I saw our wonderful baby for the first time. She looked really gorgeous with a lovely round head and with a deep tan as if she had been sunbathing. I went back and told Barbie how lovely she looked, but I don't think she was entirely pacified.

Later she admitted that, because she hadn't been able to actually see her, she had thought that the baby must in some way be deformed. Only three days later, when they finally took Nikky in to Barbie, was she convinced that she had, after all, given birth to a perfectly formed and beautiful baby. Then the nurse said 'Thank goodness she has got over that jaundiced stage'. The suntan, about which I had waxed lyrical, had really been jaundice. The beautiful round head was also an obvious feature of caesarean births.

When they were both sufficiently well, I took them home in the sidecar. 'That is the last time I ever want to take my baby in that thing' said Barbie on arrival home, and I don't think she ever got into the sidecar again. She had not enjoyed the ride one little bit. I hadn't imagined how bumpy and uncomfortable it must have been for her. How wonderful though to be home with our little girl and start life as a real family. Life could not get any better.

I had to do something quickly about transport. We didn't want to put all our savings into a new car, and then we saw the adverts for the new Bubble Cars out from Germany. These seemed to answer all the questions. They were far cheaper than conventional cars, they were economical and they were weatherproof, so off I went to Worksop to have a look.

I saw a very good salesman, but I must say that he was preaching to the already converted, because I decided there and then to buy one. The clinch came when he said that I could drive it without L-plates, including carrying passengers, on my present license. 'How is that possible?' I asked, thinking that it was a car. He then explained that there was a little bar which could be inserted to block off the reverse gear, hence it could be driven as a 'three wheeler without means of reverse'. He also gave me a fair price in part exchange. I decided on the obvious choice of the Heinkel, because the driver and passenger sat side by side in the front, and the bench seat at the back was ideally designed for the carrycot. The alternative, the Mescherschmit, had seats one behind the other with no provisions for a carrycot or any other passenger.

It was one of the first Bubble Cars sold in the district, and not only caused a stir in the village, but at school as well. As with most things, the novelty soon wore off, and we were no longer the centre of attraction when they became more common. We really enjoyed every bit of our time with XNN 211, and it answered all our questions for two years. Oh how I wished I had it now – it would be worth a fortune on the antiques market.

Our super little Heinkel

I drove it around for a long time before I took a driving test, but the inconvenience of not being able to reverse eventually persuaded me that it was time to sit the test for a full licence. The decision was made after I was following the bus taking the school football team on an away fixture. The bus stopped and started to reverse until the pupils on the back seat screamed at the driver to stop because I was right behind him. The driver couldn't see my little car.

I finally condescended to take the test and duly turned up at the examination centre, and after the examiner had given me the theory part of the test we walked out to the car.

'Is this it?' he said.

'Yes' I replied.

'Where are the L-plates?'

'Inside the car, I was a bit late and didn't have time to put them on.'

'Who came with you?'

'No one, I came on my own.'

By this time I could see that he was not very pleased. He must have been really peeved that I had been able to drive a virtual car with only a motorcycle licence, but yet stay within the law. I fixed on the L-plates and began to realise as we sat inside, that I ought to have given this a bit more thought and preparation. I then made an exaggerated show of taking out the bar governing the reverse and we proceeded with the test.

I'm quite sure that I handled it like a veteran, after all, I had been driving it for the best part of a year, but I was equally sure that he wasn't going to pass me. Sure enough he found some flimsy excuse to say 'Sorry.' It only meant that I had the inconvenience of having to go through the process of another test, which I passed this time. I had learned another important lesson. Not only is preparation very necessary in teaching, it is also equally so in other aspects of life.

Ernest asked me to be his best man. He was finally settling down and marrying Wendy. It was a lovely day and a lovely wedding, and it was also without 'Top Hat and Tails'. We still remembered our working class roots, and money was too precious to waste on show. It meant that we saw a lot more of each other, for Killamarsh was not far away, just south of Sheffield.

Ernie had a different philosophy about cars. He was into second hand bangers and I enjoyed a couple of his experiences with them. He told me about the time when he went to get into his car when leaving school. He opened the

Barbie and cat outside the front door at Ivy House

door and stepped onto the running board, present on all earlier cars, in order to get inside, but this one was very rusty and it promptly fell off. He said he was so embarrassed he simply jumped into the car and drove off as if it wasn't his! We had a good laugh about it.

On another occasion, we were driving in different cars to the same function. Barbie and I were in our Heinkel and Ernie and Wendy were following behind. I was slowing down for a left turn when Barbie cried 'Look out Ken!' I looked to where she was pointing and saw a wheel rolling along and overtaking us. We both stopped, and when we had stopped laughing we discovered that Ernie's rear offside wheel had somehow come adrift to wander along on its own.

On yet another occasion they had come over for dinner when there was a knock at the door. 'Is this your car sir?' said Bobby Cannings, the local policeman from up the street. When Ernie said that it was his, Bobby Cannings told him that he had no off sidelights on. 'Oh, sorry' said Ernie, who promptly jumped up, went outside and proceeded to turn the 'frogs eye' sidelight through 360 degrees. 'It's a bit temperamental' said Ernie as the light came back on. 'Yes, well you'd better get it fixed before you come again' said Bobby Cannings, hiding a smile as he walked off. Oh for the old time village copper.

During the first four years in Dinnington we managed to take four school holidays abroad. This was made easy by a company called Gentours who specialised in organising school trips. It was a means by which we could give the schoolchildren a treat, and have a family holiday on the cheap. It wasn't difficult to recruit up to twenty-five schoolchildren each summer, and it was indicative of the times that we took a mixture of boys and girls from 1st up to 4th year pupils. They all turned out to be wonderful holidays for all concerned.

We saw other squads from other schools walking along in crocodiles, all well regimented, but we adopted a different, more relaxed, attitude. It is a mark of the respect that they held for both Barbie, yes especially Barbie, and I, that we never had one incident during any of our holidays in Ghent, Blankenburg, St Malo or Skerries. No quarrels, fights, cheekiness or misbehaviour of any kind. We had a happy, joining-in-together atmosphere the whole while. When we took Nikky with us to St Malo, the older girls did their best to 'mother' her too.

It was on our first school holiday when we were all on the beach and heard a French mother calling her for child. 'Nicola, Ni-co-la' she called, and it sounded so lovely that we decided, if or when we had a baby girl, we would call her Nicola. We had been very restricted in our choice of names, because Barbie had always said that she did not want a name that reminded her of any of the children that she had taught. That narrowed the choice down somewhat dramatically.

We often went to visit our parents, but mine in particular as we could always stay overnight at Ivy House. There was so much space, with the lawns and the gardens, and then there was the added bonus of the fruit and vegetables in season. Though there was only Daisy living at home now, mum was always baking tarts and buns and making mouth-watering, fresh bread. How could we forget what we called flapjacks, which were rolled out dough like large naan bread? These, straight from the oven, oozing with butter, were to die for.

One day mum put her hands on Barbie's waist and said 'Are you sure this isn't fat with feet on?' That was the first indication that Barbie was pregnant again. Having been a nurse and a midwife, mum was always the first to know when someone was pregnant. None of us ever knew her to be wrong about guessing the sex either.

Rosalind Carol was born on Friday 13 March 1959. It might sound unlucky to some but to us it was and still is one of the two luckiest days of our married life. Unlike Nikky who wanted to come before her time, Ros was more reluctant and overstayed her welcome. Barbie had once again to go into Jessops, to be induced I guess. Like Nikky though, she had to be delivered by caesarean section because she would have been another placenta previa. That occurs when the placenta is in front of the baby and would have to be delivered first, and hence cause complications.

When I went to see them both, because this time they were not kept apart, Barbie began to be so apologetic. She assumed that I would have wanted a boy. I assured her that if Ros turned out to be only half as good as Nikky, then I would be happy. I just wanted another healthy baby and the sex didn't matter. We were blessed with two wonderful children and the gender of either was of no importance. It is sad that some people yearn for a specific sex, for how could one be disappointed in a child created between husband and wife? Nikky and Ros have both had their adventures, but they are still two wonderful people. We must have got something right in their upbringing.

The Bubble Car was very close to the ground, and this led to quite a surreal experience. I had gone to collect Barbie from night school, so it was after 9 p.m. and quite dark. It also became quite foggy, but that was the surreal part, because we were driving along under the fog, which was forming a blanket about 3 feet above the ground. We had perfect visibility in our bubble car, in fact it was enhanced, because the headlights were reflecting down from the blanket of fog, making it extra bright. Had I opened the roof and put my head out, it would have been in the fog, and in a conventional car I would not have been able to see very far. It was possible to drive with my head out of the roof, by the way, because I had done this in the daylight for fun. (Please don't tell the police!)

The Bubble Car was perfect for a while, but as soon as Ros was crawling it didn't really fit the bill. We embarked on a number of second hand cars. The father of one of the girls who went on the holidays with us owned a garage and because of that I think I got reasonable deals from him.

The first was a Vauxhall Victor Estate. I hadn't had it long, but one evening after school I left the gym to get my car, but it wasn't there! My first thought was that someone on the staff was playing silly B's, so I went back into the staff room to confront the few who were still around but, eventually, I had to accept that they knew nothing about it. I had to phone the police to report it stolen. When I arrived home I told Barbie not to mind as all the police in England would now be looking for it. That was a laugh, even if I did believe it at the time. It was found abandoned in a pub car park near Rotherham two weeks later.

Isn't it strange how, after having something stolen, one changes one's mind about it? We used to love the car, but now we just felt uncomfortable in it, and I hated driving it, so I exchanged it for a Hillman. This didn't last long either and we decided to have new cars after that and exchanged that for a brand new Mini Minor, only recently introduced onto the market.

It was time that Barbie learned how to drive, so I set about letting her get behind the wheel as often as possible. When I thought she was ready we duly applied for a test. What a difference it was from my driving test. I have no doubt that Barbie knew the highway code from back to front, but when they had gone a little way on the driving section they had to stop at traffic lights. Unbeknown to Barbie the engine had stalled, so when the lights turned green she put her foot down on the accelerator and let out the clutch and of course nothing happened. Without more ado the test instructor put his hand on Barbie's knee and said 'I would start the engine if I were you my dear.' They continued for a while until he told her to head back to the office. She had completed the test and she had passed! Well she was a very attractive young lady, and it was during the era of the miniskirts.

CROWGATE AND COMPREHENSION!

In 1960, with the children both mobile, the cottage was becoming just a little too small. We had not been actively looking for a move, but one day Barbie came home from school with the news that Crammie was selling her house and moving. Miss Crampton was an elderly teacher at the primary school who was notorious for keeping pets, especially dogs. She lived in a large, stone-built semi, adjoining Bobby Cannings. It was high off the road and had steps leading up to the front door. It had a good sized garden both to the side and to the back which was largely taken up with dog pens and nettles. There were three bedrooms and a bathroom upstairs and two very large rooms and a toilet downstairs, with a hallway to the front door. The kitchen was the first of the three outhouses adjoining the lounge but there was a door leading to it from inside. Each of her dogs had its own bedroom!

We didn't take long to make up our mind. The building was solid and we didn't even go upstairs to look at the bedrooms. We guessed what it would be like from the state of the downstairs. We knew that we would have to completely redecorate throughout.

I went up to see her later that night and offered her the asking price of £1,300 which was accepted. I doubt if we needed to have been so quick though because most people would have been put off by the doggy rooms.

Up to that time we had never had a bank account because we had taken the option of being paid in cash at the end of each month. We had now to open an account in order to obtain a mortgage which was never a problem in those days. We had to agree to have our salary paid into the bank too, which was a relief.

The very last month before we opened an account at the bank, I was paid cash, as usual, and stuffed the cash in my shorts pocket. Without giving it a thought, because anything discarded by me went straight into the laundry basket, Barbie put them in the washer. 'Panic stations' was the best way to describe it. I remember Nikky being quite intrigued at the line across the front of the fireplace with banknotes pegged out from one end to the other. Fortunately we somehow managed to save them all.

We organised the removal ourselves to save money but had the help of one of my night school men who owned a van. He also did a bit of plastering on the side, so after the whole house had been fumigated and washed down to get rid of the doggie smells, we set him on replastering most of the house.

We all learned how to do D.I.Y. jobs because most of us could never afford to employ professionals and I continued in this vein even when I could afford to employ help. Barbie and I were brought up to be frugal and we remained frugal all our lives. This does not mean that we didn't have a good time or lacked luxuries in any way, but we could never be accused of wasting money. I can honestly say, too, that I was never the last to buy a round, but usually the first, so we could never be accused of being mean, we just hated waste. I think most of us who had grown up during the war were the same. When the time came to plaster the kitchen, I had learned enough to be able to tackle it myself. I can't say that I did it as well as my night school pal would have done it though. It wasn't quite as easy as it had looked.

Among all the other activities we had to do, I began to paint and decorate the house. I was always proud to challenge anyone to find the joins in the wallpaper. We fitted the curtains which Barbie made and I hung and covered the floors in carpets or linoleum. Two of the wooden windows were starting to rot, so I simply took out the frames and bought new ones to our design and plastered round to finish them off.

I started outside to dig the garden at the back which I planted with potatoes. I had been told that this was the best way to get rid of nettle roots. I left the side garden because I planned to make a driveway up to the back.

Again my night school pal came to the rescue – he was getting tax-free pay I suppose, but I didn't bother about that – and we used his van to transport two huge stone gateposts and a load of flat stones from a stone quarry with which to make the driveway. The only professional I had to hire was the farmer with his digger with which he dug out the sloping driveway for me. The stones from the wall that was removed on the roadside were used to build the sloping walls at the sides of the drive, which I made to look like a rockery.

Every spare daylight hour was taken up with this work, but when one is working for oneself it doesn't seem like work but truly a labour of love. It made it all the more pleasant to relax when it got dark with the satisfaction of work well done. Nikky watched me for a while one Saturday morning and then went indoors and said 'Mummy, daddy is still doing his jigsaw' I guess it was a jigsaw too as all the crazy paving had to fit together as neatly as possible.

If anyone was to ask us how we brought up our children, I wouldn't know how to answer. I do know that in my childhood we had to be regimented into doing all the necessary jobs, to avoid chaos. In the same way, we were so busy all the time at home that there was never any time to waste, or to stop and argue, so the children learned not to make a fuss out of necessity.

I think the main reason was the way we spoke to them, which was usually in a pleasant friendly voice. We hardly ever had to raise our voice or chastise them unless what they were doing was dangerous. We also spent time reading to them at bedtime and Barbie remembers little tears welling up in Nikky's eyes as I made up stories of the big bad witch.

Nikky and Ros on my completed 'jigsaw' drive

They often came to join us in bed on weekend mornings when they woke up early. I remember talking about all sorts of things and answering questions. We even discussed fractions which I made up for them. 'If I cut an apple in two, how big is each piece?' 'A half', 'What if I cut each of those halves in two, how big is each piece then?' 'Quarters' said Nikky. This was at four years old. No wonder she went on to get a maths degree. That was when a degree recognised you as one of the top 5%, rather than one of the top 80%. It puzzles me to hear everyone clamouring for a degree nowadays, when all that you can boast is that 'I am not one of the bottom 20%' I apologise to the graduates, because it isn't their fault, but the fault of the governments who downgraded the British degree. It is an insult to those who got a degree which put them in the top 5%, to say that now 80% are as intelligent as they were. One only has to ask employers to find what the worth of a degree is nowadays. I shall mention this when talking about American degrees later.

We never lied to the children and we never said anything to them that we didn't mean or threaten them without carrying out the threat if they didn't conform. Believe me under those circumstances you have to be very careful what you threaten, and because of this we hardly ever remember having to do so. Like the slipper in the corner of my gym, we never had to use it.

Life with Nikky and Ros was always fun and we were always playful with them. I didn't actively impose gymnastics onto them, but we often did handstands against the wall. They loved doing somersaults with me holding their hands through their legs, and they loved balancing in various positions while I lay on my back supporting them. I think we just acted naturally with them and made sure that they knew that we loved them. Most of all, we taught them that people other than themselves had always to be considered, and I tried to

Nikky practising somersaults

be scrupulously fair, and always treat them equally. No doubt Ros thought we favoured Nikky because of her academic ability, but I'm sure Nikky also thought we favoured Ros because of her athletic skills.

They responded by being exceptionally good children. It was rare in our day to hear children screaming and making a fuss in public. In our experience, when children are badly behaved it usually reflects on the parents. That doesn't mean that the parents are necessarily bad people. It just means that they don't educate their children to live in a society. I can only say that Barbie and I are, and have always been, justly proud of our children.

You will notice that I have avoided any use of the word 'KIDS' nor will I ever use this awful import from America. Just remember that if you stoop to referring to your children as kids, you are relegating yourself to being a GOAT. A kid is the offspring of a goat and nothing else. There used to be a saying 'give a dog a bad name, etc', but I'm sure that there are some of the children who do not deserve to be called little goats.

Yes, it is one of my pet hates, and one of the things I am passionate about, like the degrading of the English language by the modernists who accept anything if enough people say it. What rubbish. To me it will always be different **from** and compared **with**. To use the word 'to' in these cases, for us members of the old school, is, and always will be, just slovenly English.

What has happened to BBC English? This used to be the hallmark of correct speech. Why do foreigners always speak better English than we do? I cringe every morning when one of the weather reporters appears. Instead of 'Good Morning' it is anything ranging from 'Gid', 'Gird', 'Ged', 'Gerd', to 'Gyerd' and even 'gewd'. Of these, I could only find 'gird' in the dictionary and that meant to gird up your loins. I guess the word causes nightmares. I want to tell her to say Robin **Hood** lived in a **Wood** and that **should** be **good**. Four of these words have the same sounding vowel. Gird, rhyming with bird, is now universally used by the media presenters, and I have to endure '…to make you feel gird' repeatedly on my favourite programme several times an hour. It makes me cringe even more when the men say it. It certainly doesn't make them sound posh to me. It's very simple, because one only has to remember that there is no r in good. I blame their teachers who don't want them to sound northern, and hence they lose the u sound altogether, but one doesn't have to push the lower jaw forward and produce the northern u. Please don't start calling our northern hero Robin Hird. Actually it is very simple:

Step 1. Say the oooo sound.

Step 2. Now say gooood, accentuating the ooo sound.

Step 3. Now say the same but make the ooo sound as short as possible. Good, easy isn't it?

Remember - THERE IS NO R (OR, I, E OR W) IN THE WORD GOOD.

By now I had been rewarded once again for my industry at school by being awarded a grade II allowance, which helped the bank balance a bit further. A new P.E. teacher was appointed to help in the department of this growing school. Gordon was also a young teacher like myself and married with two children and was a big help, especially with the growing number of out-of-school activities which I had started.

I can't think of him without feeling somewhat guilty. I had completed the garden and drive and had set about building a garage out of manufactured stone blocks to try to keep it in character with the house. I built the shell, together with its castellated top with concrete balls interspersed, using up the spare concrete I had left over.

All my own work!

The roof was supported from the inside and hidden from the outside. I then dug out an inspection pit and put shuttering up around it. All I needed now was to concrete the floor and I needed help for that. Gordon agreed and we invited them over for the day when it was delivered.

I thought the shovelling of the concrete, delivered by the cubic yard, was easy enough, and the 'floating' of the floor relatively easy too. It did entail quite a bit of bending I must admit. Alas though, I don't think

Gordon was as work fit as I was, for although he was fine when they eventually left for home, he didn't turn up for school for a few days afterwards due to having a bad back. We became good friends in spite of this beginning.

I had successfully applied for the post of Youth Leader, which meant that I would have to give up my night school classes. The Youth Club was to be held on three evenings each week, but it did offer better remuneration. I put a great deal of effort into making it a success. I added a few more courses away at Woolley Hall, near Wakefield, to the ones I had attended on the 'modern' approach to P.E., and during the second year a lady assistant was appointed to help.

I don't understand the thinking of whoever makes these appointments. She was a good and enthusiastic teacher but she was not local but lived in a different catchment area. I was to experience later in life at Walworth that local leaders are far more effective in influencing children. The Youth Club was by no means a failure but I have to admit that we could have been a little more effective. Maybe I set my targets too high, but the members obviously enjoyed it.

Comprehensive schools were becoming fashionable and avidly pushed along by the Labour party. It was openly rumoured during the latter part of 1963 that ours was to follow suit, especially as we were in a mining village and thus in a Labour stronghold. It is strange to me that most teachers are left wing too. I can understand why other branches of the civil service were left wing, being union led, but teachers were supposed to be able to think for themselves; after all, they don't have to rely on a sympathetic Government for their wages and pensions structure like other civil servants. I realise that I was also a teacher, but I guess I always had a commercially-oriented mind. The country, like any business, cannot be run on a deficit.

With comprehensive schools, I wondered what was going to happen to the secondary modern prefects, games captains and house officials? Ten to one these will now come from the grammar-school types. What about the brightest of the secondary modern children? They are now going to feel backward by comparison. Imagine being in the eighth 'stream' or 'set'. So much for comprehension being for the benefit of the academically less able. I was against the principle from the start because I did not think that it would benefit any of my secondary modern boys.

Sure enough, at the beginning of 1964 all the staff received a letter saying that our school would be combined with the technical school next door to form a comprehensive school. All local children would attend instead of the grammar streams going to nearby grammar schools. Also, as it was going to be a new school, it would be advertised nationally, and so we were all invited to reapply for our own jobs.

Personally, I was not concerned about any local competition, but nationally, it was another matter. We all expected applications from the top universities for the plum jobs. On principle, all the heads of department therefore applied for posts elsewhere. It was a real worry to all those members of staff who lived in the area and didn't want to move, but as I have explained before, by the very nature of my subject, any change of school meant a change of location, for which I had always been prepared.

We drew a line across England from the Wash and deemed anywhere south of that would be too expensive for us to live there comfortably. It soon became evident that there wasn't much going north of the Wash, either, so we agreed that we would begin to look for posts overseas.

We saw a double post for a married couple in Kingston, Jamaica which looked ideal for us. We sent in our application and soon had a letter back inviting us for an interview. We thought that the interview was going very well too until he asked us if we had any questions. Barbie had been to the library doing a bit of research and remarked that unless we had accommodation provided for us in our contract, the salaries would hardly put us above the subsistence level. The cost of living was heavily influenced by the American presence and thus was very high.

The man who was interviewing us then said something very strange. He said 'Yes I understand, but as the man in charge of P.E. there would always be the receipts from the school cricket matches' I hope that I concealed my shock. Was I hearing correctly and was it being suggested that I should do something illegal or not? Either way I did not dare ask. We were still pondering over this for days afterwards, but I had made up my mind that unless there was a drastic change in the pay structure, we would not be going to Jamaica.

We didn't have to wait long. We got a letter in the post within a week, offering us a joint contract at the said rates. Things hadn't changed. However at the end of the letter was a 'p.s.'

If for any reason you are unable to accept this offer, would you be interested in a posting to The Bishop Stuart Teacher Training College, Mbarara, Uganda.' Initially it would be a two year contract with air travel provided. Housing with hard furniture was included on site and a more generous salary was offered. There would be a 20% topping up allowance paid into a UK bank as an incentive, and also, education would be provided free at a school of our choice, with free air travel for the children at Christmas, Easter and in the summer.

The education offer would not apply to us of course unless we stayed long enough for them to need secondary education, because there were good primary schools in Uganda for expatriates. Some of the commercial people did send young children back to boarding schools, but we never contemplated that. At that time we never even considered the possibility of a boarding education for our girls, primary or secondary. How times would change.

There was one request they made. Could we go within the month as the college was desperate for staff? This meant that we would not have time to attend the induction course, normally held at Farnham Castle, to explain to those new to Africa any monetary or political and social concerns. This was to become an important issue later but we didn't even know how important at that time.

Teaching had, up to now, been a stable occupation for us and at times we had thought that we would never need to move. Little did we envisage however, the number of moves that this initial one would precipitate.

PART THREE
Africa, here we come

I T DID NOT TAKE LONG FOR US TO MAKE UP OUR MIND TO GO. The obvious rise in salary, the apparent elevating of status to be lecturers at a T.T.C. and the additional perks attached were too tempting. The obvious downsides were being separated from our families and the sheer gamble of travelling into the unknown.

There was a lot to do now to prepare everything. New summer clothes for us all, and the small matter of our house. Our luck had not deserted us because the Woodwork master was eager to buy the house for £3300. It began to dawn on us that a guardian angel was guiding our life for us. We discovered we had a generous luggage allowance on the ship for all our soft furnishings etc., and it even included the car. We had recently exchanged the Mini for a V.W. Variant, which was a new model on the market, but that should not make its suitability for African conditions any more speculative than that of the Mini.

My siblings thought we were quite mad. They often told friends 'Our Ken has a good job, his own house and car, a lovely wife and two adorable children, and he is packing it all up and going off to live with them in Africa.' I am pleased to say that mum was more understanding, especially when I was going to a T.T.C. Neither of us knew though, at that time, how different it would be from a T.T.C. in the UK. Never mind, mum was happy for us.

Just before our scheduled departure, my dad was diagnosed as having duodenal ulcers and had to go into hospital. When we went to visit him he was very cheerful and told us not to forget to bring a banana back for him. He always had eyes that twinkled and I remember they were still twinkling as we left him in the hospital. I like to think that I have inherited that twinkle from him too, but was that twinkle going to land me in trouble?

We hired a reputable company to transport our goods. We bought two second-hand trunks and packed our special belongings and effects that we thought that we might need in Africa into them. The remainder of the larger items, together with the trunks, were packed into three huge wooden crates. These, together with the new car, were collected a few days before we travelled to ensure that they were on the same ship on

71

which we were to sail.

Our farewells to the family were, for them, quite emotional, but we just felt a sense of excitement to be starting on a new venture. It wasn't as if we were going to war or something and it was only for two years – we thought.

After quite a long and tiring journey to London Docks, we embarked on the S.S. *Uganda*. We didn't know this at the time of course, but this was to become the hospital ship in the war in the Falklands and, later still, it became an educational ship. We were to sail on the night tide so we had a few hours in which to explore the boat and find our bearings. We had been allotted two adjoining cabins on A Deck which certainly lived up to the title 1st Class.

The children had a separate restaurant for their dining and we were able to take them for dinner before we needed to prepare for ours. All I can say is that they were never unhappy with their meals. They had always enjoyed their food and had never developed any food fads, so it wasn't difficult to satisfy them. They were naturally quite tired after a day's travelling and all the excitement, and by the time we had dressed and were ready to go to dinner, they were comfortably tucked up and fast asleep.

No one had told us that the dress code on the first night was always informal, so when I turned up in D.J's (dinner jacket) we had to withstand the embarrassment of our ignorance at that first meal. We had been placed on the Purser's table to make matters worse, together with an ex-Mayor of Johannesburg and his wife. After the initial teasing they all turned out to be good company however and were to remain so throughout the voyage. I doubt though if Barbie and I ever got rid of the feeling of being from working class stock amongst the upper class.

The food was spectacular and was, and continued to be, fit for comparison with any top-class hotel. We began to save the menus because we doubted people would believe us without seeing the evidence of all the seven-course meals.

Barbie and I had also had a tiring day and we decided to go to bed rather than stay up to experience the ticker tape send off. I remember that we slept well and were awakened in the morning when the children came through to us.

I felt quite ill and asked Barbie if she would take them to breakfast because I felt a bit seasick. A few moments later I heard her laughter as she opened the curtains. We had apparently missed the tide and were still in dock and here was I feeling seasick. I felt that I had to get up, but I still didn't feel well and hardly touched breakfast. We were now able to watch the send off after all, and so started our adventure.

The crew were all from Goa and dressed immaculately. On the first morning, after breakfast, Nikky told us that the Captain had been in to run their bath water. The Captain was quite amused as we shared the thought with him when it was our turn to have dinner with him at the Captain's table.

Playing shuffleboard on the S.S. Uganda

That first day was far too short because there was so much to see, explore and do. We saw where it was possible to play shuffle-board, table tennis and deck quoits, and of course as soon as we saw the pool we had to go and fetch our swimming gear, complete with life belts for the girls. My hours in the swimming baths at college and the certificates I gained certainly came in useful.

Ros was very tentative at first, but with us beside her and Nikky making good progress, we mixed play with instruction. By the end of the first week Nikky wanted to try without the life belt, and Ros, spurred on by this was not far behind. In no time at all they were jumping in and swimming across unaided, which made life very easy for us and a lot of fun. During the second day, my queasiness suddenly disappeared and we settled down to enjoy the best holiday of our lives to date.

For two days we sailed through the Thames and the Channel and were fascinated by the sights of the white cliffs etc. about which we had read so much, but after we had left the Channel we had a few days at sea when all we saw were seagulls.

We got into the routine of playing all the games we could, but we were careful about our exposure to the sun. Consequently we made the transition to a tan without getting burned. It was good, too, that Barbie could match me at in all the games, as she had at tennis previously, for it had taken me quite a while to catch up with her skill in that department. Our competitiveness seemed to rub off on the girls too because they too enjoyed some ding-dong battles.

The whole ship began to get excited. One could feel it running through the veins because we were nearing Gibraltar, our first port of call. How thrilling to catch the first sight of the 'Rock' and I could now explain why we couldn't see the 'Pillar' at the other side. I had seen the 'Rock' before, when sailing to Malta, but Barbie and the girls hadn't, and even for me it was different from viewing it from a troopship.

Suddenly there were dozens of other ships of all types and sizes either passing though the straights, turning into the port as we were, or even anchored offshore to send their boats in as tenders or to trade. We then watched what seemed to be tiny, midget-sized tugboats manoeuvre us gently into the berth allotted to us. We were then able to disembark in order to explore this small enclave of British territory which has played such an important part in the UK's past history.

Main Street, Gibraltar, is just like any other street in a provincial town, but the great attraction was its tax-free status for anyone wanting to buy goods there. We went up the Rock on a lift and walked among the Barbary apes which live there and appear quite tame. At that time they were confined to the Rock and had not ventured down into the suburbs to present a nuisance to the residents, which they apparently do now.

It was on a later visit when we actually went on a tour of the caves and tunnels dug into the Rock. There were purported to be three miles of tunnels in total, most of which is controlled by the army. Presumably it contains ammunition dumps and defensive weaponry, and is thus prohibited to the public. There was still sufficient tunnelling left to satisfy the tourists, with lookout posts, recorded information and simulated wartime experiences interspersed along its length.

It was a tiring day walking around Gibraltar and it was quite a relief to board ship again. We now had another opportunity to watch those amazing little tugs do their work and manoeuvre us back into the open channel. Leaving the port we had a much closer look at the Rock and we could actually see the open ends of the tunnels high up where the defences were positioned.

Soon we were back in the open sea and nothing to see until we reached our next port of call. Naples was a shorter stop and we didn't bother to go ashore, but we regretted it afterwards because it is such a beautiful city. It was also a pity that we passed between Italy and Sicily during the night, so we saw nothing but the 'Swan ink blue' Mediterranean until we approached our next port of call at Port Said.

This was a completely different experience. Long before we docked we were surrounded by dozens of small boats, some of which were piled high with goods to sell. They sold anything from small purses to raffia shopping bags and camel stools. Soon there were ropes from deck to the boats with goods on one end and a purse for the money on the other end. It all worked like clockwork without a hitch, with bargaining shouted from both ends. I guess if one transaction had gone wrong it would have ended the whole procedure, so it was in everyone's interest to be honest.

While this was going on, small boys in the other boats invited the passengers to throw pennies into the water which they immediately dived for and retrieved. This was an indication of how clear the water was and how skilled they were at swimming, for I am sure that they didn't lose any. They always came up with teeth gleaming and holding high their prize.

This then was our first glimpse of Africa, and what a start. We were now torn between the activities and games that we were used to and the sightseeing of what was happening on shore, for now we were going through the Suez Canal and there was always something to see. We were made aware of the site of the Anzac Memorial, commemorating the Australian and New Zealand cavalry during the First World War, which had been destroyed during the 1956 riots. Then there were the camels and the distant pyramids to spot through the binoculars. These were in constant use now and passed from one to the other between the four of us because Nikky and Ros were equally keen to see all the new sights.

When we docked at Cairo it was a repeat performance of Port Said and by now the new travellers like us became braver. We actually bought a colourful shopping bag for each of the girls and a camel stool for ourselves. We were scheduled to stay overnight here, but again we did not venture ashore. There were optional trips to the pyramids and the Cairo Museum, but I think it was a mixture of not having the right currency and not a little fear of the unknown which held us back. This was our first experience of Africa and we had children with us, so no apologies for our apprehension. Of course we were to regret not taking the opportunity then because, as so often happens, the opportunity never happened again.

Only one more stop to go before Mombasa. Now it really was sinking in that we were nearly there and the anticipation was getting to us all. The competitions were starting in earnest too, and of course we entered everything. It was all eyes on the notice boards to see when and against whom we were playing. Once again there wasn't anything to see as we passed down the Red Sea except water and the occasional liner or fishing vessel. There were no distractions from the competitions and enjoying the sun and life aboard a liner. The 'Captain' still continued to run Nikky's bath and make the beds daily and the food and service was impeccable.

Notices were posted for the impending Children's Fancy Dress Ball. We wracked our brains for inspiration and soon found out that all the seasoned travellers had brought their fancy dresses along with them in their luggage, 'Not fair', we thought, but hey ho, let's get on with it. We dressed Ros up as Father Christmas and Nikky as a pirate and they looked OK. One of our friend's girls won, however, appearing as '9 carat gold', dressed in a gold costume and bedecked with golden trinkets and nine fresh carrots strung round her belt. A deserved winner, truly, but all the children were given a present so none of them felt disappointed. Our Fancy Dress Ball was to take place after the next stop in Aden and we had no idea what we were going to do.

Aden, what can we say? Very dry and arid, like the atmosphere. I had no local currency but our new-found friend and his wife and three daughters pressed us to go ashore with them. He said I could always pay him back at the bar later.

It was something quite new, and something we had to get used to, walking where we 'whites' were in an obvious minority. I was grateful for the experience and being with someone familiar to that situation. It felt as though I needed to be protective of my children rather than any personal apprehension.

We shall always remember stopping at an outside café for refreshments, but we remembered it not for what we had to drink. When the waiter brought back Fred's change on a plate, with hardly a glance he said 'Please go back and bring me the correct amount.' Our reaction was quiet horror, as it appeared to us to be so rude. However, with no more ado the waiter turned round and came back later with the correct amount. 'They always try it on with tourists' Fred said, and I'm sure I saw a glint in the waiter's eye, thinking 'Pity, I didn't get away with that one.' We were on the start of a learning curve.

It was the semifinals of the men's deck quoits and to say I was surprised is an understatement. The man standing at the other side of the net had artificial legs. I began a series of throwing it straight to him, backwards and forwards, but he wasn't returning them straight to me and I soon found myself four down. It was no good feeling sorry for him and being beaten, and I really had to pull out all the stops from then on. I only just beat him in the end after a really good game and we then enjoyed a refreshing drink together.

We crossed the equator with all the ceremonies of King Neptune. A chair was erected with its back to the pool and 'victims' were sat in and daubed with buckets full of coloured foam and shaved with a huge cardboard cut-throat razor. They were then unceremoniously tipped backwards into the pool while another 'victim' was hauled up to be 'shaved'. The pool was soon deep in multicoloured foam and we all laughed and laughed.

The horse racing turned out to be a bit of a fiddle, or astuteness on the part of the Purser. It was a knock out competition amongst the ladies. They were seated, six in each heat, in front of a winder which had a string threaded round a spool and attached to a horse on wheels at the other side of the room. At the sound of a whistle they had to wind in their horse along the deck and the first horse to cross the line won. Odds were laid and serious bets were placed. Afterwards, someone told us that the Purser had a stop watch on the heats so it was no surprise when he ended up winning. Technically he had done nothing wrong, but we thought it was a bit sneaky. Although heavily backed, Barbie was beaten into second place by Sylvia, our friend and the mother of the three girls. She never stopped apologising to the friends we knew who had backed her to win.

We still had no idea what to do for the Fancy Dress and were thinking of not entering. On the morning bulletin, however, it was announced that Elizabeth Taylor and Richard Burton were being sued for 50 million dollars by the Film Studio. Bingo! I borrowed a cap and gown, brief case and a rolled up piece of paper. Barbie dressed in a sheet with all the gold we could find and borrow draped around her, and we went as the 50 million dollar law suit. We won too, more because of the topicality than anything else I guess.

I was surprised that we beat the team which came second. They were four young men bronzed all over and walking with a single canoe around their midriffs. They each had a placard on them. – No. 1 Skin – No. 2 Skin – No. 3 Skin, - No.? . All the adult prizes were in vouchers and I was pleased to find that all our winnings in the Fancy Dress and the other competitions paid our bar bill at the end of the trip.

Tomorrow, when we wake up, we should be entering Mombasa port, so we were planning to get up very early. I don't think any of us had slept very much. We raced through breakfast just in time to see the faithful little tug boats do their job, and in no time at all we saw men start to unload the cargo onto the docks. We had plenty of time to watch because we had already packed our travelling effects and had been given a specific time to disembark for the train.

I then heard someone ask for Mr. Pidcock. I turned and saw a ship's Officer who handed me an envelope and told me it was a telegram. In those days there was no ship-to-shore communications whilst at sea so it could have been sent at any time after Aden. It was not good news. My dad had died in hospital! There was nothing we could do as by that time the funeral had already taken place, but it made us very sad that we had not been there to grieve and comfort mum.

We said our goodbyes to our friends who were going to Geita Gold mine in Tanzania. They would stay aboard and disembark at Dar es Salaam. Other friends were travelling with us on the train to Kampala, the capital of Uganda. We were destined to meet many of these friends later on in life, either when they visited us or we visited them.

We then had another huge surprise. There were our crates being off-loaded with the name PIDCOCK on the sides, and then a larger crate with our name on it was lowered onto the docks, the front of the crate removed, and our car was wheeled out and pushed along, presumably to the goods train.

The station and train looked like any other station and train we had seen. They had been manufactured in the UK, so it should not have been a surprise. What was a surprise was when we were shown our compartment – we had one all to ourselves. It had four beds, two on each side, one above the other, which were folded back during the day into the seats.

By now it was time for lunch and we went down the corridor to the dining car to find our allotted places and were then treated to silver service of the highest standard. In those days East African Railways were second to none, probably including the Orient Express. This standard of service was new to the girls and was good for their education.

After all that had happened in the past few days the girls could hardly hide their excitement, especially as we started to move off, for no sooner had we left the station than we seemed to be out in the country among the banana trees and African dwellings. That was soon replaced with what we were to call the 'Bush'. Grassland and different species of trees we didn't recognise. We didn't see many animals because they didn't like the noise of the railways, but we were told that they wouldn't be far away and would be out there somewhere. It was still exciting to see vague shapes in the distance, half hidden, and guessing what they might be. Only the elephants we were sure of because of their size.

It took two days and two nights to reach Kampala. The train had to wind down the Rift Valley and sometimes on the tight bends we looked out of the window and the rear of the train looked to be going in the opposite direction. We also had to stop in Nairobi, but a train station is a train station, and this one was also an import from the UK.

It was different here though, for as soon as the train stopped, dozens of food vendors descended on the train selling all different kinds of food. There was a third class section of people who hadn't had access to the Dining Car, and they were looking for someone selling their type of tribal food before journeying on to Uganda. This was the only chance of hot food for them and for the rest of the two days they had to exist on what they could take with them.

It is remarkable how quickly one can adjust to situations. When we finally arrived in Kampala, we were met by a man from the Ministry and taken to the Imperial Hotel – at that time the best in Kampala, and later to have its name changed to The Grand Hotel, because of the connotation attached to the word Imperial.

It was no longer strange to be dealing with people of a different colour. The hotel certainly stood up to its name and the first class service continued. We were to be met in the morning by the Principal of Bishop Stuart T.T.C., hence we went to bed early. I was awake before the others and as I glanced down from the window, I was surprised to see six brand new 'Citroen ID 19' cars. At that time they were the top of the range car, all with OXFAM written on the top.

Should I have been surprised? I don't know, but it made me ponder on where a lot of donations had gone into providing them. Surely a less expensive car could have done the same tasks equally well? As I write this I hear that some executives of charities award themselves salaries of over £100,000. Probably the man wasn't a cynic who told me the easiest way to make money is to find a good cause and open a charity, then you can award yourself what salary you wish. This will surely make some people more selective about donating to the charities of their choice. I will have more to say about this when we get to Kano, in Nigeria. Meanwhile, the start of our adventure was certainly reaching its climax.

The Principal was a small man who certainly looked as if he had been in the sun a long time. He was obviously pleased to see us, as we were to meet him, and we had lots to talk about on the way down to Mbarara.

We were soon out of the city and now had a better close-up view of the plantations and shambas and small villages, mainly composed of mud huts with thatched roofs. Occasionally there would be a car parked outside one, and we even saw a new Mercedes by the side of one of the mud huts. We were to learn that the status symbol of a car was considered more important than that of a home for many of the Africans. One would be seen more in one's car than one would be seen at home.

We wondered why we began to slow down, and then we saw them. At each side of the road was a vertical concrete circle on which were printed the letters N and S in large letters. There was a broad white line painted across the road too. This was the equator which also divides Uganda in half. We had to wonder about the accuracy of this line across the road, but we were to believe it more before we left the country because an English University, doing a geological survey, had calculated that it was a number of yards out, and they took the trouble to move the whole of the structures that number of yards to their true positions.

We passed through the small town of Masaka then more scrub land until we passed a sign saying Mbarara where we turned left. We were now on a murram road, which is called laterite in other parts of the world. It is rock found in the tropics which has been weathered and broken down into a powder and its condition is dependant on the weather and the proportions of the various elements from which it is composed. It was prone to deep ruts in the rainy season, similar to a muddy lane, and we soon discovered it was very, very dusty in the dry season. We didn't find out about the corrugations until later.

Mbarara Main Street, 1964

BISHOP STUART T.T.C.

The large sign BISHOP STUART T.T.C. heralded our arrival. At the end of a long driveway we were greeted by the rest of the staff and treated to welcome refreshments after a short prayer thanking God for our safe arrival. We were then taken to our new home and to our surprise our crates were already outside which was a mark of efficiency entirely unexpected. Our car had to be released from customs, so we had to wait until the weekend to go up to Kampala to complete the paperwork and other formalities to enable us to collect it.

The bungalow was set in a fair sized garden and, we were to learn, was the standard design for most of the government quarters. It had a large living room, two bedrooms, a bathroom, toilet, a dining room and a kitchen. At the back was a concrete building where the houseboy was to live.

It was quite old but better than we had imagined. A new one was under construction and we were promised a change to that before the next term started. All the furniture was made from Mvule, a local hardwood, similar to but harder than mahogany, and was solid and heavy. The two armchairs and settee had separate cushions and I particularly liked the design of the arms which were flat and ideal on which to rest a cup or glass. They were going to be well used.

The floor also deserves a mention. I was to learn that they 'floated' the concrete so that the top mixture was strong, smooth and level. Then, when it dried, they poured on a mixture of paraffin and floor polish, let it dry, and the houseboy would then buff it until it shone like glass. It was to become a common sight to see houseboys skating around with their feet covered in sheepskin pads.

Carrying goods the African way. Economical, and it teaches balance

We didn't have to have a houseboy, but it was expected of us, because it was considered a major form of employment for the local people. In fact, we, like most government expatriates, had a cook/houseboy. Only the commercial expatriates had separate cooks and houseboys. They were paid for by the company and a lot more would be expected from them. Most of the commercial set had a shamba (Swahili word for compound or garden) boy to do the garden as well. There was always this divide between government and commercial. Our remuneration was better than in the UK but still it nowhere near matched that of the commercial personnel. Their houses came equipped with absolutely everything, so they needed to travel with only their clothes.

I get help to open the crates (Two of five)

We set about unpacking the crates and sorting out the house and it soon became to look like a home. The garden was in good shape too, thank goodness. Whoever had been in before had looked after it well.

On Saturday we were taken up to Kampala to collect the car and sign all the necessary papers at the customs department. What a difference that made. We were now free and independent, ready to start our new life and it was good that we still had to drive on the left.

We made sure to stop at the equator signs on the return journey and take photographs with Barbie straddling the line holding hands with one child in the northern and one in the southern hemisphere, plus many different combinations of the same. We did a bit more shopping at the Dukas (local stores) as we passed through Mbarara town on the way back to the college, and now we were stocked up and ready to start.

Sunday saw all the students arrive amid the great excitement that usually creates. It was especially so because we were new to them as they were obviously new to us. Every new face we saw was split by a beaming smile showing the rows of white teeth that they are famous for. It was an encouraging beginning to say the least.

Straddling the Equator

We took Nikky to the Mbarara Primary School which was of mixed race and where all the expatriate's children went. Unfortunately Ros wasn't old enough yet and had to stay with us, which wasn't entirely satisfactory for her, having to tag along with Barbie. We quickly had to buy a uniform for Nikky for the new school. We were quite surprised to discover that even the smallest of schools way out in the 'bush' would each have their distinctive uniform, which they would wear with obvious pride.

The college was run on very religious lines. I had an idea that we were the first members of staff who were not recruited from missionary sources. Daily prayers and services were the order of the day but we had both been confirmed into the C of E. so this posed no problems for us.

Teaching was a dream. The students were so keen and eager to learn that discipline was never a problem. What a difference the UK would be with the same attitude towards learning. We would also find that, without exception, the parents were equally keen and supportive.

As I write this I have just returned from church in England. The vicar, in her sermon, referred to the joy experienced by children in the UK on the first day of their holidays. Things were different in Africa where the reverse was true. The children there looked forward to school commencing, not ending, and I shall keep referring to the poor attitude towards education, prevalent in the UK. I have come to the conclusion that when one has had to pay for something, one values it all the more. Certainly it is true that if something is free it is less well appreciated.

One morning during the first week, after we had finished breakfast, we heard a knock at the door. I went and opened it and for a fleeting moment thought that no one was there. Then I glanced down and saw one of the older students on her knees with a message from the principal. 'Please stand up' I said, 'You need never be on your knees when you speak to us.'

I have to admit that the episode left me with more than a little disquiet. It certainly made me wonder if this was a one off or if this type of subservience was to be expected. As the newcomers, we never questioned this nor mentioned it to the rest of the staff. We were to learn that whites who had been in Africa a long time were more likely to feel superior. That could never be attributed to us, nor, indeed, to the majority of the new teachers who were also newcomers to Africa.

African friend with home-made toy

I do think that our informality was like a breath of fresh air to the students and I believe we were popular for it. I soon became the man to go to when any D.I.Y. job was needed, so I was often called upon to mend a toilet or a light switch.

The college had an old harmonium which Barbie played for assemblies and there had been a leak in the bellows for as long as could be remembered. I had a vested interest, therefore, in repairing that because Barbie's knees used to ache after having to pump twice as hard as was necessary to get a reasonable volume from it.

The college also had a 'demonstration' school which was a primary school in which our students could practice their teaching skills. The principal came up with the idea that Ros could go to this school because it would solve the problem for her and help the other pupils with their English. Like all bright ideas though, it didn't quite turn out like that.

Ros, in front of the demonstration class at Bishop Stuart T.T.C.

After the first day we asked her what she had done and she said that they had all learned a poem. We asked her to recite it, and she started 'Polla pu da kettal on.' This we didn't mind so much. At least we could work on the diction. On the second day, however, when she came home, she was obviously upset and told us that all the children were crowding around her to stroke her hair and touch her skin all the time. One couldn't blame the little Africans, for they had never been in contact with a young white girl with long, blonde, silky hair before, but we did think that Ros should have had a little more protection from the teacher.

The whole experience had obviously been a bit too much for Ros to handle. Off we went to see the Head Teacher at Mbarara Primary School who promised to take Ros during the next term as a special favour.

We didn't keep Eriasafu, our first houseboy, long. It must have been his first attempt at work and he could not speak any English. It might have worked had Barbie been home all day to show him what and what not to cook – he had boiled the lettuce for one dinner – and train him, but we were as new as he was and without much communication between us, we had to let him go. We were then extremely fortunate because a family were leaving and their houseboy came looking for work. He was called Rutiri, Tiri for short, and turned out to be absolutely Heaven sent. He had obviously had a very good Memsaab to teach him how to cook, and rather than having to teach him, I am sure that he could have taught us a lot about cooking.

Tiri's son carrying baby brother African style

Our houseboy's wife bathing the baby

As in all settlements where there was a significant expatriate population, there was a club. It was originally a club for expatriates, but with independence all the clubs became multinational. The club consisted of a large hall, with a committee room, ladies and gents side rooms and toilet facilities. Mbarara Club had a kidney shaped swimming pool with diving boards at one end, a tennis court and a nine holes golf course.

Tennis in Mbarara

Trophies in Uganda. A couple might be mine!

We applied for and became members right away. Even if we had not been keen, we would have joined for the sake of the children we were keen though and we began to spend a lot of spare time there. Nikky and Ros would have lived there if that had been possible, and soon became like little fish in the water along with all the other children. It wasn't long before they were asking me to teach them back dives from the sides, and it wasn't long before they were doing them on their own.

We soon made many friends, including an Indian Didar Sagoo who often took picnic parties on his boat from which we swam off-shore in Lake Victoria.

Preparing for a picnic on Didar Sagoo's boat

I would guess that we were the first members from the college to have joined in the club life, but we had no qualms about it as we knew we contributed a great deal to college life. We played tennis at weekends and I began to teach Barbie how to play golf. I later cut down some old golf clubs and started teaching the girls how to play as well, but we never felt that we neglected our duties towards the college. We were the first couple with their own children to teach at the college, and we had to share duties between the college and the needs of the children.

The 'chit' system was in operation at the club, which meant that we could sign for drinks and pay at the end of the month. What a good idea, we thought. At the end of the month though, when we got our bill, we were given a stack of 'chits' signed Ros Pidcock, with a few for Nikky Pidcock. We found that we had two very generous daughters. That, I'm afraid, stopped very quickly, and the stewards had instructions only to accept 'chits' from Barbie or me. The girls had to learn to budget from their pocket money or ask us to get them a drink.

The academic standard at the college was not particularly high. These students had been chosen from the students who had not got into a Senior Secondary School after their 11+ type examinations. In the S.S.S.s they would go on to take Cambridge School and Higher School Certificates, but Universal Primary Education had only just been introduced, hence teaching ability was considered more important in the selection of our students, rather than their academic achievement.

Up to the introduction of Universal Primary Education, parents would have had to pay for children's education and so it was not unusual to have over twenty year olds in the Primary Schools. That resulted in the situation where there were mature students who wanted to teach, but had not been selected for entry into a Senior Secondary School and who did in fact make good teachers. Those constituted the majority of the students whom we inherited.

I took the Maths and the little P.E. they needed, which was mainly games training. The Maths was most enjoyable because of their obvious enthusiasm, and it was a joy to see rows of eager smiling faces looking back intently. They were highly amused when I went on a cross country run with them. They were well accustomed to the altitude, as Lake Victoria was well over 4000 feet above sea level, hence all of Uganda had to be higher than that. I think I went up in their estimations though when I kept up with them. A number of them beat me easily on the run in of course, but nevertheless I was a middle-aged white man to them, and they knew that I couldn't have trained for months.

One day a group of students came to us with a bundle in a sack. They said that one of them had stepped on it in the banana plantation and they had killed it. They then proceeded to empty the sack onto my front lawn and out dropped a 5-feet-long puff adder. It is a good job that it was a puff adder too because it is one of the more lethargic of snakes. Had it been another species, that student might not have been able to jump out of the way quickly enough.

Students present us with a snake

Was I interested? Yes, I was, but what could I do with it? That wasn't a problem, they told us. One of them had a brother who worked in the Museum in Kampala and was a bit of a taxidermist. We were to learn that whatever the situation, there was always someone amongst them who 'had a brother.' He may have been no relation, but there was always a commercial aspect involved in the transaction.

The next time we saw it, it had been transformed into a cured snake skin which then decorated our wall. I feel sure that a commercial transaction had taken place, as I had expected, but it was only a few shillings to us and well worth it.

We were often invited home to meet parents, which usually meant a trek through the bush, often to a mud hut surrounded by banana trees and a garden. Most families in the Bush would be self-sufficient to some extent, and we usually returned with a hand of bananas or some sort of gift. We were always given a good welcome and it was lovely to feel so appreciated.

We visit a Student's home near Mbarara

During the summer holidays other expatriate children came from their various boarding schools in the UK, to join their parents. This added a change of scenery around the pool, and often resulted in the girls making new friends. These friends were to have quite an influence on their decision making when they were older.

We also made our first trip to the coast with friends. We called at the Kahawa Barracks near Nairobi which was an old Army station which had been converted into a school. There we met up with friends we had made on the S.S. *Uganda*. We then travelled to the coast on murrum roads. These needed to be graded regularly, for if they weren't graded they became corrugated.

Corrugation, which I mentioned previously, was an intriguing phenomenon, and it is difficult to explain how it happens. It is easy to imagine ruts being created along the road when it is wet. If you can now imagine corrugations appearing in a regular pattern across the road, at right angles to the ruts, similar to driving from the top to the bottom of a scrubbing board, then that is how it became after a long period without rain. It was quite an art to drive over such terrain. If one went too fast or too slow it was like driving over a scrubbing board, however if one went at the optimum speed for your car, you had a reasonably smooth ride. It must have been related to the strength of the shock absorbers on your particular vehicle. Our optimum speed turned out to be just under 50 m.p.h. which was a reasonable speed. The roads were not too busy, and at that speed we enjoyed a reasonably smooth ride.

We spent a night on the coast at a camp site called White Sands, but then we were awakened by baboons in the morning, and then we were troubled with them on top of the toilet roofs. The female members of the party did not appreciate baboons interfering with their toiletries, so we decided that it would be wise to move on to our real destination of Malindi. Yes, I was secretly glad about the decision too.

This beach at Malindi was paradise. It was protected by two reefs. Up to the first one it was safe to bathe from sharks. Some people said it was safe up to the second reef, but we didn't tempt providence. We had brought a tent from England with a

Man carrying fishing baskets. A typical scene.

living space and two bedrooms, which was perfectly pitched under the palm trees above the high water line.

A German couple had opened a small beach cafe and the girls soon became friends with their son and daughter of similar ages. They still remember the time when the slot machine kept paying out winnings after every penny gambled. That didn't last very long though.

I also went fishing, but this was deep sea fishing and only for men. Six of us hired a boat and the skipper took us right out to sea before we cast the lines overboard. We used live bait, but all that was prepared for us by the crew. The first one to get a 'bite' was helped into the chair in the stern and strapped in. The rest of us had to reel in our lines in order not to get them entangled.

This was real sports fishing, for the fish didn't just give up, but fought to the last breath, initially going straight down, and then zigzagging in different directions. It was a good job therefore that the other lines had been reeled in, and it was really backbreaking work that could take up to half an hour to reel in each one. I am pleased to say that I was one of the lucky ones to experience this; in fact we arranged it so that we each of us had a chance. When we returned we had caught five sailfish and a Barracuda. The total weight was 374 lbs.

Inspecting the catch of Sailfish. Notice Nikky exposing the dorsal fin, whereby it gets its name 'sailfish'

The best was to come. Custom had it that the skipper then sold them on to the market and he told us that there was more than enough to pay for the boat, so we had just had a whole afternoon's sports fishing free.

For Nikky and Ros, the highlight of the holiday must have been their introduction to dabchicks. These were like surfboards with a sail, a jib, and a centreboard. Several of the families had come equipped with them, including one of the families from Victoria Nile. All the children naturally congregated together, and they were very generous in sharing.

Sailing a dabchick was meant to be a single handed affair, hence it was quite a skilful art to sail one. One had to understand how to use the wind and sails to move and change direction, and how to use the centreboard. It was also possible for two children to sail on one at the same time, so in no time the competent ones were soon teaching the newcomers, and I do remember that both Nikky and Ros were able to sail one on their own by the end of the holiday. We understood that they all had to be built by the owners, either from raw material or from a kit, and it was our vowed intention to purchase a kit for ourselves in the future. Unfortunately, we were never in a situation where we had either the time or conditions to do so.

The children loved the dabchicks.

Often, men would come along the beach selling small fish or fruit of all kinds. We have memories of all of us with our faces buried in juicy slices of melon, or barbecuing small fish over a charcoal burner. We had fun finding shells of all kinds too. That was before it was made into a National Park when, quite rightly, one wasn't allowed to collect anything from the beach or from the reefs. Sadly though, the time came when we had to pack up the tent and make our way home.

During the rest of that holiday we were also able to fit in a trip to the Queen Elizabeth Game Park, entering at MWEYA Lodge where we stayed for a few days. This was our first experience of a game park, and the excitement that it was always going to produce. We saw a wide variety of animals and soon learned their names. Elephant and buffalo of course we knew, but there were Uganda cob, waterbuck, bushbuck, warthog, hippos and of course the beautiful lions. There were many other species of course, but we had at other times to hire rangers to teach us their names and where to look for them. Some species were particular to different game parks, for instance we didn't see Thomsons or Grants Gazelles in the Q.E. Park. They were found in the Kenya and Tanzania parks. We kept our distance from the elephants, buffalo and hippo, but the others seemed unperturbed by the cars and we could even get quite close to lions if they were resting. The cars smelled of fuel which obscured any smell of flesh, and they assumed therefore that cars presented no problems.

Before we set off on our safari, a friend asked us to bring him back a set of horns if we came across any. I replied that I would have to find some for myself first. While driving through the park, I looked ahead and thought I had struck lucky. I could see a perfect set of buffalo horns.

There were few established tracks in the game parks, and one followed foot trails or mostly drove carefully anywhere. I made a beeline for the horns, therefore, feeling great, but when I was about 30 yards away from my prize, I got a huge shock.

A buffalo jumped up out of a dust hole and ran away together with my prize horns. We never actually found any horns lying around during all our many visits to game parks. It seems everyone else was looking for them too.

On the last day we decided to make the trip up to Murchison Falls National Park on the way home. We set off early but it was a longer journey than we had anticipated so we decided to stay at Chobe Lodge in the Murchison Park for an extra night. That gave us plenty of time to take a river trip on a covered but open sided boat. What an experience! The first scary bit was when we saw the many Hippo swimming, snorting and cavorting about ten metres away. Then on the other side where we were nearer the bank, we began to see crocodiles. They seemed to be basking with their mouths wide open, but as we passed their mouths snapped shut and they slithered into the water where we guessed that they felt safer. We were told that they slept with their mouths open to breath, which was something to do with the absence of an epiglottis. They looked enormous, and are apparently the largest in the world except for the sea crocodiles off Australia.

We then chugged as near as we could to the foot of the falls, but rapids prevented us getting too close. As we turned round we went close to a relatively calm and shallow bay. This was where the crocodiles lay their eggs, and indeed we did see many little baby ones swimming around. Looking at the Volume of water rushing down, no wonder the crocodiles grew so big. They fed on all the fish that were stunned as they crashed over the Falls! We wondered too about the Crocs and the Hippo living so close together, but realised that they both had tremendously powerful jaws, hence had mutual respect for each other. That did not prevent the Crocs eating a dead hippo which had drifted downstream however, which we were to witness later.

Of course we had to go round to view the Falls from the top, passing a huge pool with dozens more Hippo hiding from the sun. We didn't know what to expect, but Health and Safety would have had a fit! There was a fence near the edge in places, but I warned everyone not to lean too hard on it! That did not detract from the incredible spectacle though. It is beyond words to describe, not that any words would be heard because of the thunderous roar. When we were standing between the sun and the Falls we could see the perpetual rainbow, which just about put the icing on the cake.

What a wonderful safari, and what wonderful education for the girls – and us. As I usually say, holidays always have to end though, so back home we had to go. Home was now in the new bungalow which had been completed, and the next few days were taken up with removals and settling in.

Barbie's progress at golf was amazing. She soon won a bottle of VAT 69 whisky, which was awarded to anyone who recorded a net 69 or less in an official tournament. Her handicap kept coming down monthly and the trophies mounted.

We met an American couple with a three-year-old boy called Tom. We were invited one day for tea and discovered that Tom never wore any clothes at home, and was let do whatever he wanted. When we arrived, Brian was painting his boat with a grey undercoat and said that it wouldn't take him a minute to finish off. We then saw that Tom also had a paint brush, but he was painting mainly himself! His tummy was grey, and so were his private parts! Every time we think of this, we cringe at what he went through when mummy had to remove the marine paint from his body! However, we had tea and they discovered that we had always been fascinated by sailing but had never done any, so he invited us to go for a sail in his rubber dinghy on the following Saturday.

A nearby Crocodile from the boat at Murchison Game Park

Looking for the elusive Leopard with the Ranger

Elephants have the right of way

Who is going to argue?

We duly turned up and Brian took us to a nearby lake where we saw the dinghy moored to a tree. After he had set up a small sail, we all got in and off we went to enjoy beating up and down and across the lake. It was while we were somewhere near the middle of the lake when Nikky suddenly said 'Oh look, there is a thorn here sticking out of the side of the dinghy!' Sure enough, we looked and there was a 3 inch thorn sticking through the side. 'For goodness sake do not pull it out' said Brian, 'or we will all be swimming back to the shore!' – How good to be so laid back in life.

Barbie woke me up one morning and said 'Ken, don't look at me because I think that I'm changing into a monkey' she wouldn't turn over, and I asked her what was wrong. 'My lips are like sausages' she said. I got up and walked around to her side and yes, her face was so bloated that I could hardly recognise her, and her lips were indeed like sausages.

We dressed quickly and I took her straight round to the doctors who took one look at her and immediately sent her to hospital. This meant a drive to Masaka because we didn't have a hospital in Mbarara. She was admitted, put to bed, and the doctor said that it must be an allergic reaction to something. Could we think of anything she had taken? I told him that she had a touch of diarrhoea and had taken a tablet of mexaform which a friend had recommended.

Barbie had to have a tube down her throat through which to be fed and when the doctor lifted her mouth open, one could see the impression of her teeth imprinted in her cheeks! I had to leave but I was told not to worry for it would not take long to reduce the swelling.

I went back to see Barbie the following day but there was no change. Barbie was in fine spirits, or I would have been far more worried than I was, but they didn't seem to be able to get the swelling down. It was another troubled night for us all.

She was seen by a young Polish doctor on the following morning, and seeing no change he simply said 'Cease all treatment.' By the time I arrived in the afternoon she was all smiles and the swelling was visibly reduced. Either the treatment was aggravating the situation or the allergic reaction had run its course. Whatever the reason, she was getting better and was able to come home on the following day.

What a relief. We would never know, but one of the problems in underdeveloped countries, apparently, is the lack of strict control over drugs. One has to beware of copies, or even substitutes, in authentic looking packaging. It could have been the mexaform, or it could have been a copy.

The Tennis Captain left and I was appointed in his place. That meant that I would automatically be a member of the Club Committee. Unfortunately I made a big mistake at the first committee meeting because I turned up in my tennis attire. I was told in no uncertain terms that dress was formal for committee meetings.

Collar and tie and long sleeves were also compulsory in the clubhouse after 6 p.m., and this was true all over East and West Africa. Our African friends were the most keen to keep this rule too. It was not introduced for their sakes and was carried over from before integration, but it was rigidly enforced by the Africans. They too loved the formality.

We were quite happy at Bishop Stuart, but we were obviously different from the rest of the mission-oriented staff. As I have said, it wouldn't have made much difference had we been on our own, but we had the children to consider and give a life to. Nothing was ever said, nor could it be, because we were so popular, useful and helpful. There was always the issue of subservience at the back of my mind though, but nothing more at which I could actually point a finger.

We were told that a new couple were coming to join the staff at Christmas, which we were looking forward to. We hoped that they would, like us, be more outward going and companions for us. The situation never arose however, because at the same time we saw an advertisement in a daily paper about the opening of over twenty-five new S.S. schools, and they were looking to recruit suitable headmasters.

I was always on the lookout for advancement and especially if it meant more money. We had a little debate and decided that we couldn't lose anything by it, so I added my application to the list. I never expected anything to come of it because, let's face it, I didn't have a university degree which most of the other teachers had.

We became friendly with the manager of one of the multinational stores. He was a keen fisherman and invited us all out for a day's fishing. We travelled early morning further up the Nile and hired a small powerboat and set off. We saw a notice at the entrance to the fishing area saying 'All fish under 25 lbs must be returned to the river.' We remarked at the time how the anglers in the UK would be interested to see that sign.

Tony provided the rods and lures. No live bait, just the plastic imitation fish with hooks on. We spent a few hours trolling before we hooked anything, but then Nikky felt a tug and we helped her to reel in a 35 lbs Nile Perch. It wasn't long before I was lucky enough to hook one of over 70 lbs.

What a contrast to sea fishing! After one attempt to leap out of the water and try to shake off the lure, these fish didn't even struggle but just gave up the ghost, so that there was not the excitement or expectancy while hauling in the catch, wondering what it was on the end of the line. It was still exciting to see such big fish being brought in over the side of the boat, however, but my catch was nowhere near the record of over 360 lbs, yet it was still very satisfying for us.

Nile Perch restrictions!

Got you! - Nile Perch trying to shake off the lure

We had to rush back then because the fish decayed notoriously quickly in the midday heat, and we had to keep it as wet as possible as we sped home. Tiri was well up to this though and had them filleted and in the chest freezer in no time at all. The fillets were almost as long as Ros was tall. Tony took his share, and there was sufficient left for us to enjoy it fried, baked, poached or curried for many weeks. We had never had fish cooked in so many different ways. Tiri was also happy because we naturally gave him his share too and he loved demonstrating his cooking skills.

Tiri filleting the smaller catch

Tiri was a genius at cooking. If he couldn't understand what we wanted, Barbie had only to show him a picture in a cookbook and he would produce it. We spoke a little more Swahili than he did English, and between us, we were always able to make ourselves understood. I am certain he would have done well on the TV programme *Masterchef*.

We met friends who played bridge and between us we taught Barbie how to play. There weren't many dances, so everyone entertained through dinner parties or bridge parties. I worked out movements for two or three tables so that either one never played with one's wife, or was never even on the same table. That way we never had any fallouts or cross words.

Well one couldn't be ungentlemanly to another guest, could one, especially if it was a lady.

Back at Dinnington I had been doing a little turning on a lathe, and so was familiar with the tight curls of metal produced. I was puzzled one day, therefore, when I thought that I saw a pile of such turnings under a tree, and wondered where there could be a lathe. I was very embarrassed when I found out that the tree in question was where the students gathered to cut their hair. I do apologise for this error, but I have to admit to what I saw and thought, and at least I hadn't voiced my thoughts to anyone else except to Barbie.

We had also realised soon after we had arrived, that there were no hairdressers for the white population in Mbarara. I had always cut the children's hair, so when Barbie asked for her hair to be cut, I told her that she could either have a trim just to straighten round the bottom, or I could cut it short, similar to the girls. With the hot weather, and frequent games of tennis or golf, she chose the shorter option. When it came to cutting mine, it was trial and error for her, but we had brought some hand shears with us and she soon got the hang of it. I must say that we were quite proud of the results. That was to save us thousands of pounds over the years. Barbie did try hairdressers later in the UK but was never satisfied and always came back to me. I'm afraid I was a spendthrift and went to professional barbers when we returned to the UK. The most I have paid to date is £5 (plus a tip). With her shorter hair style, I realised that she looked extraordinarily like Audrey Hepburn, one of the current glamorous filmstars.

MY FIRST HEADSHIP, AND K.P.S.

It happened! I received a letter offering me the post as Headmaster of Kinyasano Senior Secondary School, Rukungiri, in Kigezi. This left us with a major issue to consider which we had never contemplated. Rukungiri was an African township twenty-five miles from the nearest expatriate, and he was a mission doctor who ran a mission hospital in the bush with his wife and two children. The next nearest expatriates were fifty miles away, and that was where we were, in Mbarara.

What could we do about Nikky and Ros? We were told that there was a Mission Primary School for boarders in Kabale which was also fifty miles south of Rukungiri, so off we went post haste with a very open mind, and with not with much hope of things being favourable. We had never envisioned that our children would ever go to a boarding school. If it had ever entered our minds it had been rejected immediately.

'Kabale Prep. School' turned out to be on a hillside in an idyllic setting. It was brick built with a huge lawn in front surrounded by Jacaranda trees which happened to be in bloom, spreading a carpet of blue over the lawn. We were greeted by a beaming Aunty Mary who took us to see Aunty Nan, the Headmistress.

A view from the playground (play-lawn) at K.P.S.

Apparently, when Doctor Leakey, of Oldevai Gorge fame, decided to become a missionary and explore Africa, he not only came with his own family but came also with his brothers and sisters and relatives and their families too. They landed in Mombasa and travelled on foot, across East Africa, leaving missionary stations at various points along the way. The final few reached Kabale and, being 7000 feet above sea level and with a very pleasant climate, was the obvious place to build a family school. Teachers were called Aunty because initially they were all Aunties to the families' children. Over time they decided, no doubt for commercial reasons as well as religious, to accept children whose parents worked in the bush or travelled a lot and were unable to give their children a stable education. Ever since then, they kept the tradition of calling the teachers Aunty.

Aunty Mary was the secretary/matron, and gave us a jolly and friendly welcome. We learned that all the staff members were qualified teachers as well as being missionaries, which was important. A bell rang for breaktime and between twenty and thirty children ran out to play on the lawn and began climbing ropes, swinging on swings and generating the normal playground noises. The striking thing about them was that they were all so obviously happy. We met the rest of the staff over refreshments and yes, there were places for them if we wished.

Nikky and Ros were party to all our conversations and when we put it to them that daddy had been offered this Headship and would they be happy to go to K.P.S. they both answered readily that they would. I think they had got to like adventures and they saw this as just another one, and no doubt they had mixed with children from boarding schools and been influenced by them. I assure everyone that had they shown any unhappiness at the idea then we would not have accepted the post. We were impressed with the school after our visit and were not surprised that the girls were too. I promised that we would visit them on every possible occasion that we could, but we were all mindful of one of the school rules which stated that visits were only allowed at half term and on special occasions.

When the ministry got my acceptance they wrote back straight away to say that, unlike the other S.S. schools, my school would not be starting until Easter as my bungalow had not been finished. I thought this was unfair on the students and went up to Kampala immediately to see the CEO to discuss the situation. I asked him if I may visit the school to look for alternatives, to which he readily agreed.

Barbie and I set off one morning to see Kinyasano for the first time. The fifty miles of Murram Road ran through the impenetrable forest which seemed to go on forever.

When we saw the school we were surprised to see four brick-built classrooms and four mud and wattle rooms; a dormitory block and a dining room. There was also a small concrete structure divided into four small rooms which looked as if it had been built for a houseboy.

Our unfinished bungalow stood overlooking the site and looked a carbon copy of all the other Public Works Department (PWD) quarters, which was a pleasant surprise. With only two classes of students in the first year there were classrooms to spare, so I looked at Barbie and said 'Do you mind living in a classroom for a while?' and, being Barbie, she said 'No, of course not.'

We were just in time for the minister to let the students know that it would open on time after all, and I am sure it made everyone very happy. This was another 'first' for us and no doubt a few more 'brownie points'.

Another move, and after such a short time, but never mind, we were still thinking of tours of twenty-one to twenty-seven months, so we thought nothing of it. That was a laugh.

What a busy time that meant. I was allowed an amount of money and made frequent trips to Kampala to order everything that a school needs, and it was left entirely to me. I had the help of the government stationery office, but I had to purchase exercise books, text books, seventy-five beds and mattresses, one hundred and fifty blankets, seventy-five pillows and countless sets of cutlery, desks and chairs. There was also the cooking equipment and office equipment to purchase and the hundred and one things one needs with which to run a school. One good thing was that I paid everything by cheque, so that throughout the whole time we were there, I never had to handle any money. My bursar saw to all that.

The Asian shopkeepers must have loved the sight of us, and in fact we were invited to lunch and actually stayed overnight with one trader when we were stranded in Kampala waiting for the goods to be assembled.

That was an experience in itself, because at the evening meal there was no water on the table, just a bottle of whisky. I'm not sure if that was an indication of what they thought about the English, but we quickly changed their opinion. The whisky remained untouched and water appeared. There was one more striking indication of a difference in culture. Barbie was the only lady at the table. With these particular Asians, their women remained in the kitchen to wait upon the menfolk.

Moving was no problem because it was all taken care of by the Public Works Department, or PWD. They controlled the building and maintenance of all government buildings, movement, and even fumigation at times against cockroaches, ticks and bedbugs and other nasties found in Africa.

These were never a major problem, although it might sound horrible. Mosquitoes were controlled by the boy who went round the house every night with a flit gun. Other pests such as cockroaches or bedbugs were controlled by PWD. They just came round and fumigated the house, which always worked. We were later to acquire sleeping nets over the beds as an added protection, and since our arrival in Africa we had been taking a tablet of palludrin daily as a prophylactic against malaria. There were other stronger drugs in case palludrin became ineffective, but we were fortunate never to need these.

It was sad to be leaving Bishop Stuart, especially leaving the students who expressed their sadness to see us go. We received several letters in the post from them hoping that we would meet again. We still intended to keep our membership of Mbarara Club, as we would often have to go to Kampala for one thing or another, and could incorporate a stopover in Mbarara to keep up with our friends.

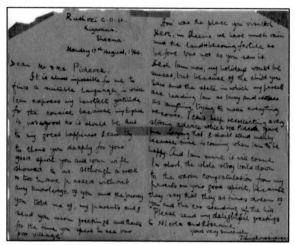

One of the letters from a student

Mbarara was only an hour away from Kinyasano, and we remained members of the club particularly because I wanted to help the newly formed rugby team. We hadn't been able to form a football team, but there were some good rugby players who had 'encouraged' us footballers to make up the squad. We called ourselves the 'Pink Elephants' which we thought was a fitting name for a rugby team in Africa. We played in an all-white strip and Barbie and a few other wives stitched a pink elephant on each shirt which Barbie had already cut out for them.

Before we finally left we stayed at Bishop Stuart for Christmas to give the girls a good time. We had already surreptitiously had a bicycle and scooter delivered from Kampala, together with books and clothing, as well as seeing Santa Claus at the club party. We tried to make sure the girls really enjoyed their first Christmas in Africa.

The second chapter of our great adventure was ready to start. I went to Kinyasano a few days before Barbie and the girls in order to organise things while they spent the last few days at the college. I met Al and Waldo, two American Peace Corps graduates, who had been appointed to the school to help us. Al Alemien was a second generation Armenian, born in Boston and educated at Harvard, while Waldo Johnson Junior was from Connecticut. He studied at Yale, and his father was the curator of the Maritime Museum there. We were lucky to have been allocated two such young and enthusiastic teachers, but we were soon to learn that they were typical of all the Peace Corps volunteers that we met.

The thing that struck Barbie and I most were the teaching regulations laid down by the Ugandan Ministry of Education. Barbie, with an English Teaching Certificate, was allowed to teach up to A levels, yet Al and Waldo, from two of the top universities in America, were only allowed to teach up to O levels. That was what the Ugandan Government thought of American degrees. I hate to think of what they might think of English degrees now.

Barbie arrived with the girls and Rinti the dog. She made fun of the journey because it was raining and she said that Rinti had his eyes fixed on the windscreen wipers. His head was going backwards and forwards like a metronome for the whole journey. What she didn't tell me, and this was typically brave of Barbie, was that the murram road had become a mud bath and they had been slipping and sliding across the road for practically the whole journey. Ros has only told me recently that she remembers it as one of the scariest moments in her life.

We had got curtains strategically arranged in the classroom/home, and somehow Tiri, who had agreed to come with us, was able to cook food for us as if he was in a normal kitchen. He only had charcoal burners to cook on, but then, that was what he was used to using for his own cooking. We then had to make the journey to Kabale to take Nikky and Ros to school. It seemed more of a trauma for us than it did for them when we had to leave.

I had made it at last. It finally sank in that I was now a headmaster, albeit of a small school of sixty students and a staff of four. That was destined to grow however, but the strange thing was that I didn't feel any different. I was still a teacher, and part of a team, but now I had the responsibility attached to it.

The students arrived on the following day and everything was hustle and bustle. They were allocated to dormitories and issued with bedding and divided into two classes. Fortunately, there were one or two older students who had obviously joined primary education late in life. They were the ones who turned out to be a great help as prefects and team leaders. It was uncanny that we members of staff did not need to take any part in selection, because the students somehow had their own pecking order and automatically looked up to certain students as their leaders. There was never any controversy this way.

Tiri off to fetch water in Kinyasano

Student taking a sewing machine to the needlework room

A secretary had been appointed by the ministry to help me in my office as I would be teaching quite a lot. We used to relate later that I had always said that I wanted a secretary, but this one wasn't a white female and blonde, but male and black. That was only a joke though, as James turned out to be very efficient and extremely helpful. Don't worry about me calling Africans Black, because that is what they call themselves. It is only the silly political correctness that has sprung up in the UK that has created the stigma attached to it. Especially in Uganda where the different tribes are described by their colour by the Africans. They say such a tribe is black, or such a tribe is brown, or even such a tribe is light brown, distinguishing tribes and regions.' Hence Tiri describes later 'Dem black men from the north'.

A bursar was also appointed from the ministry, and as I have said, I only had to sign cheques and never touched any cash. Thank goodness book-keeping was taken out of my hands. All in all, therefore, we could get on with teaching, which is what we were there to do.

Administration was not a problem for me and organising a full scale athletics meeting using unqualified teachers to supervise each event presented a far bigger task than running a two class school.

One other huge asset was the school lorry. Each out of town school had been allocated a lorry and ours in particular became very useful. It was a 3 ton Bedford and could be driven on a normal driving licence. If the staff couldn't drive one before, then they soon learned. Yes, even Barbie had, on occasions, driven it to Kampala when I was otherwise occupied in the school.

The Peace Corps boys were not allowed to own their own motorised transport, but they were allowed a bicycle if they wished. Al and Waldo didn't bother. A distance of fifty miles to Mbarara or 150 to Kampala wasn't a prospect they fancied. They both loved to drive the lorry when necessary, which was handy when taking parties of students around. It was surprising how often it was used too, to take teams to compete somewhere, or to take representatives to the Independence Day parades or other festivals.

Barbie's art room at Kinyasano.
Proof that excellence can come out of poor buildings!

The school soon settled down and started functioning as a school. Waldo was Classical and Al was Science oriented, with Barbie taking Music and Art and sharing French with Waldo, while I took care of the Maths. We all chipped in with P.E. but that was not a priority, although some P.E. was necessary if only as a recreation.

It is a dream occupation to teach in Africa. I have already pointed out their eagerness to study, and I cannot remember one disciplinary problem which occurred in my time there. If any student had misbehaved, he would have been more likely to be punished by the rest of the class. They didn't like their studies to be disturbed.

It was no surprise that I hadn't thought of everything that a school needed, so trips to Kampala for one of us were not infrequent. I had remembered all the essentials though so it was only the less important items that appeared on that list, and we were never really without the essentials. It was more the case of 'Oh, while you are in Kampala, can you get so and so.'

Waldo and Al decided to live in the small concrete building with four rooms. They christened it 'Honeymoon Cottage' and that's how we always referred to it. I have just remembered that I had slept in one of the rooms with them for the two nights before Barbie joined us. I remember that because one or two house geckos were tossed over the dividing wall amid muffled giggles from the other side. I promised them that I would get my own back later.

A house gecko is a small lizard which is found in even the cleanest and most expensive houses. They are rarely seen because, like a chameleon, they blend in with the colour of the wall, which is usually cream. They are not a pest, in fact they live off spiders and flies and other insects, and therefore have a beneficial reason for not being harmed. I think the Peace Corps boys had been testing out my sense of humour. Such was the atmosphere of fun that we could be quite informal without the students taking advantage. I think that they knew just how far to go with me because they knew that I considered study of paramount importance and nothing should interfere with that.

Waldo had brought a couple of American rugby balls with him and in spare time he taught me the 'torpedo pass'. He was also an 'even time' sprinter, so I took him to Mbarara with me on one of the trips, and recruited him into the rugby team on the wing.

I won't waste time over rugby, but by the end of the season we had won the Uganda Championships and Waldo played a significant part in that. There were only the five major towns involved in the competition, but it was some feat to win, as we were by far the smallest of all the centres.

Roadside view in Kigesi

We played baseball with the students in our spare time and they soon became more than just competent. It was very rare for us to be sitting down just resting in the sun. If it wasn't baseball they would be playing football or practising their songs accompanied by their tribal dancing. They just loved activity and most of all they were always smiling. I knew that they were thinking how lucky they were to get this chance of being educated. It made us happy too – happy, but not complacent.

We had a letter from the girls and they wrote that a sad thing had happened at K.P.S. – one of the little boys had died quite quickly of meningitis. The parents were Seventh Day Adventists, and as the girls reported it, the parents, instead of being sad, seemed more to celebrate his death because he had been chosen to go to Jesus sooner rather than later. Apparently they took him back to where they were missionaries in a box strapped to the top of their car, but none of the murram roads were particularly smooth. It must have been a harrowing journey and the whole episode left a lasting effect on Nikky and Ros. It also made us feel how vulnerable we were to be miles from anywhere.

During half term and special occasions we visited the girls and, true to form, it soon became routine to have a Mr. Pidcock's table. This was a table containing all the odd jobs that they hadn't been able to mend. Sometimes it was something bigger, like mending the swing or the toilet that wouldn't flush. I thus became a welcome visitor for the Aunties as well as for Nikky and Ros.

Typical roadside craft stall

The only reservation the girls ever made about the school was when they had to make up a prayer to thank Jesus and recite it out loud to the class. It was a mission school after all, and it didn't do them any harm. At least it made them think about religion as something more than just attending church on a Sunday with mummy and daddy. They told us of midnight feasts and climbing to the top of a fir tree, which was quite safe, but would have appalled Health and Safety in the UK and most important for us they seemed happy. What experiences they were building up too.

As I write these memoirs, I have just found out from Nikky that in spite of them feeling fine when we left them, they had become desperately homesick during that first week. However, she said, it was a good thing that we couldn't visit them then because they might never have got over that stage. She also said that later it became quite the reverse because sometimes our visits interrupted their play. That satisfied both our emotions. There was a strange sort of comfort, as parents, to know that we were missed by our children. It was also a relief that they survived that and that they were now enjoying the new lifestyle.

My staff at Kinyasano S.S.S. (2nd year) with the Bursar, my Secretary and the R.C. Father

PART FOUR
Near misses and more moves

WHILE WE WERE RETURNING FROM KABALE one half term, we had just reached the murram road leading up into the mountains when dust began to pour through the door on my side. I had to stop otherwise we would have been choked and I got out to inspect it but could find nothing wrong. It did not happen again when I set off, which puzzled us, and we started the long, steep and winding climb up the mountain.

Suddenly we saw a ball of dust about half a mile ahead and it could only mean that someone was coming down fast in a car and was in trouble. I stopped and pulled into the side as tightly as I could against the cliff face, for there was a 500 feet drop at the other side of the road, and there were no barriers. We could see the car clearly now and the driver was deliberately glancing off the cliff face in order to slow the car down. We held our breath but it just kept coming and coming.

Fortunately the car just managed to stop a few yards in front of us. The distraught driver got out and explained that his brakes had failed. He had been very lucky, and very clever to stop it at all. The side of the car was very much the worse for wear where he had repeatedly hit the

A near miss on the road to K.P.S. (Kabale) just a few hundred feet drop over the edge!

cliff face in his efforts to stop the car.We then thought of all the things that had happened in the past two years when we thought things were going wrong but it had turned out for the better. It was then that we realised with certainty that there must be someone up above watching over us and directing our lives. We looked at each other and without saying anything we both realised that if I hadn't stopped for the dust in the car, or if we had driven a few yards further, one or both cars could by now have been over the edge, 500 feet further down the side of the mountain.

It reminded us also of the time when we had a blow-out driving up to Kampala when we were still at Bishop Stuart. It was a front tyre and the car started spinning out of control until suddenly there was a loud bang at the back of the car and we found that we had stopped spinning. I then managed somehow to bring it to a stop on the correct side of the road. When I got out of the car to assess the damage at the back, to my surprise, I couldn't see any. As the car had spun around, the tip of the towbar had hit a culvert on the side of the road which had corrected the spin and slowed it down allowing me to regain control. There was merely a white paint mark from the culvert on the towbar. If that isn't divine intervention I don't know what is. Our 'Guardian Angel' was with us, and was to remain so.

During one of my talks with the head boy, he mentioned that they didn't get much meat with their meals. The staple diet was matoke, or cooked plantain. It was a large variety of green bananas, which indeed contained bulk but little protein. When they had a piled up plate they referred to it as a Kilimanjaro.

I spoke to the bursar and he told me that meat had become so expensive in the market, especially goat meat. 'Why don't we keep our own goats?' I said, 'We have plenty of land.' This was soon acted upon and we started our own goat herd, another first for us.

There were very few sheep in Uganda and the staple meat was goat meat,

Ladies pounding maize or matoke (plantain) for lunch

because goats can live anywhere and they literally eat anything. That included leather, so it was not wise to leave shoes anywhere near them. We then encountered another problem because a lot of the boys were Muslims, so animal meat had to be halal. That was soon overcome however. We just employed the right man when a goat had to be slaughtered. We had extra wide smiles from all the students after that.

Waldo always wore boots and thick socks even in the hottest weather. He thought it was the best way of keeping his feet healthy. He came to me one day complaining about having itchy feet, and they were driving him mad. I realised immediately what might be wrong, so I told him to come round to see me in my house and I would have a look. I told Al to come as well and bring a specimen jar. I had met with the problem of chigoes before and few people escape them for long. A chigoe is a small flea which lives in the dusty floors. It lays its eggs under the skin of its victim, usually in the toes. The eggs are contained in a sac, formed under the skin, and when the eggs begin to develop they itch like mad.

There is a certain technique in dealing with them so I asked Waldo to take off his boots and socks to let me take a look. At this point they were puzzled as to what I was going to do. 'Put your foot on my knee and let's have a look' I said brandishing a needle.'

What one has to do is gently break the skin with the point of the needle. This doesn't hurt because the skin has already died through lack of blood supply. Then one has to carefully winkle out the sac without bursting it. It contains all the eggs which mustn't get back under the skin to reinfect it. I think Al had eleven little sacs in the specimen jar by the time I had finished. After that we finally converted Waldo to wearing shoes. The fleas had just loved his sweaty socks.

When the drums sounded you knew that it was time to go to church. The C. of E. (Church of England) Church was only a ten minute walk away, and some of the students were involved in beating the drums to let people know that it was church time. Services were not too dissimilar from those in the UK.

Why is it, I wonder, that we always remember the funny or unusual events? One Sunday, the vicar had forgotten the keys for the cupboard where the chalice was kept, so he substituted it with a mug. This mug was not one of the newest we had ever seen, however he had washed it as well as he could. It is doubtful whether he had any soap at hand however. At some point a fly had taken a drink and drowned in the wine, but everyone seemed to ignore it when it was passed round and they were taking their sip. It was sacred wine after all! I tried to see, but was not able to discern what the vicar did when it was his turn to drink up the last few drops.

Calling to Church with the Drums in Rukungiri

We are invited to an African wedding

There were a number of Roman Catholics amongst the students, and the Catholic father was a frequent visitor. He enjoyed our hospitality many times and liked to chat over a cup of tea. It was a fact that there seemed to be an Irish Catholic father in every settlement we had known, or where ever we were to go.

The Muslims went to the local mosque and we were lucky and thankful because there was no friction at all between the different religions in those days. As we all now know, religious friction was to become a major issue in many African countries, and is now a major problem.

I can't think of a happier school, and everyone was so keen and proud to belong here. We were all determined to make this one of the best schools in the country.

We were reminded about mature pupils attending primary school when we were invited to field a team to play the local primary school at football. We had three or four mature students, but the primary school team seemed to be all men. It was good fun, but our boys didn't like to be beaten 2-1 by a primary school. We had a successful reversal of fortune when we played Kitunga S.S.S. which was the nearest of the new schools to be opened at the same time as ours. Kitunga was about thirty miles southeast of us.

Time seemed to fly by because we were all so busy. We were in constant touch with home and averaged more than one letter a week both ways. It must have been very strange reading for the folks at home and we often wondered what they thought of all our news and escapades. It was difficult to tell from their letters, but I'm sure mum would be pleased. Mum's arthritis prevented her from writing, so the news was all passed on by my sisters.

THE LION HUNT, A STUDENT DIES AND I AM INTERROGATED

It was just a normal Saturday afternoon and we were settling down to enjoy a break when news came through, presumably by bush telegraph, that a lion had killed some cattle in the village and they were organising a lion hunt. Barbie, the students and I jumped in the car and went to where there was a crowd on a hill overlooking an open patch of land.

The men were spread out, and walking in a line down the hill, brandishing spears and pangas (machetes). They surrounded a copse of trees and began to hack away at the elephant grass and undergrowth, hooting and shouting in an effort to flush the lion out. I had remembered our binoculars and was taking a closer look when I was horrified to see Al, stripped to the waist in the centre of the line, brandishing a panga like the rest and hacking away at the undergrowth. I said a quick prayer to God that the lion wouldn't decide to break out at that spot.

It made me realise what an adrenaline rush does to create all the frenzy involved, and it not only affects the Africans apparently. We watched with fear of the outcome, but then saw the lion break cover further down the line. Unfortunately one of the men nearest to the lion started to run away, but hadn't gone far before the lion chased after him and with one swipe across his back, felled the man and proceeded to sit on him, looking around bewildered wondering what was happening. This was a new scenario that he hadn't met with before.

By this time, a ranger appeared near to where we were standing. He raised his gun and fired. The first shot missed. Maybe it was a 'sighter' to make sure that he didn't hit the man. The second shot hit the lion in its thigh causing it to spring off the poor man. It was standing there gazing around, still wondering what was happening. How had that pain suddenly occurred? Why can't I bear weight on my right leg? Now the ranger had a clear aim however and the third shot killed it amid shouts and whoops of triumphant joy.

Our view was now obscured by so many men milling around, but eventually a group of men emerged from the crowd carrying the dead lion and laid it on the side of the road quite near to us.

The crowd gave deference to us *Msungus (*whitemen*)* and we went and took photographs of Barbie lifting its paw and tail before they lifted it onto a lorry to take it away. It was now the property of the village chief.

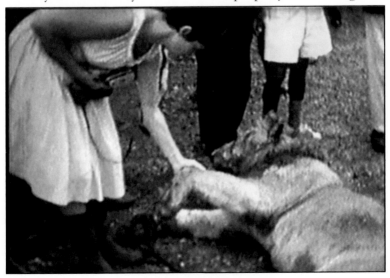

Barbie and the Lion

The crowd soon dispersed and we were about to go home when some more men appeared carrying the wounded man. We had almost forgotten him in all the excitement. No one seemed to know what to do with him, and there didn't appear to be any family members with him. He obviously needed hospital treatment, so through students acting as our interpreters, we agreed that we would take him to the mission hospital, run by the Dutch family. There were now plenty of willing hands to help us as we laid him on a blanket in the back of the car. It helped that it had a rear door and a flat boot area.

I then drove the twenty-five miles to the mission hospital and booked him in with the Dutch doctors. We had met them before at K.P.S. because their two children were also pupils there. The man was quite conscious and though he had a massive wound in his back he had not bled very much, and could speak with the doctor who obviously knew the local language.

The following week we made an effort to go to the hospital to see how the man was progressing. We were told that yes, he had operated and it had appeared successful, but then he had died. He then said something to us that at first seemed very strange. He told us that he had met this situation before and the man had died, not because of the wounds, but because he had expected to die. So strong is the belief that it is always fatal when you have been wounded by a lion that the victim goes into a type of catatonic shock and dies. The power of voodoo was still very prevalent among the remote tribes.

In a similar incident, I was teaching a class when I noticed that one of the students had a very sore arm. I went to look at it and it was obviously festering and needed treatment. Without any second thought, as one would do in the UK, I said that he should go home and get his parents to take him to the hospital for treatment. He said that he would and sure enough he did not appear for lessons the next day. I did not see him for over two weeks and I enquired about him from the students, believing that he should be back at school by now. I was then shocked to hear that he had died.

I finally worked out what must have happened. I know that he went home. The students then told me that he would have gone to see his tribal doctor. To a European this meant the local witch doctor. He would then be treated with local herbs and sometimes with poultices of cow dung, which they believe contains some medicinal properties. The arm would then become gangrenous and he would develop a fever and die. When I asked why on earth hadn't he gone to the European hospital? I was told that if he had gone there he would have had his arm cut off!

The sad truth is that unwesternised Africans usually try to treat it their way first, by going to the witch doctor, and on the occasions when it becomes untreatable, they then go to the hospital as a last resort. Here it would be found to be gangrenous and so far advanced that they would have to amputate, hence arose the myth.

I gave the whole school a talk about how easy it was to treat wounds with antibiotics. Even a simple dose of penicillin would have done the trick and saved that boy. I came away thinking that some of them would still put their faith in the witch doctor and it would take a lot of education to change ingrained customs, but I vowed never to send a student home again. If only to prove my point, I would take him to the nearby medical centre myself, where I knew that they would be treated with antibiotics.

I haven't mentioned the Peace Corps much but in fact they were a great help to us when we were organising things at the beginning. When we went to Kampala we often stayed with their members overnight and they helped in many other ways. We decided to have a party for those who could manage to find time, and in particular, those in charge.

We chose the 11 November in consultation with Al and Waldo, and about twelve were able to make it. We had a super evening and they all stayed overnight sleeping on settees and even on the floor. Tiri cooked breakfast for sixteen before they drifted off back to the north.

I thought nothing more about it, but later that week I was sitting in my office when two gentlemen came to see me. They introduced themselves and showed me cards identifying themselves as being from the 'Special Branch', in other words they were detectives. They asked me if I minded them asking me a few questions and I said that of course I didn't.

They then started questioning me about the party and why we had chosen that particular day. I explained that it was for the members of the Peace Corps in Kampala who had been extremely helpful to us. The date we chose was the date when most of them could come, but why were they asking? 'Haven't you a radio?' they asked. 'No' I said. 'Have you any idea what happened on that day?' they persisted, and I said 'No, why should I?'

I must at last have satisfied them, because they then told me that on that day, Rhodesia had declared their independence. It was the date of U.D.I. (Unilateral Declaration of Independence) and they wanted to know if it was that which had prompted our celebrations, of all the dates that we could have chosen!

I marvelled at Bush telegraph at the time, but maybe I should have thought of something more sinister and closer to home. How could they have possibly heard about our party in such a short time, and in an enclosed school? I had no reason to suspect anything was amiss or that anyone had any reason to wish us ill. I was so naive, and it would dawn on me later, when another event happened.

The prize Bull at the show. (All Ankole cattle had similar long horns)

Another frequent visitor was K.K.K. Karajesa, the local MP. (Member of Parliament.) He was what we would call a gentleman farmer, and had been educated in England and loved to talk about it over tea. I remember him as always being immaculately dressed. He always appeared as though he had just walked in from 'Savile Row'. We also remember him for one saying in particular. Somehow the conversation had got on to the breeding of cattle and I asked him if he used the latest method of artificial insemination. He replied that no, his cows liked it the old-fashioned way. He was quite a colourful character and we had lots of laughs with him.

Tribal Dancer for the Governor

Horseman in full regalia ready to charge towards the Governor at the Durbar

Horseman set for the Durbar

It was indicative of the high esteem with which principals and headmasters were held in Uganda when we were invited to be among the Guests of Honour at the retirement of the Bishop of Kigezi and again to the inauguration of the new bishop. We were also invited to a party organised by the British High Commission to celebrate the birthday of Her Majesty Queen Elizabeth, and also to 'The formal erection (The actual word used on the invitation!) of the Diocese of Kigezi.' We were introduced at these functions to the president Dr Milton Obote, and Idi Amin, as well as the Tribal Chiefs of Ankole and Kigezi. It was an honour and a very pleasant experience to have been in such company.

We could hardly believe it. A whole year had gone by and the students were preparing to go home for Christmas. It is amazing how quickly time flies. The end of term exams had been reason-ably successful, and the students put on a surprise concert for me. I think Al and Waldo had been in the know but had kept it secret.

They began with a lovely choir, which had been one of the first groups to be formed. Africans loved singing and, like the Welsh, all seemed to have beautiful singing voices. They sang some lovely African songs to which another group performed a bit of tribal dancing. Then they put on a play which was quite fun because one of the students was acting as me. It was both funny and entertaining, but surprising to me too, because I was depicted as being very severe and strict, which I felt sure that I wasn't. It was somehow satisfying, however, that they thought so. We then all said our goodbyes and before very long there was just Al, Waldo, Barbie, me and the girls left on site.

Elephants by the lake

SAFARIS

We all needed to go to Kampala, and of course Al and Waldo came with us. I remember Barbie asking me once if we could ever go for a ride in the car on our own. We didn't mind really, and we did stay with the Peace Corps members many times while in Kampala.

I had to attend a headmasters conference while I was there. After a day-long meeting, in his final speech, the most important point that the minister had to get across to us was remarkable. 'Would we please impress upon the students, who would be leaving to go to universities in other parts of the world, the importance of returning to work or teach in Uganda.' He then said that there were only four Ugandan graduate teachers actually teaching in the whole of the Ugandan education system.

It usually happened that most students opted to study at universities overseas. America, the UK, Russia and the Eastern Block were the favourites in that order. Many of the students would find a wife from that country, and those who had chosen to come to the UK often opted to stay, to which they were entitled under Commonwealth rules. The ones who did return preferred to find a more lucrative job in commerce, hence the 'brain drain' from a country that could ill afford it.

The Uganda Government could have done something about it. They could have changed the rule about the right of the students to remain in the UK, or they could have made the right to reside reciprocal. Africans from the Commonwealth were allowed to stay and work in the UK yet we had to have Visas and Work Permits and could only stay for limited periods in their countries. They did not want to lose those privileges though, which left them in a 'Catch 22' situation. Kenya and Rhodesia were exceptions to this rule.

Last off the ferry to Mweya Lodge

We find a skeleton of an elephant

With time on our hands, we took Al and Waldo into the Q.E. game park, which was new and exciting for them, but we noticed Nikky in the back seat reading a book. The girls had become quite blasé about seeing yet another herd of elephants. We then came across the skeleton of an elephant though and that soon had Nikky looking up from her book. We actually got out of the car to pick up the bones and inspect them. The thigh bones were almost as big as Nikky and Ros. Yes, don't worry, this time we had a park ranger with us, and we were a long way from any animals, with good visibility and no significant vegetation around where they could be hiding.

Friends from Mbarara invited us to go with them to visit Toni Nuti's Island. Toni Nuti was an Italian lady who had set up her home on an island in the river. To get across the very fast rapids surrounding the island she had set up a wire cage attached to a steel rope which one of her 'boys' would hand winch across. Our friend offered to help to winch when I and the girls went across. Of course, he stopped turning when we were halfway, much to everyone's enjoyment, but for a moment both Nikky and Ros were a bit frightened.

Back from Toni Nuti's Island. - Stopped in the middle!

It all looked a bit scary but was quite safe. At least there had been no accidents up until then. She had set up a sort of sanctuary for orphaned animals and also kept chickens, ducks and a number of domestic animals. There was also an extensive garden and she tried to be as self-sufficient as possible.

Trust Al to find a monitor lizard raiding the chicken's eggs. How they caught it I don't know, but he came towards us holding the 4 foot reptile up by its tail with egg yolk dripping from its mouth. After photographing him, he

Ros at a wildlife sanctuary for orphans

129

let it scuttle back to its natural habitat of course. We then had a meal there and spent some more time exploring the island and wandering among her virtually tame animals. It was interesting to see that she had built up quite a menagerie.

We spent Christmas with friends who had children whom Nikky and Ros knew from school. They lived near Kabale and while we were there they took us to the shores of Lake Kivu. Here the locals fished in dugout canoes and we actually managed to get the men to take us out in one. We had a few giggles getting into them, but no spills thank goodness.

We are given a ride in a dugout canoe

That was a good thing, although we didn't realise it at the time, because the lake was supposed to be infested with the dreaded bilharzia snails. Bilharzia is the second worst socioeconomic disease in the world after malaria, but little is known about it outside the infected areas. The snails carry a worm parasite which then infests the water and gains entry into any abrasions in the skins of animals. It then completes its life cycle within that animal, causing sickness and often leading to death.

The natives are happy to do anything for a few shillings and are especially friendly with us *Msungus*. I think that they enjoyed taking us in their canoes as much as we did. Churchill had once called Uganda 'The pearl of Africa' and, together with the climate and the scenery, the people certainly made it so.

YEAR II TRAUMAS AND WE DECIDE TO LEAVE

We had to prepare for the intake of new students during this break and on our journeys to Kampala we had ordered the next compliment of beds, bedding, stationery and books etc. for them. New classrooms and dormitories had been built and, more importantly, a new bungalow. At last Al and Waldo could now move out of Honeymoon Cottage, into a bungalow similar to ours.

Once again we had to take Nikky and Ros to K.P.S. which was always sad, but they had by now got used to boarding education and seemed to accept it as the norm along with the other children. The journey this time was incident free, but none of us knew that this would be their last term there.

The day before the students arrived back, we welcomed two new African graduate teachers, which was remarkable having heard what the Minister of Education had told us. They were newly trained and appeared to be fit and eager and looked the type we needed in this school. We needed young pioneering types with plenty of energy and vigour. I was happy that they were joining us, and I knew that they were going to be a big asset.

The following few days were hectic, but the second year students were marvellous and helped to orientate the newcomers into our routines. Once again the students chose their own leaders and the aptness of their choices was again apparent.

Several of the second year students brought little parcels to our house. They had brought us several colobus monkey skins and two serval cat skins. These were presents from the parents in appreciation of what we had done for their children. We could hardly refuse them, even though the colobus were a protected species. The local men in that district used to shoot the colobus with bows and arrows to eat, so it was only in England where they are protected. The serval cats used to try to steal domesticated poultry, just like our foxes. One can still see all the skins decorating our lounge.

Barbie was bitten on the leg by a mosquito. We were bitten hundreds of times but the irritations generally disappeared after a few days and we were more or less immune to them. Barbie must have scratched hers, however, because it became infected and turned into a tropical ulcer which was very painful. On the way into Rukungiri there was a medical station and I took Barbie there to see if they could help.

We were not really inspired as we walked into a mud hut, but the male nurse looked efficient and spoke English and after a cursory glance said Barbie should have a course of three injections of antibiotics. He had obviously seen this many times before. We became much more impressed however when he took out a portable burner and tray and proceeded to sterilise the syringe and needle. When he was satisfied he drew the antibiotic into the syringe and pointed to Barbie's arm and injected it very professionally. 'Come back tomorrow' he said and off we went.

On the morrow I was teaching so Barbie decided to go on her own. He went through the same procedure, but when he came to inject her, he pointed to her bum. When she came home she declared that she would not go on her own again, so the following day I went with her and when the time came to inject he pointed to the other arm. The motto being, 'when an opportunity presents itself, take it.' We reckoned he had never seen a white bum before and it became a joke for us to relate many times in the future. The leg, however, healed up beautifully.

If this book appears to be more about what we did outside school than inside then I must apologise. Teaching is the same the world over, and little of it is exciting enough to write a book about. I admit that not many schools would keep two snakes, a boomslang and a grass snake, in the science lab. They had been captured by students and added to Al's teaching aids. He had collected quite a menagerie for varying periods of time, which included helping a mother and baby monkey, rescuing a young crested crane, and keeping for observation some frogs and a tortoise. Al was quite a practical guy and the students were keen, eager to learn, did their homework, and did well in their exams. What more could we ask.

The students were very resourceful and organised their own groups of interest without any prompting. They formed singing, drama and traditional dance groups. They started producing their own monthly magazine of school life and the prefects instigated the rule that only English should be spoken anywhere on the school compound because they had to take exams in English. Woe betides anyone found by the prefects who were speaking in their tribal languages.

I did encounter one minor problem. The students were always asking to leave the room to 'relieve themselves'. I gave them due warning that they must make sure that they went to the toilet between lessons and not during lessons. The next one to put his hand up to go I refused. 'But I can't wait Sir' he said. 'I think that you can' I said. 'I'm sure that the indignity of doing it in your pants will overcome the necessity to go.' They all smiled, but they did manage to organise themselves after that and the habit soon died.

We had come to Africa not knowing what to expect and found that there were so many things to do and see that we took every opportunity to see as much as we could. By no means did we ever neglect our duties and we saved all these safaris for half terms and holidays. When all the students went home the place was deserted, and we just naturally wanted to see as much of Africa as we could. It was no good going back to England and saying 'I wish that we had done this or that.' There was so much of Africa to see.

Sadly, we went back to our bungalow after lessons one day and found Rinti in agony and frothing at the mouth. He had been such a wonderful guard dog, pet and companion for the girls. We assumed that he had either been bitten by a snake, or by something rabid, and so there was no hope for him. There were no vets to consult in the middle of the African 'bush' so we had to assume the worst, because if it was rabies then we couldn't risk him going mad and running amok. We went to tell Al who promised to put him out of his misery. We didn't ask how and we didn't want to know. He later came to tell us it was all over and he was now at peace in his grave. We then had to tell the girls who were heartbroken because they loved him so much and had spent hours playing with him.

In the clouds with our guide up Mhabura

133

On two occasions I had joined a party interested in climbing the volcanoes on the southern border with Rwanda. Barbie didn't fancy the climbs so I went on my own, but there were two other females in the party of eight who braved the elements. The first trip started very early.

We had to drive as near as we could to Mhabura, the tallest of the range and the most easterly. It was a straightforward hike then for seven miles to the base and a rise of around 7000 feet from the base to the top. We were told that our guide was the same guide who had taken Princess Elizabeth on a climb but that may have been sales talk. We went on tracks through the bamboo forests which flourish between certain heights, then saw giant groundsel, and lobelia plants six to eight feet in height.

Halfway up the volcano our guide suddenly stopped and was pointing excitedly in front of him. He really did seem over excited, and explained that he could see recent gorilla tracks. He then asked us if we would prefer to follow the tracks and possibly see the gorillas, or did we still want to go to the top? He was obviously disappointed when we decided to keep on up to the summit, because after all, that is why we had come, and we could possibly look for the gorillas another time. How stupid could we get? What we didn't realise was that gorillas had not been seen there for several years and it was feared that they may be extinct. What a coup it would have been if we had been the first to see them after so long. I am sure we all regretted the decision as I surely did. In retrospect, I wondered if there had been a tinge of fear behind our decision. We hadn't seen Mr Attenborough's TV shows then.

At the top was a crater lake, and those of us who had brought swimming trunks were mad enough to swim across. It was a case of diving in and getting across as quickly as possible because the water was literally freezing. All that so that we could boast that we had done it.

The second excursion was to be up the third in the range. Incidentally, the second volcano was called Mgahinga and is now one of the two wildlife sanctuaries for the gorilla. The local term for Mgahinga was 'The Pup' because it looked like a smaller replica of Mhabura.

The third in the line of volcanoes, Sabyinyo, was our objective but this time we decided that we would follow any gorilla tracks if possible. We were roughly the same group and had the same guide. We weren't to know that gorilla had never been seen on this volcano.

Proof that I swam across the crater lake on Mhabura

Sabyinyo - to climb, along the razorback and back in the day!

We soon realised that this was to be a much more arduous climb than the previous one because the terrain was more up and down and we had to hack our way through the undergrowth in certain parts where the trail had become overgrown. There was the same belt of bamboo forest at the same altitude and the same giant lobelia, together with strange cacti and lichen we hadn't seen before, together with the old man's whiskers which trailed from every branch. I wished there had been a botanist with us.

Unfortunately there were no gorilla tracks, nor was there a crater lake. The top was a razorback series of four or five peaks leading in sequence to the highest one. The term razorback was not quite as scary as it sounds as we could walk or scramble comfortably on the ridge without fear of falling either way, though as a pleasant consequence, the views at either side were stunning.

Descending from the clouds over Sabyinyo.
Pretty steep!

Coming down the volcano was another thing. We had experienced a little of what was to come on Mhabura but nothing in comparison with this. It is always more of a strain on leg muscles going down a mountain and the strenuous terrain made it worse. The front of one's thigh muscles begin to scream with pain and in the case of one of the ladies her legs went completely and we had to take it in turns to help her down. I thought that I was fit but this is something that one has to train specifically for. We were all very relieved to get to the foot of the volcano and to the cars and refreshments, but once again what a wonderful experience it had been.

At the same time, the Peace Corps *en masse* were climbing Mount Kilimanjaro in Tanzania. Waldo had told everyone that he had done some mountaineering in the States but he was mortified to tell us on their return that he, above all, had suffered from mountain sickness. Poor Waldo, I guess he will never live that down.

We had already been down to Geita in Tanzania to visit our friends from the boat with the three girls. He worked in the gold mines there.

That was when, on our way there, Nikky suddenly asked us if the Romans had built this road? We looked ahead and the road was dead straight, right to the horizon. 'As a matter of fact they did Nikky' I said. The constructers had been Stirling Astaldi, an Italian firm, who had been responsible for laying the road. Not quite historic Roman, but a clever observation on her part.

Primitive workings at Kilembe Copper mine

137

It was interesting to see how a gold mine worked. In Geita they used the method known as cyanide extraction. I can't recall any more details, except seeing the forbidden areas of highly toxic cyanide sludge, to which we gave a wide berth.

Our friends had since been transferred to Kilembe, not too far north of Rukungiri, so we went to visit them again. Kilembe was a copper mine, and very important to Uganda's economy. This was to be something new for us, but very interesting because they mined upwards.

We entered a short tunnel at the base of the mountain to observe how they operated. They weren't working at the time of course, or we wouldn't have been allowed inside. The basic principle was that they blasted the copper down from the veins in the roof, collected the ore down a centre chute and used the debris as infill around the central chute. In this way they moved in stages up the inside of the mountain. It was so simple but so very clever. All we saw, therefore, was the opening at the bottom of the central chute and the tubs on rails to collect the ore to be transported away.

After spending the weekend with them, we set off relatively early in the morning to return home, and were told to look to the left before we hit the main road south, and so we did, and there they were, the burnt out shells of the huts of an entire village. The opposing warring tribe had surrounded them during the night and set fire to them, giving the occupants the choice of burning to death or of coming out and facing a volley of spears.

That was our first encounter with the violence inherent in the parts of the country where the UK had not as yet had much influence. It was shocking to see, but it was a reminder to us to let us know where we were. Before we criticise, however, remember what happened in our world wars.

We drove on corrugated murram to the main road and turned right onto the tarmac, which was always a relief. We had not gone far, however, when I felt that there was something wrong with the handling of the car. It wasn't responding to the steering wheel as it should. I slowed down to stop and investigate, and the whole front end of the car seemed to settle down further than it ought to, in fact it seemed to be resting on the wheels. I had no idea then what was wrong until I lifted up the bonnet. I looked around, puzzled, until I finally saw that the torsion bar had snapped in two. I had to wonder. Why had it broken on a perfectly flat piece of tarmac, when I had just been on a very bumpy road through the 'Bush?' Divine intervention again? Surely it was further evidence that someone was looking down upon us favourably.

We were on a tarmac road, but we weren't out of the mire yet because technically we were still on the fringes of the game park. The animals rarely crossed the road during daylight hours but that was not to say that they never would, and they were more likely to do so at night when there would be little traffic.

There was no alternative but for me to stop a car and cadge a lift to the nearest telephone and then hope to get a lift back. We couldn't leave an empty car if we wanted to see it again and I couldn't send Barbie on her own. I had to go, although I hated to leave them, but there was no alternative. Fortunately, we didn't have to wait too long for a friendly car to stop and help us. He not only took me to the next petrol station to telephone for our friends to come and tow us back to Kilembe, but he then gave me a lift back to the car.

Mending a puncture African style – before I was politely told to get out of the way

This may have appeared to be very kind, and it was, but it was only indicative of the camaraderie that existed between drivers who are anywhere near a game park. Most drivers would have done the same thing.

There was a garage at the mine, and they made an attempt to weld the torsion bar together. It lasted about 20 yards on the road. Ours was probably the only VW Varient in the country, so we had to hire a car while spares were sent from the UK. This prompted us to change the car, which we did when we were next in Kampala. I exchanged it for a Volvo Estate car. This sounds rather opulent, but in fact, without British taxes, it was quite reasonably priced.

There was a period without a car, between waiting for the spare part from England and part-exchanging it for the Volvo. We had arranged to see friends in Rwanda just across the southern border of Uganda and in order to avoid disappointing them, another friend said that we could borrow her car. It was old and she was also waiting to exchange it, but it worked and it served its purpose.

The safari went very well until we were well on the way home. We had about twenty miles to go before we reached the next town, telephone and garage, when we had a puncture. No problem, I thought, for I had changed many a wheel. Then I discovered that the spare wheel was flat. Oh dear, I had forgotten the basic rule when travelling in Africa. Always check the tyre pressures, **including the spare wheel.** What do we do now? Africa teaches you to be resourceful if nothing else. I dredged up a memory from somewhere of someone stuffing a tire with grass, so hey presto that is what I set about to do.

It is a well known fact in Africa that wherever you travel, even if you think that you are in the middle of a wilderness, whenever you stop for any reason, within a few minutes there will be an enquiring group of the natives round you. Sure enough, before I had got very far with my task we had a group of onlookers. Not only that, two of them came forward and insisted on taking over the task from me.

They had obviously seen this happen before. When they had pushed in as much grass as possible, which was much more than I would have managed, they did something that I certainly would never have thought of. With the absence of any water around, one of the men quite unashamedly urinated on the grass in the tire before they replaced the tire back onto the wheel. All the while they were laughing and joking in their own language, which we didn't understand. They were obviously from remote regions because they didn't understand Swahili either, and Swahili was the universal language of the foreigners who first came to Uganda to work.

We offered to pay them, but they refused, and smiled their usual beaming smiles as we waved them goodbye. What wonderful people.

When we reached the next garage safely we learned that had they not wet the grass, it would have become chewed up into a powder and would not have lasted us more than a mile or two.

All these excursions had taken place during holiday breaks in the first year, but now it was January 1966 and Nikky and Ros were back at K.P.S. School rules dictated that they must all write at least one letter each week to their parents, and in one of the letters Nikky told us that Ros had been in sickbay for a day. We also had a letter from Aunty Mary to tell us that Ros had been sick too, but only for a day. After that though it seemed that every letter we received mentioned that Ros had been in the sickbay again. We obviously began to get very worried, and when we collected her at half term for the weekend she had once again just come out of the sickbay.

We had a long chat with Auntie Mary, who explained that she had not written to us again because each time Ros had been sent to sickbay with a high temperature she had recovered back to normal within a day or two. Ros was normally a very active and athletic child and 'back to normal' meant that she had regained her usual vigour. She did seem to limp a bit when we got home, but that disappeared quickly and we enjoyed a pleasant break with them.

When, during the first week after half term, we were told that once again she had been in sickbay with a temperature of well over 100 degrees, we could no longer ignore it. We were in Africa where there was a possibility of untold tropical diseases. Ros was fifty miles away with no telephone link between us in those days. We were all 150 miles from a hospital in Kampala and we had a sick daughter with an unknown disease. We could not help but remember the boy who had died of meningitis.

We could not imagine being in a happier school and everything else was working beautifully, but should we stay where we were and be prepared to risk the health of our child? One thing was certain though, we couldn't continue doing nothing about it, so we very reluctantly decided that we would have to go back to England. At least there would be first-class medical treatment there, and there seemed to be no alternative.

I wrote out my resignation and went up to Kampala to hand it in personally. The CEO saw me and asked me why I was resigning, as he thought we were happy at Kinyasano. I told him that we had been very happy indeed but I explained about Ros and her continual sickness. He asked me to stay a while so that he could discuss it with the minister.

An hour later he called me into his office and said 'We have Mulago hospital here in Kampala. It is staffed mainly by postgraduate doctors from the UK doing research studies into tropical medicine. It is very up to date and I don't think your daughter could be in a better place, even if you were to go back to the UK. What if we transferred you to Kampala where you will be near Mulago?'

He was paying me a great compliment by inference, but I asked him where there was a vacancy for me in Kampala. He replied that there wasn't one at the moment, but he had an American architect designing a new primary school for Kampala and he would like me to be the headmaster designate, and I could help in the design and be responsible for equipping it when it was built. What a compliment. I said that I was indeed interested but that I would have to have my wife's approval too. I did add that I didn't think that it would be a problem.

Barbie was as keen as I was, and with only a month to Easter we started preparations for our departure from the south. We were even more pleased to hear that Barbie had also been guaranteed a teaching post at Nakasero P.S. in Kampala. This was the large multiracial school where all the expatriate children were educated and it had an excellent reputation. We could not believe our luck.

Our two years tour was due to expire at Easter. We had thought to extend it to the end of the school year at Kinyasano, but now we could take our four days per month leave as normal and go home to the UK after the schools had broken up for Easter.

We had another big surprise for Nikky and Ros when they came to Kinyasano for the weekend. Mummy was going to have another baby. They had been having a little sex education at school and Nikky said, with her eyes cocked up looking at the far corner of the ceiling – a pose we had noticed she adopted whenever thinking deeply.

'Daddy, does that mean that you have impregnated mummy with a baby?

'Yes, I suppose so' I said.

'When, and why didn't you tell us?'

'Well you see it doesn't always work love, so we have to wait until we find out for certain' then, after a long pause:

'Well, if mummy has a baby in Africa, will it be black?'

I said 'No love, because mummy and daddy are both white,' But that wasn't the first answer that went through my head. I usually say jokingly to friends 'It had better b. . . . not be!' Joking apart, it wouldn't have been the first time that it had happened to a wife in Africa, especially if the husband was habitually away on safari, as many were.

We were very sad and excited at the same time about leaving Kinyasano. The day before we were due to leave, I was in my office and two of our cleaners came in brandishing a book and said 'Look what we have found.' It was an exercise book full of my signatures, page after page of them.

To my dying day I will regret passing this off as just a schoolboy prank. Had I had a little more time to think, I might have realised a more sinister side to it, but we were in a bit of a hurry and who would want to harm us or the school anyway? I paid no heed to the fact that it was found in the bursar's waste bin. Students were often in his office and I was convinced that everyone here was so happy. I had left a signed cheque with the bursar in case of an emergency anyway. If only I had kept the book and mentioned it to Al or Waldo, but they had already left to spend Easter with the rest of the Peace Corps in Kampala, and we were ready to leave.

We were able to stay in the Grand Hotel again for the few days it took us to get all the documents ready to leave with and return to Uganda.

We also managed to arrange an interview with a doctor at the Mulago Hospital. He had just graduated from the UK and was also studying for a further degree in tropical medicine. Sure enough he looked very young, but had that assured look as though he knew what he was talking about. Basically he told us that he could hardly diagnose anything unless he actually saw her when she was ill. It was almost as a last resort that he asked us if we were sure that there were no other symptoms which we had noticed, however small or unimportant they may have seemed at the time? I felt a bit silly mentioning it, but I recalled the limp and said that was the only thing that I could think of.

Instead of pooh-poohing it he asked us a few more details about it, and then he told us he would give us a note to recommend that she had her tonsils out while we were in the UK. 'But there was never any mention of her having a sore throat' I said. He then explained that there was something called a Tonsilic Hip. The tonsils are part of the lymph system and in some cases the infection travels from the tonsils to the lymph nodes in the hip, causing discomfort there. This, in his opinion may be what was happening in Ros's case. If she was to return to Africa it would be the wisest precaution and couldn't do her any harm.

We were soon in the air, flying home in the trusty VC 10. We had gone to Africa for two years, but without a second thought we had agreed to go back, and I was quite excited at the prospect ahead. Was this change going to be as exciting as the others? If only we could get Ros's health sorted out.

HOME ON LEAVE, AND A SHOCK!

It was as if the Prodigal Son had returned again when we arrived back at mum's where we were to stay for the rest of our leave, except that it was 'WELCOME HOME Ken, Barbara, Nicola and Rosalind' emblazoned on the banner. It was a good job that Ivy House had a wide frontage. There was great excitement, hugs and kisses, and it was a delight to see mum's face and realise how proud she was.

Sylvia was now the night superintendent at the Children's Hospital in Sheffield and after all the parties were over she arranged for us to see a surgeon who agreed to take Ros's offending tonsils out. We were given priority treatment because we were returning to Africa and he arranged to remove them straight away with little fuss. It seemed only a little time before she was up and running around as normal. It is with great relief that since that operation, Ros has enjoyed an extremely healthy life. Many thanks to that postgraduate doctor.

We then enrolled them into Norton Primary School for the summer term as we did not want them to miss any education. Our ninety-six days would end in the summer holidays and it was interesting to note that they were well up to standard in all subjects. Being in Africa had certainly not affected their educational progress.

We had been in England for less than two weeks when I had a message from the Ministry in Kampala that a large amount of money had gone missing from the school accounts at Kinyasano. I was shocked, and then remembered the sequence of events before I left.

I contacted Kampala immediately, explaining precisely what had happened during that final day, and I offered to return immediately to help sort it all out. I was told to continue with my leave as normal and return on the air tickets with which I had been issued.

It was probably a mark of my naivety that I did not feel too worried about it all being sorted out. In my mind I guessed exactly what had happened, but I have to admit that it cast a cloud over the rest of my leave and it was in the back of my mind what I would have to face on my return. Of course I had a clear conscience, but it could appear to look as if I had run off with the money. I guess if I had been a suspect however, the minister would have wanted me back immediately. Barbie did ask me if I hadn't noticed that whenever the bursar spoke to us he never once looked us in the eye, but always looked down at the ground, and I always thought that it was I who noticed attitudes. It made me wonder why I hadn't realised the significance of the book with the signatures being found in the bursar's office. I admit that, though I saw him often, he was a government employee, and he played no part in the running of the school except keeping the financial records. I can't think how I could have involved him more into the life of the school. If it was him, and as far as I know he was never convicted, then was it resentment against me, personally, or was it merely opportunism? I will have reason to discuss this in later chapters of this book.

When we were in Kabale we were particularly friendly with a couple who had a car in the UK. When I said we would have no transport in the UK he at first offered to lend it to me and then to sell it. It was an Austin Metropolitan, made for the American market, and was a convertible. Only a few had been sold in the UK, but what a super car it turned out to be. It was quite old, but very nippy, and I decided to buy it. We just loved zooming around the country in it. The girls especially loved it when the hood was down, and being a wonderful summer, it was hardly ever up. How I wish that I still possessed it. Together with the Bubble Car, what antique value they would have held between them.

Our lovely Metropolitan in the drive at Ivy House

It was nice to relax and rest for a while. One of the friends whom the girls met at school had a pony which she used to bring round for them to ride, and later in the term she entered it in a gymkhana with Ros riding it. Nikky was good at riding but not quite as confident or daring as Ros.

It was a lovely sunny day and, as the first annual gymkhana the village had attempted, the event was quite successful. Ros didn't win anything of course, but it made it an exciting day watching her.

We had kept in touch with Gordon, my assistant from Dinnington Modern, and we arranged to meet them, with their two little girls, at Butlins, Skegness, over the half term break.

We will always remember the ride there in the sun with the hood down, and at one point me having to tell the girls to get down. We were singing along with the Mamas and the Papas on the radio and they had their feet on the back seat and were sitting on the hood. That was obviously long before the advent of the seat belts. It was a different sort of holiday for us all, and for that reason alone we thoroughly enjoyed ourselves. For no other reason than the distance which separated us, we were destined never to see Gordon and his family again.

Barbie was twenty-seven weeks into her pregnancy and we arranged to see a doctor in Sheffield for a checkup before we went back to Africa. Having driven to Sheffield we parked the car and walked to the surgery quite normally, unaware of the drama that was to follow. 'Mrs. Redcock' the receptionist called. That was not the best start to begin with. Barbie had a 'thing' about our name, so no wonder what was to follow happened. Barbie went in, not best pleased, and I waited, and I waited, and I waited.

It was well over a half an hour later when the receptionist asked for Mr. Pidcock to go in to see him. Barbie had obviously had time to put them right on the name. When I entered I was surprised to see the doctor was alone. 'Where is Barbara?' I asked. 'Please sit down Mr. Pidcock; I have to tell you that you have a very sick wife.'

Apparently at some point while seeing the doctor, Barbie had suffered kidney failure and collapsed. He told me that they had rushed her to the Royal Hospital and that I was to go there immediately for the latest information.

I was devastated to say the least, but knowing that Barbie's first thought would be for the baby I asked, 'What about the baby, doctor?' The doctor, thinking no doubt that I was putting the baby's wellbeing before my wife's said quite heatedly, 'Mr. Pidcock, our first duty is to save your wife. The doctors at the hospital will decide what to do when she gets there.'

With that ringing in my ears, I somehow got to the hospital in a daze.

We had walked into the surgery feeling quite normal and now here we were with Barbie desperately ill. I was taken into the ward, but they were already wheeling Barbie out for surgery, so I only had a fleeting glimpse of her pale face as she passed by. Then a long wait, a very long wait.

A doctor came to the waiting room and told me that Barbie had undergone a double operation. Firstly they had performed a partial Pyelo nephrectomy. They had removed stones which they called a staghorn calculus which had completely blocked the tubes leading from the kidney to the bladder. They had then performed a caesarean section, but after the trauma and high temperatures that Barbie had endured, the baby was stillborn. Barbie had been put on the 'danger' list, and to mark the severity of the situation they said that I could stay overnight if I wished.

The hospital had a room with a bed to accommodate me, and I was told that I should be able to see her in the morning. I was very sad of course about the baby, but so immensely relieved that Barbie had survived the operation. Unlike everything the G.P. had thought, I had hardly considered the fate of the baby and my thoughts were all focused on Barbie's survival.

When morning came I was led to the bedside to find Barbie asleep. Well, she was in fact in a coma and would not come out of it for another two days. For the whole of that time she was on the 'danger' list. It was with great relief therefore when she did emerge from the coma but she was still quite delirious for a while. In the middle of her delirium, though she couldn't speak, she somehow motioned for a pencil and then scrawled 'Baby?' all across a sheet of paper. Miss Platt, the surgeon was with us at that time and explained to Barbie what she had done, and Barbie then slipped back into her delirious state.

The big medical news on the media that week was that the first ever successful kidney transplant had just been performed, albeit in a different hospital, and we were to learn that Barbie's operation had been one of the first of such operations as well. The new techniques had been developed just in time for us.

I stayed by her bedside for the next three days and was thankful to see her become fully awake. Perhaps it had been good that she had learned the situation as she had done, while she was semiconscious. She was able to get over most of the shock during her delirium. Even so she took it very badly and apologised to me as if she had let me down. I reassured her as well as I could, and I told her that I was so happy that at least she was alive.

147

Barbie now had a massive scar across her back, and the one down her tummy which had now been used for the third time. The new method of cutting the caesarean section horizontally had been devised by then, but as Miss Platt, the surgeon, said, 'You would have looked like a hot cross bun if I had cut horizontally.' It was typical of Barbie that she often made a joke of that afterwards and typical too that she made a remarkable recovery and was soon up and walking again. As a result though, she was to be on sulphadimidine as a prophylactic for many years to come.

Being Barbie though, she did not let the experience affect her, and her greatest sporting achievements were yet to be accomplished. We both thought that this was another example of divine intervention. Our guardian angel was still present. I know that we were both devastated about losing our baby, but what if the appointment had been on another day, or even an hour later? That she should collapse at that precise moment in time when actually with a doctor, and when the necessary surgery techniques had just been developed, was surely miraculous.

Norton School had swimming lessons in their curriculum and it was while Ros's class were having their session that the Yorkshire Swimming Coach happened to be there. I have to explain that the rest of the class were only learning how to swim, while Ros could do any stroke she wished.

The coach then contacted us to ask if there was any possibility that Ros could stay in England so that he could give her specialist training. He must have thought that he had a budding Olympic champion in the making. He would have been even more impressed had he seen Nikky too. Nikky and Ros knew they were good swimmers, but they were also aware that they were probably not so outstanding amongst the other expatriate children in Africa where they practically lived in the swimming pool.

They didn't want to stay in England though, and we certainly didn't want them to stay either. Training for Olympic athletes was bad enough, but nothing compared with the rigorous routine the swimmers have to go through.

BACK HOME - IN AFRICA

Our families had more or less accepted that we were to work in Africa for the foreseeable future and probably now understood that we weren't quite so mad after all. We flew back to Entebbe and were met and taken to Kampala and to the hotel once again. We had been allocated a bungalow in Coppice Road, a small group of houses amid the trees on the northern outskirts, and our crates were duly delivered from PWD and we were soon organised once again.

When we were still in Rukungiri and had asked Tiri if he would come with us to Kampala, he had said 'No Bwana, dem black men up dere.' The Africans differentiate one another according to the colour of their skin too, but it ranges from Fair (Light Brown) to Brown and Black. They are certainly not hung up on describing someone with their colour, and they can see the subtle differences in each other. They can usually guess which tribe a stranger comes from, merely by looking at them. Imagine a Geordie seeing a stranger and being able to say 'Ah, you must be a Liverpudlian' without him having spoken.

Just as we were leaving though Tiri came to us and said 'I come Bwana.' He obviously thought that our need was greater than his. We breathed a huge sigh of relief because having a good and trusted houseboy was so important. On top of that we genuinely liked him, and I am sure that our informal and relaxed attitude was better than he would get from most other Memsaabs. We got on very well together and had become quite attached to him.

When I went to the ministry it was as though nothing had happened in my absence. I was expecting a grilling over the disappearance of the money, but in fact it wasn't mentioned. I did not ask any questions because it was up to them to bring up the subject. We had learned that we shouldn't question their politics. I guess I was a little afraid, but as long as they had faith in me I was satisfied. I was introduced to the architect and we soon struck up a friendship and a working relationship. I suppose I was his 'gofer' for a while because my contribution to the project was mainly in the future. With a nine-to-five job however I found life far different from the constant pressure of a headmaster's duties.

Barbie and the girls soon settled into Nakasero too so we could settle down to an orderly routine for a while. We joined the Kampala Club and had time for football and tennis once again. The girls were delighted with the prospects of swimming again, and this time there was a coach for them. He wasn't official but was one of the parents who did it as a hobby in his spare time. I helped him a little on the two weekly sessions but left the instructions to him as he had started the class and had vastly more experience than I had.

He provided two cups to strive for each week. One was for swimming and the other for diving. It was awarded for a different discipline each week, i.e. a different dive or a different stroke, or sometimes he awarded it to the most improved swimmer. The children absolutely revelled in the competitive atmosphere. Whoever said that competition was not good for children?

Nikky diving for the cup

They also practised Personal Survival for which there was to be an examination on a certain date. Many of the adults also wanted the Personal Survival certificates, and it was interesting to see both adults and children practising getting undressed in the water and swimming through hoops etc. especially when the adults were struggling more than the children.

It was not long before Nikky or Ros came home with a cup, and once, just once, they achieved their goal. They both won one at the same time, and proudly stood for their photograph with the two cups between them.

During the first month back we decided to take a trip down to Kinyasano to meet the students and staff again. I was interested to find out what had happened. We set off on a Saturday morning and had just about reached Masaka when we saw a lorry in the distance. Surely that was

Once, just once, they got the diving and swimming cups together

Barbie's golf and tennis trophies - I shared one!

the Kinyasano lorry? Yes, we recognised it before it had reached us and slowed down to a stop. Al and Waldo had also recognised our car and stopped opposite us.

We hugged and shook hands and marvelled at the coincidence. They were going for a meeting of the Peace Corps personnel, but they had hoped to see us in Kampala as well, and had brought some mail for us. Some of it had been opened, but that was during the investigation they said. Waldo was his usual self, but I had a feeling of a little reserve in Al's demeanour. He never had been as open-hearted as Waldo, so maybe it was nothing.

We were all conscious that we were illegally parked, so we couldn't just stand and chat for long. They had no conclusions to offer on the money, so I motioned to Barbie that we were ready to continue on to Kinyasano. It was then that Al advised us not to go, since they were not going to be there. That is probably what was bugging him. The bursar was driving around in a new Mercedes and some of the locals must still think that I might have had a hand in the embezzlement. A lot of money was involved from an African point of view, and certainly sufficient for a few bribes to have been dished out. I was very upset that this should be so, but if the bursar was still around I could understand what the situation might be. What I couldn't understand was why he was still around, but maybe we were wrong and it wasn't him. I didn't wish to open that particular can of worms, and didn't comment. We said our goodbyes and reluctantly turned around and made our way, rather unhappily, back to Kampala. Was our meeting with them just a coincidence, or again was someone watching and guiding us? I have mentioned that we were brought up to care about 'what people might think' and I am still haunted by the thought that some people back in Rukungiri might think ill of me.

We missed having a dog and when we saw puppies for sale we went to look and brought Suki back with us. She was a lovely Golden Labrador cross and a super pet. The girls adored her. I remember when she came into season during the following year we took her round to a neighbour who had a Golden Labrador male. We put them together in their garage but he didn't seem interested at all. It made an amusing tale to relate at later get-togethers.

We soon managed to find another suitable mate for her and she duly produced eight gorgeous little white bundles of fluff. It was very good education for Nikky and Ros and they gave us hours of fun playing with them on the lawn. Suki was such a good mother too and we sometimes felt sorry for her with eight big boisterous bundles fighting over her teats. She just lay back unconcerned as if it was no trouble at all.

We couldn't possibly keep them all, and after they were weaned we sold them all except Brumas, the biggest one and the girls' favourite. Yes we sold them, but not to make money. There is a theory in Africa that if one pays for something then it is treasured. If one gets something for nothing then it is not particularly valued and has a greater chance of being neglected. How true I have found this to be and it has become one of my pet theories applicable to other aspects of life too.

With Tiri cooking for us, we have never eaten so well, but that didn't stop us experimenting. We regularly went to the African market where one could see things one would never see in Europe, such as fried grasshoppers and fried flying ants or termites.

Jinja market

During certain seasons the grasshoppers congregated in their tens of thousands around the street lights in the city. Why, I never understood, but all the market traders had to do was to stand underneath with a huge sheet and collect them as they became exhausted and fell. I have seen them collect a barrow full in one go, and what a good source of protein.

The white ants built huge ant hills in the bush, sometimes 10 feet high, and again, during a certain season, the traders would simulate rain by drumming on the ground, attracting the ants which flew out in their thousands, and were then duly collected.

Eventually we had to try them. Well, they had been fried. The grasshoppers actually were not dissimilar to shrimps. Ros decided that she was going to buy some for lunch at school the following day, but whether she just overdid it or whether she ate a bad one we don't know. All we do know is that she had to leave the classroom that afternoon to be violently sick.

We had a football team at the Kampala Club and played a few games against local teams and local S.S. schools, but at that time we had no organised leagues. On one occasion we were due to play a local African team and for some reason I had forgotten my boots and it was time to play.

Now for ten years in Dinnington I had taken gym lessons and night school classes with bare feet, and this included the occasional game of three-a-side indoor football. Most of the African teams played in bare feet in any case, including the one we were due to play, so yes, I took to the field barefooted.

Immediately there were hoots and cheers and much merriment and laughing from the crowd who were mainly African. This was a first for them, a *Msungu* (white man) in bare feet. Every time I touched the ball there were whoops and cheers, all good natured, and I don't think it affected my game much. I never repeated the performance though, not with a real football. The one in the gym had been made of felt, and I have to admit that playing with a leather ball made my feet somewhat sore afterwards. It all added to the entertainment though, and that is what it is all about.

We played a lot of tennis in our spare time and it was the lead up to the national championships. All the tennis players entered because it was the natural thing to do. Most of those who played were from Kampala but all the best had entered from the provinces.

Finals weekend arrived, to be held in the Lugogo National Stadium, and Barbie had won through to four finals. I thought that I had started rather well too. A young American lady had seen us play and asked me to partner her because she had just arrived and had not had time to find anyone else. She had been a junior champion in the states and was very good. After the first round, which we won, we began the second round and I remember that early in the game I missed an easy shot at the net. After that I don't know what happened to me, but we were annihilated. I have never been so embarrassed on a sports field in my life. I don't think I returned one ball over the net. My arm felt paralysed. I've experienced the yips in golf, but this was something else. Anyway, I never saw this young lady again.

Unfortunately Barbie and her partner lost the 'Ladies Doubles' on the Saturday, but that left three to be played on the Sunday. She saw one of the organisers to explain her predicament and he said, in his broad Australian brogue, 'Tough titty'. That was all the sympathy she got.

We were entered in the 'Married Couples' competition, but she had entered the 'Mixed Doubles' with another partner who was better than me. The top men players were always vying for the better lady players to partner them. They duly won too after a thrilling match, so two down and two to go. Barbie just lost out in the 'Ladies Singles' however, but it was a tight match, and she gave a good account of herself, so the spectators got their money's worth. Maybe she was thinking about the next match that she had to play.

The last event on the programme was the 'Married Couples' final. Mr. and Mrs. Pidcock were playing Mr. and Mrs. Batcup. What a mouthful for the umpire, who to his credit after a bit of initial stuttering and stammering, managed to get through without too much trouble.

I hope it was entertaining for the crowd. It should have been, for there were no tie-breaks in those days and the final score was 4-6, 6-4, 26-24 in favour of the Pidcocks. We were the 'Ugandan Married Couples Tennis Champions'. Barbie must have been exhausted at the end. They had played on Barbie most of the match thinking that she would be the weaker player. How wrong they were, but at least I was able to play my normal game, without getting the tennis version of the 'yips' again.

Ugandan Television was still in its infancy and I was surprised to be approached one day to give an interview on TV as headmaster designate of the new school. I had not been given any advice, or information on what was going to transpire. I turned up at the appropriate time and was just walked to a chair and put straight under the spotlights. I remember being half blinded by the lights, and without any preamble they started firing questions at me. I told them about the needs for another school and my hopes and aspirations for it. I remember that I just had to ad lib throughout the whole programme.

In retrospect, I wondered if the whole episode had been a mistake. It was soon afterwards that the opposition party tried to make politics over whether or not an African headmaster should have been appointed. I had assumed, wrongly, that it had been organised by the education ministry, and was left with the feeling that I had been 'set up.' I still considered that I had given all the right answers in order to promote the school, but maybe I had inadvertently given the opposition party sufficient ammunition to fire at the government. I remember that at the time I was very upset, but in retrospect, we have no regrets about the outcome. We were convinced again that there was someone above guiding our lives.

Nikky was now ten years old and it was time to start thinking of secondary education. We received notice from the Nakasero School that those wishing to take the 11+ examination should attend the school on a certain date. Yes, it was the same one that was set in the UK at the same time. Nakasero was well prepared and had organised this for many years and it was therefore no surprise or shock for the pupils. The date was fixed for half way through the spring term.

I happened to mention over lunch that I ought to be handing in my notice and applying for jobs in the UK soon. Immediately the girls looked up and said 'Why?' This surprised me somewhat, so I explained that Nikky was nearly eleven and there were no secondary schools for European children in Uganda. 'But all our friends go to boarding schools, and anyway we want to keep coming out here on our school holidays' they replied. I had to be frank and said as gently as I could 'But Nikky love, you know you are a bit shy, and I don't think you would be happy on your own in a new school.' Again they both made their position clear, but it was Nikky's situation that we were concerned about at the time.

We had another dilemma to resolve, not just for the girls, but for my situation. Should I attempt to further my career by going back to the UK? I didn't think that I should leave it too late. Or should I stay where we were both happy in our jobs and where we really thought that we were doing some good? Eventually we reached a compromise. I said that we would have a trial period and stay, but should Nikky go to boarding school and be at all unhappy in her new situation, then I would resign immediately and we would return to the UK where I could take my chances.

There was still the question of where. If Nikky was to go to boarding school, to which one should she go? Our contract allowed us to choose wherever we wanted, so we began to ask friends for advice, and we are glad that we did. Roedean and Millfield had been mentioned, among others, but we were warned to beware of the cultural differences that might exist. It could be hard for a girl from a working class background, who was placed among the rich upper classes where they had all been to private schools and had elocution drilled into them. Not that our speech was not good and correct, but I could understand their argument. The reverse had also been known too, when it had eventually created a cultural gap, and the child had become ashamed of his or her own family's speech.

We then had a talk with a couple who were also teachers. He was the headmaster of one of the Senior Secondary Schools in Kampala. They were as down to earth as we were and told us that their daughter went to Lady Manners School in Bakewell, Derbyshire, and described what a good school it was.

We could not apply directly to schools but only to the counties, so we added Derbyshire to our list. Each county by law had to provide boarding facilities for families overseas, and we knew that Lady Manners fit the bill for Derbyshire. Very quickly we heard back from Derbyshire who offered us a place at Lady Manners, providing Nikky passed the 11+. Nothing was heard from any of the other counties at that time.

Meanwhile I was making a matchstick scale model of the new school, and lists of requirements. It was precise work but hardly very demanding. I felt that I was just marking time. Never complain about working hard because it is more preferable than not having very much to do.

VICTORIA NILE SCHOOL - ANOTHER MOVE!

I was not destined to mark time for long however because I was summoned to the ministry. They had a crisis but didn't tell me what it was, but I suspected that it was political, and related to my television interview. There was a chance that it was nothing to do with me, but rather concerned with events in Jinja, but I was always careful to avoid politics, and didn't ask the reasons why.

I was just asked if I could help them to solve the problem they had by moving to Jinja. Whatever the cause, it represented a huge amount of trust that they must have had in me. They were asking me to take over as headmaster of what was probably the second largest and second most important multiracial primary school in Uganda. The present headmaster from Victoria Nile, Jinja, was seemingly to do a swap with me.

Of course, things are not always straightforward. Nikky had to take her 11+ at Nakasero, and hence study in preparation for it there. It wasn't an ideal situation, but two of her friends agreed to let her stay with them for three weeks each. It was the best solution that we could come up with. Ros, of course, came with us to Jinja, but she too missed the company of her big sister.

Jinja was a town on the northern shores of Lake Victoria and the last stopping place before crossing over to Kenya. Victoria Nile was a multinational school of around four hundred primary children and certainly where all the expatriate children of that area attended. I would guess that 40% were African, and 30% each of European and Asian children. There was stiff competition amongst the Africans to get their children to pass the entrance examination in English which they needed to gain admission. The staff were also a mixture of English and Asians with one African lady member.

Barbie's top Infant class at Victoria Nile School, Jinja

There were two main compounds. The main area was where my office was situated, and the classrooms which were built round a quadrangle. A short distance away was a smaller replica where the first two years and the remedial class were taught.

Barbie and the girls were obviously reluctant to leave Nakasero School and all the friends we had made in Kampala, but I could hardly refuse an offer like that. We made our fifth change of residence and Nikky and Ros their sixth change of school, and they were still primary children. When they were at Norton school they both seemed ahead of their classes, so we had no reason to believe that another move would affect them adversely.

It may sound a cliché but again we settled down very quickly into the new environment. This is obviously what we were good at, adapting quickly into new situations.

Four new members of staff had been recruited to Victoria Nile from the UK so we were not the only newcomers. Barbie taught over in what we referred to as the infants department, as unofficial head of that department, while I was, of course, mainly in my office because, being a larger school, I did little teaching. My time was fully occupied with administrative duties. I did have a senior mistress too; a very able Asian lady, and I also had an equally capable secretary – again male and African.

Only one week into the term had passed when a delivery lorry drove up the drive to the school. Several large crates were delivered for which I signed. I had no idea what they were and I was keen to see what was inside them. One of my handymen opened the first one which contained five identical boxes. They were polished boxes and had a well fitting lid. We still didn't know what they were when we lifted the lid up to inspect them. They were obviously electrical with dials. Were they something to do with radio? All the rest were the same, and there were three more crates. Twenty boxes was just more than one for each classroom. It then dawned on me. This was a two-way talking system between the headmaster's office and each classroom. Talk about Big Brother is watching you. This certainly wasn't my style, so I put them in the store room and wrote a letter to the ministry, informing them that we had the twenty boxes which were surplus to requirements. I would certainly not need them.

I never set out to spy on my teachers, but on my travels round the school I could tell at a glance what was going on inside the classrooms. I was always pleased with what I saw. I don't think the pupils even saw me passing. There was no nudging and sitting up straight. They all appeared to be engrossed in either the teacher or the work they were doing, which was a good indication of industry.

Without me lecturing them, the teachers knew that I expected excellence and they duly responded and passed this on to the children. One young male member of staff was keen on apparatus work and usually had ropes and pulleys on his desk to interest his class. It was a delight to go over to the infant department too with all the walls bedecked with the children's drawings, charts and paintings.

Our Ideal home, but a bit noisy when it rained!

The entrance to our house on Nile Crescent, lined with cypress trees

The first house we were given was not really satisfactory. A local official had fancied the previous headmaster's house, but we were soon offered a bungalow on Nile Crescent. It was quite old and looked from the outside as though it was in danger of collapsing, but if there is such a thing as an ideal building for the hot climates then this was it. The outside obviously badly needed a coat of paint, but it was never to get one while I was there. It didn't matter because the inside was ideal, and we were more interested in the functionality of the house rather than its looks.

It was very simple. Four large rooms side by side with a 3 metre wide veranda all the way round. There were two bathrooms, one at the rear of each side veranda. We therefore had two bedrooms, virtually en suite, a dining room and a lounge. The veranda wasn't glazed but had mosquito proof metal netting fitted. The back veranda had been converted into a fitted kitchen and a laundry room.

The girls loved to sleep in the side verandas when we had guests staying. I was able to tell friends that I could practise my bowling at cricket on the front veranda because it was 26 yards long.

The first term went surprisingly well. It had been well run before and there were no problems for me to sort out. The new teachers had adapted very quickly and there was a satisfying atmosphere of industry and enjoyment. So there should have been too because they all had a good life in the excellent weather outside school time.

Just before Easter, Nikky joined us, having completed her 11+. Thankfully we didn't have to wait long for the results. She had passed, along with most of the others, and her place at Lady Manners was secured. During the previous year the local university had set an intelligence test for all ages in Kampala, and Nikky had come top, so we would have been surprised had she not passed, and she was always near the top of the class or actually at the top. It is always a relief though to have the future sorted out.

Weeks later we received a rather curt letter from Mr. Clegg, Yorkshire's Chief Education officer, asking why we had chosen a school in Derbyshire to send Nikky to. I had to reply that they were the only authority at that time who had answered our application. Apparently, wherever Nikky went, Yorkshire was responsible for the cost of her education, because our permanent residence was in Yorkshire. In that case, one would have thought that the Yorkshire officials should have been much quicker in responding to our application. This once again demonstrated how we were being watched over and guided. Bakewell proved to be a very good choice.

Camping on the beach at Malindi, Kenya

During the Easter holidays we decided to go to Malindi once again. It had been so lovely when we had last been there. Two of the new teachers, one with her husband who taught at one of the secondary schools in Jinja, came in their Dormobile. The journey there should have been made a lot easier because they had now concreted the road to Mombasa. It was irritating to go from Mombasa to Malindi on the road which was still murram, when we could see the parallel concrete road which looked all but finished but not yet opened.

It was also disappointing to see that the sea had eroded 20 metres of the shoreline and we had to pitch our tents much further back. At first we mistakenly thought that meant the water was deeper over the reefs which made them less sharkproof, and that would have curtailed our swimming. This turned out not to be true of course, and we were able to enjoy the warm sea as much as usual.

We continued to enjoy the holiday at the seaside with all its added attractions, and especially with the company, but somehow it did not seem quite as exciting as it had during the last holiday there. For my part, there wasn't the group of men to share another fishing expedition with, and there was not the group with the dabchicks for the girls to share and enjoy. Even just watching the children enjoying themselves had been fun. So, we decided to call in at Tsavo National Park on the way back and didn't stay in Malindi quite as long as originally intended.

The entrance to Tsavo National Park

Tsavo was not much of a detour from the road home and had a huge cut-out rhino advertising its entrance. We arrived early in the morning because we did not intend to camp there. As soon as we entered we encountered baboons on the road. They were crafty devils and just sat there, deliberately blocking our passage. As soon as we stopped a couple hopped onto our car and wouldn't budge. The Dormobile was a little too high for them with no bonnet to use as a step-up

We now had no option but to drive on, and had no alternative but to keep the windows well closed, otherwise little hands would have reached in and taken whatever they could grab a hold of. One naturally drove slowly in a game park in order to look for game and I think the baboons knew this too. At least they understood the how, if not the why. We followed the track for a while and came to a pond around which there were many more baboons. As soon as we stopped the baboons jumped off and joined their friends. They must have played this game all day and every day, who knows? Probably they took it in turns to have a ride to the entrance and back, but we will never know. Talk about clever monkeys.

We spent another few hours driving around admiring the game, some which we had not seen in the Q.E. Park, like the giraffe, both Grants and

Thomsons (affectionately known as Tommies) gazelle, zebra and the largest antelope of all, the impala. We always saw lion, but we knew that there were cheetah and leopard around but they evaded us and were very rarely seen.

When we saw vultures circling around we knew that there had been a kill and we would drive towards it. When we did reach a kill, we would also see the hyena, vultures, marabou storks and jackals lurking at a distance, waiting to take their turn to clean up. There is never any disease from waste or rotting carcasses in the wild, because every last morsel is consumed by some carrion eater or other. Among the ugliest creatures on earth are probably the vultures and marabou storks while they are on the ground, but in the air, they look absolutely majestic and so graceful in flight.

A male giraffe. They are huge. An average man could easily walk under its tummy!

Sure enough we were stopped once again on the way out by the baboons to cadge a lift back to the gate where they hopped off without even a thank you. If it was possible to detect a smirk on a baboon's face, then I'm sure we saw one.

Three important events in the school calendar happen during the summer term. The first was open day when parents are invited to see the work of their children. Maybe this was the proudest time for all for the staff, me included. The practical displays in the junior classes were good, but those in the infant department were spectacular. The drawings, paintings, knitting, needlework and craft displays were so beautiful, and were a credit to all the staff. What a lot of work went into it.

The next big event was sports day, and this was my department. This was my forte, for I had assigned teachers to each event and given them sufficient instructions for them to know the rules. The finishing judges, timekeepers and scorers were all in place and the programmes distributed. It really did run well, the like of which had not been seen in many primary schools at that time. I am a great believer in competition, and I think I was vindicated when even those not participating were cheering their team on. Football supporters may not be able to play well themselves, but boy, don't they want their side to win, and so it was with our children. We tried to work it so that all the children took part. We introduced fun events like the egg-and-spoon, potato, or sack races for them, so that even the less athletic could score points for their House.

To end the term off, we had the yearly examinations results delivered on Speech Day. Yes, and we did publish positions in the children's reports too. None of this nonsense about upsetting the children's feelings. I know for a fact that the children know who are the brightest, and who find it the most difficult, long before the teachers do. If it upsets the parents then maybe that will give them the incentive to help and spend more time with their children's education. This is a complaint for the UK though, and one that cannot normally be levelled in Africa, especially against the Asian, Lebanese or African parents. Their positive attitude seemed to have rubbed off onto the European expatriates in Africa too.

I also believe that red marks hurt nobody, for they certainly didn't harm me and I had more than most in my books. That was how I discovered what was correct and what was incorrect spelling etc. Look what the 'modern' system has produced, just an appalling drop in standards of literacy (and probably numeracy too.) The modernist's theories have a lot to answer for because Maths is an exact subject, I suppose I expect English to be the same.

School ended for the summer holidays. We had enjoyed eighteen wonderful months in Jinja, and we had just a week before our next leave was due. We had heard of the Tree lions in Ishasha, at the southern end of the Q.E. Park, but we hadn't found them on our other visits, so we resolved to go down to try to find them. We made our plans and were surprised when we were ready and Nikky said she didn't want to go as she wanted to stay with her friend. She hadn't long to see her friends before we took our leave and so it would be a long time before they saw each other again. The family were quite trustworthy so we reluctantly agreed to let her stay. It was only a day trip, and we never really expected to find the lions. It would be like looking for a needle in a haystack, but off we went, forever optimistic.

As usual there were lots of game about and Ros got a bit frightened as we went round a bush to find ourselves confronted by a herd of elephants to our front, and, when I looked to the right there was another small herd there too. As I stopped I noticed they had calves with them which made the situation much more dangerous. I had to think quickly and slowly reversed away from them. The big bull elephant guarding them lifted its trunk as if to charge, and gave a little bellow, but by that time he could see that I was a lot further away and the crisis was over.

One never knew what might be round the back of bushes and small clusters of trees, but only elephants with young were a real threat. Buffalo and rhino were much less common in the Q.E. and hippos were only to be found near or in water during the daytime, because their skin was surprisingly sensitive to sunburn.

We continued south, searching all the while and came to an area with hardly any trees at all. Thinking that we were out of luck we were almost prepared to turn back, and only drove onwards as a last resort. We had still got a little time on our hands.

We saw a small copse in the distance, and decided to go as far as that and then turn around. Hang on, what was that over there? We could see dark shapes in one of the trees from a distance. Was it just vegetation, or were we going to be lucky after all?

We approached slowly now because we were certain that they were the lion we had come to find. Approaching from behind, and about twenty yards from the trees we saw a gory sight. It was the top half of a buffalo, just as if it had been cut in half through the waist. All the inside of its chest was empty and exposed and was glistening as if it had just been rained upon. I then took what was professionally probably the best photograph of my life, catching the drops of water on its innards beautifully. Of course I can never display it because it is so gory, but I do still have the slide. We never saw any sign of the bottom half of the beast and assumed that it must have been the lions' breakfast.

Tree lion's lunch. (Water Buffalo)

Tree lion and cubs. - May I pass please?

We then inched our way round the tree, and there we saw a male, female and four cubs resting on a big horizontal branch, about 20 feet high from the ground. I took photos with my telescopic lens mostly, because even if we were virtually beneath them they would appear small on an ordinary camera. We watched for several minutes in awe of these splendid creatures.

Tree lion resting after lunch

They had obviously grown accustomed to cars. They just took no notice of us at all. I imagine that they wouldn't remain so placid if anyone had been foolish enough to get out of the car and expose themselves as flesh and blood, although I was leaning out of the window to take the photographs. Then again, it might have been safe. They had already eaten their fill, and lion usually only kill to eat. There are only a few animals, horrible foxes being one of the worst, who kill just for the sake of it. We were never likely to test this theory out of course.

We were not to be left on our own for long however because we heard the noise of an engine, and another car came into view. Our car would have been obvious from a great distance, and had attracted company. It was driving rather too quickly in my estimation, but fortunately it didn't seem to disturb the lions.

The female decided to stand up and started to urinate, so what did the other driver do? He drove under the stream of urine so that he could say that a lion had urinated on his car. At the time we felt somewhat disgusted, but I suppose we had to admit that it would be a future talking point for the occupants. I don't know what it was that made us feel as we did. Maybe it was because they drove under deliberately and that it hadn't happened naturally, or was it that it was somehow demeaning to the lions?

I am sure that we could have stayed watching them for hours, and no doubt would have stayed longer had we been on our own. We had achieved what we had set out to do however, and taken some wonderful photographs, so we turned around and drove back to Jinja.

Poor Nikky wished she had come with us as we related the story to her when we arrived home, and she was even more upset when she saw the photos.

SAFARI TO THE UK, VIA SOUTH AFRICA

It was possible to take what was called our 'final entitlement' once, and once only, after or during any number of tours. Just as we had travelled to Uganda First Class with unlimited freight, we could claim the equivalent of the First Class fare on the return journey. We put our heads together and decided that, as this was to be our last journey together as a family, we would take the final entitlement now.

We decided to make it a family holiday and fly down to Durban, take a tour of The 'Garden Route' to Capetown, and sail home from there. It was organised for us by a very good travel agent, and what a super job they made of it. I suspect that they had organised the same holiday many times before for expatriates in a similar position. We didn't travel First Class of course and the difference in the fares meant that we had nothing more to pay.

The flight to Durban was just a normal flight, but it was spiced by the excitement and anticipation of what was to come. What a shock when we landed in Durban, for here we were more or less in our summer outfits, and it was cold. We hadn't thought that it would be winter south of the equator, and that Durban was so far south.

The first thing we did when we settled in the hotel was to go shopping to buy clothes, and especially duffle coats.

The second shock was when we approached the doors of the stores, because without touching them, they just opened in front of us. We were so tentative at going through them that first time. We had never heard of automatic doors, let alone seen them. We so enjoyed that first shopping spree in those stores, because they were like the ones which one would see in London or Paris. It also felt so much better when we walked out of the stores with our new duffle coats on.

The whole trip was just spectacular, but it would take me too long to describe it in detail. I would advise any tourist, however, to take the tour if they can.

We called at Pietermaritzburg, and had a lucky escape at Kokstad, the next overnight stop. We knew it was bitterly cold, even in our new winter wear, but I say we were lucky because when we arrived at East London, the next destination in our tour, we were told that after we had left Kokstad, it had been cut off by a blizzard.

We also stayed overnight in Port Elizabeth before reaching Capetown. Long before then Barbie kept us laughing by imitating the courier when he announced 'and now we are stopping for morning refreshments' in his very clipped South African brogue. He was also very good at directing our attention to the right-hand side of the coach when passing a view of a 'shantytown' or other unsavoury sights on the left. It had been a truly superb tour and one to be recommended.

Capetown was of course the show piece, and we just had to go up to the top of Table Mountain in the cable car. I warn you now though. If you are afraid of heights give it a miss. When we were half way up I was standing in the exact centre of the cage and imploring Nikky and Ros to 'come away from the edge.' It was quite safe of course but I have to admit that I was scared. To make matters worse the conductor said that we shouldn't worry as there hadn't been an accident on it for over forty years. I thought that now must surely be the time for one to be due.

What a relief when we stepped out at the top. The views over the harbour and surrounding countryside were

The cable car over Capetown.
(Wouldn't you have been scared too?)

breathtaking. Strangely with my feet on solid ground I felt no fear at all. We had an hour to wander around and we ended up going into the only shop at the top.

We couldn't believe our eyes. The shopkeeper looked just like Old Father Time. How fitting to find him on the top of the world. We did buy a few souvenirs and then it was time to go down, which I endured far better than I had on the upward journey. Crazy I know, because any mishap would have been just as disastrous. What is amazing is that Barbie, who suffered quite badly from vertigo later in life, did not display any signs at all during the whole trip. She must have acquired it at some time later.

All the hotels had been first class, but unfortunately that could not be said about the one we stayed in while in Capetown. I realised that this hotel had had to fit into the budget, whereas the others had been part of the packaged excursion. That didn't bother us much because the following morning we embarked on the S. A. *Vaal* which was to take us home. It was a one class ship, so Nikky couldn't complain that 'One of those third class children had been sitting in her place' as she had done on the S.S. *Uganda*. It was a pleasant cruise though and once again we experienced the ticker tape send off.

A cruise is a cruise however and not a subject for this book. We did go through the 'Crossing the line' ceremony again, and called in for refuelling in Madeira before we berthed in London Docks. The big difference from when we sailed out to Africa was that now we were travelling north, and after passing the equator we felt the drop in temperature day by day. It had the curious effect that it always felt chilly.

Sylvia met us in Doncaster when we arrived there on the train, and drove the nine miles home. We got the same warm reception all over again and it was a joy to see mum looking so well in spite of her arthritis.

Did I detect a tinge of jealousy from some of my siblings over the obvious adoration mum showed towards me? Strangely, we both detected a slight reticence in some of our friends too, when we talked about our travels, or even when we were just answering their questions. It was as if they were just a little jealous of our apparent success and exciting travels and safaris, even though we had made a point of trying not to boast about our experiences. That isn't as easy as it sounds, and we had to make a real conscious effort not to prefix our sentences by 'When we were in... '

We now had no home of our own in England, but we had the prospect of Nikky going to Lady Manners to look forward to and prepare for. It was only natural for us to think that it might be a good idea to buy a house in Bakewell.

We had never been to Bakewell before and found it to be a beautiful little market town, with all the nearby attractions of the Peak District as a bonus. It was a real beauty spot, but what we found not so beautiful was the price of property there.

We went to all the estate agents, and in spite of the price there wasn't very much available at all. It was obviously a very desirable place to live. We did find a two-year-old link house for sale. It was on a new estate backing on to one of Lord Beeching's defunct railways. It was ideal, but way over the price bracket we had budgeted for. We could not possibly afford £7,500. Still, it was what we wanted and where we wanted to be, and the bank manager would agree to give us a mortgage on it, so we bought it.

The estate was in the form of a short stemmed T with our house at the head of the stem with a lovely view down the road and across the river to the town. A short driveway led to a garage and the front porch. The front door led into a large lounge with an open staircase leading from it. Through the lounge was a large kitchen and dining room with a picture frame window looking out onto a fairly large lawn and garden. Upstairs were two bedrooms, a bathroom a toilet and a box/bedroom.

Most of our holiday was spent moving in, furnishing it and getting to know our neighbours. It was ideal for many reasons. It was quiet, it was only a short walk into town and the boarding house to Lady Manners was just round the corner on the same estate. The only minus was that it was quite a trek from the boarding house to the school, which was on the other side of the town at the top of a long steep hill. It was one of the few things that the girls ever complained about.

Nikky was asked to go for a courtesy interview with the headmaster of Lady Manners and we were to accompany her. It was an imposing school building, but in the dismal weather looked a bit on the bleak side. It was rather embarrassing when he asked Nikky what her favourite TV programme was. There were very few televisions in Uganda and not one of them belonged to us. Thank goodness she didn't say that it had been *Steptoe and Sons* which would have been true, but hardly the answer he would have wanted. He really hadn't been prepared properly to interview a pupil who had spent the last four and a half years of her life in Africa.

Before we returned to Uganda we needed to rent out our house because we didn't want to leave it empty. We can only thank our good fortune again when the estate agent came up with the solution. He let it on a yearly basis to four of the teachers at Lady Manners. They were delighted and so were we. We could arrange leave during the summer holidays so that as they left we could take over, and as we left, they could move back in.

With all that organised we could breathe a sigh of relief. We drove to Norton to say *au revoir* to the family, but this time it was not going to be easy. We were going to have to say goodbye for a while to Nikky, who was to stay at Grandma's until Lady Manners started the autumn term. Of course, she had boarded before, but this was the first time that we would be in different countries, and Nikky would be on her own at school. We prayed that she would soon make friends, and that they were a happy lot in the boarding house. They now had a telephone at Ivy House, so she could get in touch with them if she needed to, and we would all keep our fingers crossed.

We said our goodbyes to everyone, and though Nikky looked unperturbed, we wondered what was going on in her mind. When something has to be done, then one has to do it, so we drove off and waved until we were out of sight.

All that was left now was to say our farewells to our friends in Bakewell, and we returned to Africa to start yet another chapter in our lives.

MUM COMES TO AFRICA

Once again, as we stepped off the plane, it felt like walking into an oven. It was with very mixed feelings, however, because this time we travelled without Nikky. It was a strange feeling to have left her back in England. At the same time we felt happy, because, not for the first time, we felt as if we were returning home, and this feeling lasted for the whole time that we were in Africa.

Yes, Africa was growing on us. It was going to be good to reunite with the friends we had made, and to get back into the routine of life at school. It was also especially nice to see Tiri again, for we had grown quite attached to him having stayed with us during all our moves. Of course it was also so good to find Suki and Brumus so well and so obviously happy to see us again.

We had arranged for Sylvia to take Nikky to Bakewell. I hope that I repaid them well for all the trouble they took on the many occasions that the girls needed transporting from one place to another. I'm sure I did because it had been ingrained in us from childhood not to expect anything for nothing. That never stopped me from wondering though.

We had access to a telephone by now and had devised a system of communication between us and Ivy House to save money. Telephoning overseas was very expensive in those days. We arranged for them to telephone at a certain time and we would not answer it for four rings. If it stopped after three rings we knew that all was well. If it went on for longer, then they had something important to say, and we were to pick up the phone. Fortunately the phone stopped after three rings on that first day at school, so we knew that everything was fine, and we would get the details later by post.

I might add that it was agony waiting for that first letter, but when it came we needn't have worried. Nikky had made friends with her room-mates in the boarding house, one of whom was still her best friend forty years later. As for schoolwork, she said she had done it all before.

One of the mothers of a child at school was a qualified nurse and came to see me about the possibility of testing the children and staff, if they wished, for trachoma, which was endemic in the tropics. I was all for it, from both a medical point of view, and I guess I was just curious.

We organised an inspection throughout the school. It was a fairly easy procedure, and merely meant flicking the top eyelid back over a matchstick and inspecting underneath, looking for the telltale white spots. We would all become experts at doing this after a while.

The results were not only quite surprising, but quite scary too, especially to the parents. Nearly half the school showed some signs of the disease, and that included many white children and a few of the staff. Thankfully the treatment was simple. Three consecutive daily applications of penicillin cream did the trick. This woke us up to the simple fact that we were all vulnerable to African maladies in spite of how clean and hygienic we tried to be. The following three days were noted for the queues of children along the corridors outside each classroom, having their daily smear of penicillin cream in their eyes. They were all advised to have their individual towels to use too. Although the school was not involved, most of the parents whom we knew also had the tests and treatments.

We had another dabble at sailing and joined the sailing club. We bought an old dinghy in partnership with a young nurse who had just arrived because we knew we wouldn't be able to devote much time to sailing. Our venture into sailing was not to last long though. It must have been on our first trip out when the rudder snapped off! We were literally rudderless, and drifting towards the coffer dam, which wasn't dangerous, but rather humiliating as we were spotted and someone had to come out in a powerboat to rescue us! That was the end of our adventures with sailing!

Victoria Nile started a new year. New nursery children were allocated classes and teachers also allocated to their class and classroom. Some mothers asked if their child could have the same teacher as in the previous year, but I left the teachers with the same year as before. To move up with the class would mean eventually dropping from the fourth to the first year, which wouldn't suit most teachers. There are also benefits to be had for children to have a change of teacher, and the teachers should actually progressively teach better the second and subsequent years, having already gone through most of the work.

The post arrived one day with the weekly letter from home. Sylvia had written it and she mentioned that mum had jokingly remarked that she would like to see 'our' Ken in Africa. I thought 'what a good idea' but didn't say anything. That was going to be a surprise.

An Asian trader had started a business chartering planes to fly to and from the UK, so I went and bought two return tickets from London to Entebbe to coincide with the holidays and sent them back by return. I knew that if I had asked, mum would have said 'no' because of the expense. I also knew that having sent the tickets, she would put all her fears aside because she couldn't possibly waste 'our' Ken's money.

When the time came, mum was given a tranquilliser just in case she was afraid during the flight, and of course Sylvia came with her. I had a wheelchair waiting on the tarmac in Entebbe, where there was a 100 yards walk to customs, because of mum's rheumatoid arthritis. All the Africans gave way to us. It was unlikely that they had ever seen a *Msungu* over eighty years old with her white hair. African hair sometimes did become grey, but that was unusual because they didn't normally live long enough. In those days their life-span was much shorter than ours.

Mum didn't say much on the journey home, but I could see that she was taking it all in, and was looking around with keen interest. She had actually been thrilled by the flight.

When we arrived in Jinja over an hour later she sank back into a chair and gave a big sigh. It had obviously been a tiring journey, but she said what an exciting one it had been. I was wondering what she was thinking when she met Tiri, who then brought in tea, on a tray, just as she liked it.

I remembered her saying at home in England 'I don't know how you can sit there and be waited on, 'our' Ken.' Well two days later I saw her sitting under a tree on the lawn ringing a little bell and saying 'Can you bring me a cup of tea Tiri please?' I hid a little smirk, and made sure that I would remind her when we were next in England. I didn't say anything then of course because I didn't want to spoil the moment, and certainly didn't want to put her off from repeating it.

Mum on the equator

When we were sure that mum had become acclimatised to the heat, we thought she was fit enough to visit the game parks. We decided to go to Tsavo first because of the wider range of animals to be found. I had taken mum round the school of course, and quick trips around Jinja, but this was the first journey of any length. We had our passports ready too, because Tsavo was in Kenya and hence we had to cross the border.

We met the same set of baboons at the entrance, or was it the turn of another troop to have free rides? It made mum jump, and Sylvia too, when they leaped onto the car, even though we had warned them and made sure that the windows were tightly closed. They duly left us at the water hole however to let us drive into the more exciting part.

We soon saw a herd of vague grey shapes in the distance, and mum said 'What are those animals Ken?' 'They're zebra' I replied. 'What, without stripes?' said mum. 'We'll see' I said, and sure enough the stripes began to appear as we got nearer. Such is the clever camouflaging effect of the stripes. One naturally expects that the stripes would make them stand out, but in fact from a distance they make excellent camouflage.

Mum had seen almost all the types of animals which we had expected to show her in Tsavo, but after an hour I had not seen any sign of a lion, and so I turned to mum and said I was sorry but I hoped we would see one soon. I was surprised then when she said 'Well there is one over there' pointing ahead.

It took me quite a while to see it, perched on a rock and half hidden by bushes. 'Gosh mum, you have still got very good eyesight' I said, and was truly amazed. We edged nearer to have a closer look, and that really made our day.

I don't suppose mum had seen many of these animals at all, even in a zoo, and to see whole herds of hundreds them just roaming around grazing must have had quite an effect on both her and Sylvia.

We still had time to drive around, but eventually we had to call it a day, and to start our journey back and give the baboons a lift to the gate. They couldn't get over the baboons, and the fact that we were prepared, and knew what was going to happen, amazed them.

Rhinos and Gnus - note the scar on the rhino

We waved goodbye to the cut-out rhino at the entrance and began to wend our way back into Uganda, stopping for a well earned cold drink at the Crested Crane Hotel as we rode into Jinja. I wanted to give mum and

Sylvia a taste of standards in Africa because some of the hotels are equal to any in the UK. The crested crane, by the way, is the national emblem of Uganda, being a bird similar to a peacock and having a large golden crest, but a much less spectacular tail.

I haven't mentioned Sylvia, but she was obviously enjoying being here too. She has always tanned very well and by now was as brown as a berry. We were all exhausted when we arrived back to Nile Crescent, but Tiri soon had a welcome cup of tea ready, and dinner was not far away.

Both mum and Sylvia were fascinated with the abundance of game in the parks so after a few days rest we decided to take them into the Q.E. Park as well. How marvellous it is to wake up and know that it will be another fine sunny and hot day. The rainy season was still a long way off.

This safari had to be organised more carefully because we wanted to show mum the Q.E. Park and Murchison Falls. We knew that we could not do both in the same day, so we would have to take our sleeping gear and stay at one of the safari lodges overnight. Which one would depend on how well we travelled and what we saw, so we would resolve that when we had seen what we wanted. It would be either at Mweya Lodge in the Q.E. or in the Chobe (Pronounced Chobi) Lodge in the Murchison National Park.

Murchison falls. – Note the spectator fence by the view point on the top right by the trees

On the way to the Q.E. Park there is a viewing spot where the road runs close to the edge of the Rift Valley. This was an ideal place to rest and have a coffee break, which Tiri had prepared along with a picnic lunch for us to take with us. We could sit and gaze over the almost sheer drop in front of us to see the massive plain below. I do not know how many feet below, only that trees appeared as dots and animals, even elephants, were too small to spot with the naked eye. This was the park, and we then took the road which meandered down, taking us to Mweya Lodge at its entrance.

We soon saw herds of Uganda Cob, the most numerous of the small antelopes and the favourite food the big cats. There were plenty of the cattle-like Waterbuck too with their distinctive white flashes down their flanks. We then found an isolated tree under which to have our lunch, and were surprised by a family of warthog. Something must have startled them because they ran along characteristically in single file - father was in front with the little ones in the middle and the mother bringing up the rear! What made us smile was that each had its tail sticking up straight and vertical!

Approach of the dry season. - A crowded Hippo pool in Murchison Game Park

We had forgotten where to find the hippo, but knew we would see them in Murchison, so we made our way to find the elephant skeleton to where we had remembered it to be. I guess this impressed mum the most, to stand and hold an elephant's thigh bone which was almost as big as oneself. We then made our way down to the Ishasha end of the park to show mum and Sylvia the tree lions. This time we knew exactly where to find them! I could see that mum was a little bit apprehensive when I drove nearly underneath them, but soon began to enjoy the experience once she had realised their complete indifference to our presence.

All this had taken longer than we had anticipated, so we made our way back to the entrance and booked in at the lodge for the night. This was another first for mum because we could not have imagined that she had spent a night in a rather basic log cabin. Darkness comes very quickly on the equator, so there is very little dusk. We were able to enjoy watching the various animals come down to the feeding areas though, which were specially prepared for the guests to view from the safety of the cabins. Then an early night for us all to prepare for a long day ahead.

We had enjoyed a late dinner and an early breakfast at the lodge and were on our way shortly after dawn. It was a few hours drive to Murchison. We had drinks with us as always, but it was still approaching midday by the time we arrived at Chobe Lodge, so we decided to have an early lunch there first, and after satisfying our tummies, we set off to do the two main objectives of the trip. Of course we saw many animals on the way, but we made a beeline for where the river trips started. We did see Roan antelope, which was new to us, and much bigger herds of buffalo, but they had become incidental. We had come for the river cruise. Unfortunately when we arrived there it became obvious that mum would never be able to negotiate the hazard of getting onto the boat. She declined even to try, hence we could only view from a distance the banks where the crocodile were. Barbie and I had been before of course, but how disappointing that mum couldn't see the crocs from close quarters, but we did see the hippo in the river and later found the overcrowded hippo pool. Because we were approaching the end of the dry season the pool was drying up, and soon the hippo would have to find a different stretch of water to submerge themselves in to protect them from the sun. At least that was half of our first objective achieved, so we then set off up to the viewing area of the Murchison Falls.

After only a short walk we came very close to where the vast river had cut into the rock, and was cascading over both sides of the gorge. What a majestic sight. We kept well back from the pathetic little wooden railing which had been placed on the edge. This must have been well before tourism started in a big way and 'Health and Safety' had to be taken into account. It was impossible to hear each other speak above the thunderous roar of the water, and any communication had to be done through sign language.

I am quite sure that mum had never experienced a sight like that in her life, and was so pleased that Barbie had thought of it. Watching the sheer power of cascading water is fascinating and can become quite hypnotic, and with the sun shining on our backs, the ever present rainbow looked as bright as ever. It is possible just to stand and watch it for ages, but eventually we all had reluctantly to drag ourselves away and drive home.

The ever present rainbow

It was a well satisfied family who finally arrived back on Nile Crescent, but it isn't possible to describe my emotion of complete satisfaction and joy through being able to provide mum with all these different experiences. I have never stopped feeling gratitude for the sacrifices she made for me as a child.

We began to notice that mum was not using her walking sticks as much as usual and we thought maybe she could manage a walk round the shops in Kampala. We therefore drove to Kampala, parked the car and locked it and began strolling along looking in the shops which were not unlike those in any British town. Suddenly there was a cry from mum and I looked round and saw a man running off with her handbag. He had just snatched it from her shoulder.

I set off after him, but a man ahead had also seen what happened and jumped in front of the thief and grabbed hold of him. We caught up with them and retrieved mum's bag and thanked the man profusely. He was a very polite African who apologised on behalf of his country and wished us well, saying he would see to the thief. We were all very grateful, especially me, as I envisaged time spent in court and filling in statements etc. which I could ill afford. That episode illustrates that there is good and bad in every country and we had just experienced both.

Nikky flew out to us for the Christmas holidays, which was good that we could spend mum's last few days together. We all went to Entebbe to meet her in the car and it never ceased to be an emotional sight to see our little daughter getting on or off the plane. In this case it was of joy, but on leaving it was always sadness. We never liked being separated from our children.

It is difficult to describe how Nikky must have felt. She was no longer a tiny tot who would come running towards you and jump up into your arms. She suddenly seemed older and sufficiently mature to take things in her stride. We all hugged her and the rest of the time we all seemed to be asking her questions at the same time.

Nikky couldn't wait to get home to see Suki and Brumus again and even Tiri appeared to be really pleased to see her again. Then she was eager to go to the club to meet her old friends and swap stories. It was hectic and an exciting time for her. This period of reuniting was to happen over and over again, and in a way it was what made boarding in the UK worthwhile for them. It was like having three extended holidays for them every year.

All too soon the time came for mum and Sylvia to fly back to their home in the UK. We had witnessed just how powerful the sun was, and how healing it could be. Not only did mum look better, but she said that it had made her feel ten years younger. By now she had discarded the sticks completely and would not need to use them, even after arriving back in England, for several years.

When we arrived at the airport we queued with them at the gates to the tarmac. In deference to age, she was allowed to go to the front of the queue. It was always at least 100 yards to the plane, and when they opened the gates it became a free for all. Incredibly she was still near the front of the hoard by the time they queued at the steps to get on board, and without her sticks.

We felt sad seeing them leaving, but we also felt so proud and happy for mum. She had wanted to come and see us in Africa, she had seen sights that she could never have dreamed of and her health had improved immensely. How could we not feel proud? At last I could feel that I had repaid her just a little bit for the sacrifices she had made for me.

MORE SAFARIS AND TRAUMAS

We continued to be happy teaching at Victoria Nile. The school could not fail to impress all who came to visit, especially on the Open Day, Sports Day and the Annual Prize giving.

We now had to have a nanny, since Ros was on her own with Nikky being in the UK. It was almost unknown for any teachers to be burgled or harmed, so we felt quite safe leaving Ros with the nanny to baby-sit. We also bought a little Fiat 500 so that if I had to go away on school business, and I often had to go to the ministry of education in Kampala, Barbie had a means of transport. We didn't reckon on anyone else using it though.

We had gone to play in a golf competition at the club and Ros had elected to stay at home and invite some friends. It did not dawn on us why she had decided to stay behind until afterwards. The little madam told Tiri to push the car up to the top of the drive so that they could practise driving by freewheeling down to the bottom of the drive. We wouldn't have known anything, except one of the boys couldn't steer very well, and stopped it by running into one of the badminton posts. Apparently Tiri had been very cross anyway, and had threatened that he would tell Bwana, but he didn't need to because the evidence was there to be seen.

We had been on many safaris, but there were two more that we wanted to do. Before mentioning these however, I must relate an incident which occurred on one of our previous safaris which will ever be imprinted in my memory. We had set off to visit the Masai Mara Park in Kenya and had arrived on the edge of the park approaching dusk. We often stayed in the lodges for safety reasons as well as the provisions they afforded in providing guides and information of the latest happenings and the whereabouts of certain species etc. The lodge was still some distance away however, so we decided to rest at a small campsite which had been set up specifically near the entrance. It consisted of a large bonfire which was kept burning throughout the night by Askaris (night watchmen) to deter the game, a few tents and a wooden structure like a phone box which housed a 'long drop' toilet.

We enjoyed the usual barbeque and sat around chatting and enjoying the sense of being completely alone in the middle of a wilderness. When bedtime came, early since we wanted to be up early, Barbie said that she would sleep in the car, while the girls and I opted to sleep in a tent. That lasted until we began to hear the sounds in the stillness of the dark. First the hyenas with their er... ough, (doh... soh) er... ough, then the roar of a lion in the distance. It wasn't long before first one of the girls, then the other, decided to sleep in the car, closely followed by me. We had air mattresses, and one of the girls lay across the front seats while we other three squashed into the back. With the back seats down there was a flat area at least 5 feet long.

We did manage to sleep because we all wakened up with the onset of dawn. We couldn't see much because the car was so steamed up. We hadn't dared to leave the windows open too much during the night. It was the sight that met our eyes that I will always remember. A lady was just emerging from the 'toilet' box, still sleepily rubbing her eyes. She looked around, as one would, and that is when we witnessed the most rapid transformation in a person that I have ever seen. Standing about 30 yards on the other side of the 'toilet' was probably the biggest bull elephant we had ever seen. It was simply massive, with large tusks. Now she wasn't the youngest or the fittest lady in the world, but if we'd have had our stopwatch handy we would have been able to record the world record for the fastest 30 yards dash back to her car. We were all able to laugh at the incident later, and the elephant maybe wasn't dangerous. They are only a threat if they feel threatened, or if they have young near them to protect.

The first opportunity we had, we arranged with friends to go to the Kidepo National Park. This was on the northern most tip of Uganda on the border with the Sudan, and to get there we had to go through the district of Karamoja.

Here, the men went about naked – well, they wore a cloth or a piece of sacking round their shoulders in case it rained. When it rained the cloth was to protect their hair, which was permanently bouffant and set, or almost glued, in one of the tribal fashions. All they did wear was a purse and a neck rest, usually on a thong around their waist. The neck rest was important. When they lay down, they had to keep their hair from touching the floor, which would be impossible without it.

Barbie answers questions from the Karamojong

Karamojong girl

Karamojong girl begging by the roadside

The karamojong normally carried a spear or a bow with arrows in a quiver slung over their shoulders. They were quite willing to sell these for a few pounds, and we actually bought a normal spear, a fish spear (with a double pronged head), a bow, and a quiver of arrows. We did not bargain, because they were cheap enough, but no doubt they would have thought they had done one over on us.

While buying these, we had our photos taken with them, which was also unusual. Normally the tribal Africans object to having their photographs taken because they believe that their spirit goes into the photograph, but this sometimes changed when money was involved. Ros, who stood hip high to these tall slender men, remarked to Barbie 'Mummy, has that man got three tailies?' I leave you to work that out for yourselves.

My mum, when we showed her the photos later, said 'Our Barbie, I don't know how you can stand there and have your photograph taken with nude men.' It was noticeable however that none of the family averted their eyes from the photos.

The ladies on the other hand wore a skirt around their waist but were entirely topless. Many of them also had steel rings round their necks. It occurred to me that they may have put one on every year, because they were of various sizes and some of them were obviously too small for them ever to be taken off. This gradually elongated their necks, but not to the grotesque degree that some tribes practised.

When we dragged ourselves away, we motored on up to Kidepo. As we were leaving we saw the men just turn and run into the scrubland. We wondered where they were heading off to. Were they going hunting or were they going home? Whatever, they had miles to go because we could see no signs of any huts or houses or any signs of habitation.

We had been told that there was no camp site in Kidepo, so we stayed in the safari lodge which, as always, was basic but adequate. We went around with one of the rangers in a Land Rover because it wasn't deemed to be safe to go alone. Poachers had actually shot and killed two of the rangers recently and we were reminded of this every time we passed their freshly dug graves which were beautifully laid out in front of the lodge for all to see.

We were surprised by the number of giraffe up there. We had never seen them in such numbers. It was fascinating to watch them drink with their straight front legs splayed out in order to get their head sufficiently low enough down to reach the water.

The arteries in their long neck were specially adapted in order to get the blood up to their heads. The anatomy of the circulation of the blood in giraffes is complicated and intriguing, involving valves in the arteries, which doesn't occur in other animals, and special elasticity in certain of the vessels. Apparently our heart would never be able to pump blood to our heads had our necks been half that length.

Giraffe at Kidepo National Park.
Note the splayed front legs when they wish to drink.

It had only been a brief visit because apart from the giraffes, and the fact that we hadn't the usual freedom of movement, the journey had been more interesting than the park. We could say, however, that we had seen part of Sudan.

We did play some football because I remember someone at the club had a friend in Eldoret, Kenya, and had arranged a match against them. The school in Eldoret was the school some parents opted for instead of a secondary boarding school in England. We had contemplated this for Nikky and Ros, but we reckoned that the education at Lady Manners would be more English orientated, and we would see them just as often, even though they were further away. I think they preferred the flying experiences too. We still had in the back of our minds also, that at some time we would be going to live back in England.

I only remember that football match for two reasons. We had just returned from leave in the UK and I had not done any training so I had been reluctant to play. I had finally agreed to play only because they were short of players. Secondly, during the game the ball was put through to me with only the centre half between me and the goals. I feinted to go left but went right, and with all the strain on my left knee it suddenly gave way. Our goalie told me later that he had heard the crack as my cartilage split, and he was at the other end of the field.

That was the only time in my football career that I, as a centre forward, can ever remember being given a foul in my favour when the defender was indeed innocent. Yes I had plenty given the other way. Forwards are always under the impression that defenders get away with murder. The referee must have thought he had kicked me though, for it to make a noise loud enough for our goalkeeper to hear. It was a classic 'bucket handle' tear, and it was surprising that after the first week, I was still able to participate, with care, in golf and tennis.

I could only hobble on it for days afterwards, but I did manage to drive OK because my left knee didn't have to move much. Barbie could have driven of course, but she rarely did when I was in the car. Not that I didn't trust her because she was a good driver, but she preferred to sit back and leave it to me. Maybe she made a better passenger than I did.

Lake Nakuru was a few miles further away from Jinja, but being so near, we couldn't miss the opportunity to see the thousands upon thousands of flamingo on the lake. When we arrived there, the lake looked a vivid pink for as far as the eye could see. It was a sight that we were glad that we hadn't missed, and we sat and gazed for hours. We had seen herds of thousands of animals, but birds seem to abound on a different scale entirely. Thinking about locusts and ants which we had also seen, I guess that insects are even more numerous, so the theory must be 'the smaller they are, the more numerous are the gatherings'.

I managed that year by being very gentle on my knee and clicking it back into place when the cartilage slipped out. I was to have my cartilage removed in Doncaster on my next home leave.

The second safari we were keen to take was realised when friends decided to go to the Ngorongoro Crater in Tanzania and asked if we would like to go along with them and of course we said yes. That was the last, and probably the most important, of our ambitions. The shortest way from Jinja was to cross into Kenya, bypass Nairobi and travel down the eastern side of Lake Victoria to Arusha, in Tanzania. The crater was not far away from there. Tanzania used to be two separate countries, Tanganyika and the island of Zanzibar. I remember Tanganyika because of the vividly coloured stamps I once had in my modest stamp collection.

Border control on the Tanganyika (now Tanzania) border,
before East Africa split into three

Once again we were caught out because we didn't take warm enough clothes. The hotels are situated on the rim, which is 2000 feet higher than the extinct volcano's floor. They were shrouded in mist when we arrived and it was bitterly cold outside. We were thankful to stay in the hotel that evening where it was warm.

The morning brought clear weather and spectacular views over the 100 square miles of the crater floor and the surrounding cliffs. It was still cold, but we hired the obligatory ranger and a Land Rover to take us down to the floor of the crater where we once again felt the normal African heat.

Private cars were not allowed in the crater, and rightly so because it must be the most popular destination on the map and would have quickly become overcrowded. Imagine any other tourist resort being able to ask tourists to limit their stay to 'two nights only' in order to give other people a chance. Anyway, in spite of the short time allowed and whatever the cost, it is well worth it.

Almost anything you wish to see is there. One can see all of the 'big five' and most of the smaller game, and the animals are so used to Land Rovers that it is possible to get quite close to whatever you want to see.

We had two cameras and I happened to be taking stills with a

189

telephoto lens. The driver told us we were approaching a rhinoceros, and what a beauty, but by the time I had the right setting on the lens it was far too close. I took shots of it anyway, so if anyone wants to see a close-up of a Rhino's eye, I have just the photo for you.

Both Nikky and Ros were with us which could have been embarrassing. It seemed to be the mating season for the lions because we saw many prides and every time we approached a pair they started mating. We knew that they mated more than once while she was in season, but it was as if he was staking his claim and saying to us that she was his wife and his alone.

Lions mating in the Ngorongoro Crater. Does she look interested?

We had to smile because the females looked quite indifferent during his performance. We wouldn't have been surprised to see the females yawn through the act. I had learned the facts of life on a farm and I thought that this was another chance for Nikky and Ros to see the practical side of sex too.

It is difficult to say which game park is the best, because they each have something special that others probably don't have. The Ngorongoro Crater would certainly have the edge if the number of separate species in one area is the deciding factor. This then must have been one of our best safaris.

Ostrich family

Surreal gnus

Ros's eleventh birthday came. We always had parties to celebrate birthdays and festivals. It was so easy, living the outdoor lifestyle which we were able to enjoy. We tended to overcompensate on presents too, so they always had good memories of their birthdays. Being eleven also meant that she would be joining Nikky hopefully at Lady Manners.

First she had to pass the 11+ exam, and as headmaster I had to arrange it. I sent to England for the details and appointed two of my staff to adjudicate so that no one could say that I had been involved in any way. I wanted to see if she was really capable of passing, and I didn't want to subject her to grammar school education if she wasn't suited to it. I need not have worried though because when the results were returned she had passed.

One Sunday we decided to take the dogs for a walk after lunch and set off as a family with Suki and Brumus prancing around alongside. We crossed the road and walked across the fifth fairway of the golf course which brought us down to the banks of the Nile.

We strolled along to see the cofferdam which had been placed there to dam the waters back while they constructed the Owen Falls Dam a mile downstream. All the time we were tossing sticks for Suki to chase and retrieve, with Brumus trundling along behind her, and we were all having such fun.

When we got near to the coffer dam we saw that it was constructed of huge steel cages, 2m x 1m x 1m, made of thick, wire netting and containing stones. These obviously stretched right across the river, and at that time the water was about 2 inches deep flowing over the top of the cages. At first I was wary of going near with the dogs, but crocodiles here were unknown, and hippos had not been seen since the dam had been constructed. The river looked just like a millpond, so I said 'OK Suki', and with obvious excitement she jumped in and swam around and Brumus soon followed.

For ten minutes we threw sticks for them to fetch and we were all having a good time, oblivious of danger. Suddenly, maybe we threw a stick too far or maybe too near the coffer dam, but we saw that Suki started to struggle and then they both disappeared, pulled down apparently by an undertow.

We were horrified but helpless. We kept looking and looking, and suddenly we saw a little head near the bank under a sheet of metal. I was just able to get down and lift the metal and grab Brumus who was just about to give up. The others kept looking and hoping Suki had managed to do the same but we never saw her again. Meanwhile I squeezed all the water out of Brumus's lungs, improvising on a dog the artificial respiration I had learned about as a child in the SJAB and he started breathing again. We wrapped him up in a towel and a very sad family went home.

I was still fearful that he wouldn't survive and remembered we had two antibiotic tablets left over from a recent throat infection from which one of us had suffered. I gave him one as soon as we arrived home and the other on the following day, and by the third day he was running around as if nothing had happened. It took us all a long time to get over that ordeal, but happily Brumus had survived, and was to die naturally of old age back in England many years later.

Our traumas weren't over however because I had to go to Kampala on business and Barbie had nipped over to the club to put her name down for the weekend competition, leaving the girls with the nanny for five minutes. The girls were playing as girls do and then it happened. Nikky was doing the chasing.

Ros ran along the veranda, through the door at the end and slammed the door behind her. Nikky put her hand out to stop it but missed the wooden part and her hand went straight through the glass. She looked at the massive gash across her wrist and then the blood started to spurt out! We later saw splashes up the wall and on the ceiling. She grabbed her wrist with her other hand and told us later that she shouted 'Now look what you've done Ros, you've killed me!'

With the blood still oozing out through her fingers, she told Ros to get something to wrap round her arm tightly. The only thing on hand was a ball of wool, so between them they tied the wool round her arm sufficiently to stop the bleeding. Meanwhile Tiri had run across to the golf course and luckily one of the teachers was passing and he came in to help. At the same time Barbie arrived back home and they all jumped into the car and set off to the hospital which was on the other side of Jinja. Almost at the same time I arrived home to find Tiri distraught and he told me that Nikky had just a few minutes ago had an accident and they had taken her to the hospital.

I dashed off and arrived at the hospital just as the doctor was examining Nikky. He had unwound the wool and put on a proper tourniquet, but Nikky, remembering the blood, refused to let go of her wrist.

I then tried to pacify Nikky and explained that it would not bleed anymore because of the tourniquet, and the doctor had to inspect it to decide how to treat it. I feel so humble to think this, but like Barbie, the girls had implicit faith in me. I held her hand and she reluctantly let go and I nearly fainted. I thought 'Oh my poor little girl' I could see a massive gash with white bits of what looked like string hanging out and I had visions of her being crippled for life. The doctor immediately covered it with gauze and said that they would need to take her into the operating theatre. I don't think that Barbie ever saw the actual gash, thank goodness, because Nikky had never let go of it until we were with the doctor, and now she was at the other side of him.

Nikky was visibly petrified and said she didn't want to be put to sleep. The doctor, recognising this said 'Ok but you have to keep it perfectly still and we will try to do what we can under a local anaesthetic, but if you can't keep still I will have to give you a general anaesthetic.' They then took her into the operating theatre.

Nikky later related to us that there were two doctors, one African and one European and she heard them talking all the time, saying things like 'join that white one to this white one' and 'join this to that one over there' etc.

After what seemed like many hours, she was wheeled back to us returning our smiles, not that we felt like smiling, but it was such a relief to see her alive and so calm. Her arm was now in a plaster. I'm quite sure that the doctors had explained everything to Nikky before they brought her out to us, which was why she could raise a smile. She had endured the procedure without needing to have a general anaesthetic.

The doctors explained to us that they would like to keep her in under observation for a few days. Two tendons, the ulna artery and the ulna nerve had been completely severed, and there was a little muscle damage, but that would soon heal up. They had sewn everything together and were optimistic that the operation would prove to have been successful, but the severed nerve which had been repaired meant that there would be no feeling in at least the little finger for some while, and she should take special care because of that. They estimated that feelings would return at the rate of half a millimetre per day.

Twice she forgot the warning. She was absent-mindedly sucking her little finger on one occasion and suddenly tasted blood, she had bitten herself. On another occasion she rested her arm on a radiator and later saw a blister along her finger.

The prediction of a half mm per day proved to be remarkably accurate, however, because it took about six months, representing about 9 cm. Thankfully, what we had feared, that she would have a crippled arm, never materialised. Thank you again our guardian angel, and thanks most of all to the doctors and medical staff at Jinja Hospital.

Both the girls had to fly back to the UK to start the autumn term at Lady Manners The doctors were reluctant to discharge Nikky from the treatment, but relented after giving her a comprehensive written account of what they had done, to give to the medical people in Sheffield.

Ros was excited because she was going for the first time, and it was a relief for us that they could now travel together. We were extra sad now to see them both walking up the steps onto the plane. Little did neither we nor they realise that it would be their first and last time to travel to England together from Uganda.

I must explain more about Victoria Nile School's position in the education system. We were, in fact, governed from the Ministry in Kampala, while all the other primary schools in the district of Jinja were governed by the Local Education Authority as in the UK.

While we were there a new African District Education Officer was appointed to Jinja, and he invited me to see him in his office. He was a jolly fellow and had been trained in Yorkshire, so we got on very well. He could also joke about the Yorkshire dialect, mimicking his landladies saying 'Ee cum in lad an sit thisen darn an put thi coit on't peg and mek thisen at home.'

Victoria Nile School, Jinja, Uganda

Because the school was run directly from Kampala, I never had the need to see him, and during working hours I was always busy, but he was always free to visit our school. In fact I never saw him again. I can imagine now how he felt when the plum school in his district was not under his jurisdiction. At the time I didn't give it another thought. It was their system and I could do little about it, but on reflection it would have been natural for him to want it to be included within his domain.

We were due another visit from the nurse, who this time concentrated on pests, and in particular bedbugs. These were bloodsucking insects which not only infested beds, but also furniture, especially chairs. Their bites were very irritating, forming distinctive sores. One of our young ladies teachers had been badly bitten on the backs of her legs without realising what they were, but clearly their chairs were infected. The remedy was simple. PWD came to fumigate the house, end of story.

The inspection, carried out by the nurse, brought to our attention that there were a number of children also with the telltale signs, and I felt it my duty to send letters home to their parents explaining the situation. I wrote one letter which I duplicated to all the affected families.

It was not long after I had sent the letters out that I, myself, had a letter from the ministry saying that they wanted to transfer me back to Kampala. I immediately went to see the CEO in Kampala to ask what it was all about, and he mentioned the letters that I had sent to parents about bedbugs. Without being specific, I had sent the same letter to both Black, Asian and White parents, but someone had obviously taken offence. It was obvious to me then that nothing could be done. This was another example of someone with a chip on their shoulder about a person from another country being in a position of responsibility in their country. I was unlucky to have had it happen to me three times now, but Uganda was an emerging country and had just gained their independence. We had to accept some adverse reactions. We also have to learn that it is not always prudent to try to treat everyone the same, and obviously I had slipped up and someone had taken it as a racial slant.

Basically there were three groups of Ugandans. Firstly we have the peasants who were desperate for education and literally worshipped the expatriates who came over to teach them because they recognised that we had travelled thousands of miles just to help them. Then we have the Elders who were in power, and who realised that the transition to self-governing was best taken slowly and would take years, and they recognised that expatriates, at the moment, were indispensable. The young intellectuals, on the other hand, were aspiring and ambitious, and thought that they could just take over and do what we did as well as we did. They were the ones who resented foreigners having administrative positions, especially when they thought that they were capable of doing the job themselves. There was an important difference though. We expatriates had no reason to let this so-called power corrupt us. Unfortunately, the young Africans had not the maturity to resist this happening, as we have come to see all too clearly. We were in Africa and that was the situation, so we just had to accept it and move on. If it hadn't happened over this, I'm sure the District Education Officer, if in fact it was at his instigation, would have found another excuse.

Unfortunately, Uganda as a country would find this out to its cost after Idi Amin came to power. He took control when Uganda was a net exporter of all the staple crops, sugar tea and coffee, whereas, a few years after he had taken over power, Uganda had become a net importer of them all. They had expelled almost all the Asian landowners and shopkeepers.

The story of the coup was interesting, yet tragic for the country. This was the story as it was related to us after we had left the country, so can only be taken as hearsay.

While President Obote was at the Commonwealth Conference in Singapore, he had a message that ammunition had gone missing from the armoury. He sent a message back instructing his police to put Idi Amin under house arrest until his return. Unfortunately the telephonist who normally received messages was ill and it is understood that Sergeant Musa had filled in for him. Sergeant Musa happened to be a member of the same tribe as Idi Amin and instead of relaying the message to the correct authority, he took it instead to Idi Amin himself, who then successfully instigated the coup. What a tragedy for Uganda. President Obote had his antagonists, but he had united the country and we all thought he had done a good job.

I was quite convinced in my mind that the school was running exceedingly well and that the incident had been used as a political excuse. We both thought long and hard and arrived at the decision that after nearly seven years it might be someone telling us that it was the right time to take up my career back in the UK.

I declined the move to Kampala and sent in my resignation. As a postscript to this, when we were back in the UK we heard that the only African member of staff at the school had been appointed in my place.

Please do not consider this to be a racist statement. There are many Africans for whom I have great respect and whom I regard highly. I think, however, that I had learned how to evaluate the competence and potential of all the staff with whom I had worked for over three years. It was just unfortunate that this particular African was not the best candidate in my opinion, and it appeared to have been purely a political move. I had, after all, left an excellent deputy head in the school.

We were given an amazing farewell, and the staff had clubbed together and bought us a beautiful crystal decanter and two sets of glasses, all engraved with David Shepherd animal engravings. It was so sad for us to leave Uganda for we had enjoyed the experience so much, and we had always found the people so happy and friendly. We did not forget Tiri, and suitably rewarded him for looking after us for so long. Little did we know though that we would be back in Africa after just over a year had elapsed. I began to think that we were a couple of Lord Tebbit's disciples because when things weren't right, we 'got on our bikes.'

Sadly we prepare to leave Jinja

As soon as we arrived back in the UK, I applied for and was accepted almost immediately, to become the tutor/warden of Walworth School in south London. The post would combine part-time teaching and the rest of the time would be devoted to my position as Youth Warden.

PART FIVE

The Swinging Sixties and aftermath

I WISH TO BACKTRACK NOW TO COVER Events over the previous year and the next two. This is an episode in my life of which I am, and forever will be, deeply ashamed. I will feel guilty to my dying day, especially in the circumstances in which I now find myself. I have therefore separated it into a chapter on its own, because, although it might have affected our life, I do not think it affected our professional lives, and to intersperse it among the other events that happened would have magnified its importance and would have detracted from the main theme of the book. It may sound as if I am attempting to make excuses, but I can assure you that I am not, because there are none to be made. I am guilty as charged and a true life history has to include it.

I have already mentioned that I had always thought of myself as looking a bit gawky, with slightly prominent teeth. It wasn't until the girls were having treatment from an orthodontist that I made a concerted effort to keep my lips closed. He had told them that it was called 'lip control' and as I had already had half of my back teeth removed, it worked very well for me too. The girls must have inherited my teeth as well, for they had to have back teeth removed and wear braces for a while. He helped me and did an excellent job on the girls.

This was the time of the 'Swinging Sixties'. Barbie and I had only ever known each other sexually, and we were quite satisfied in that knowledge. It was called the swinging sixties because of the loosening of morals and censorship, which produced films like *White Mischief* and *Out of Africa*. The general conversation in Uganda at that time was about the goings on in the 'happy valley' in Kenya and the wife swapping that went on etc.

When ladies danced a little too close, or held on a fraction too long, or said 'Oh, I imagined your cheek to be smoother' or 'You have no idea what an impression you make when you walk into the pool area', I put it down to a woman's natural attraction to power. It was during the time that I was a headmaster, but if this sounds as though it went to my head, I didn't think that it did, because I did nothing about it. I remember Barbie often used to say to friends 'Of course, all the ladies have fallen for Ken', and I think that she was proud to say it, whether it was true or not.

I remembered a saying from that time. Dancing is the vertical realisation of a horizontal intention. Some of the ladies made this pretty obvious, and it is sad to say that in my eyes, contestants on 'Strictly Come Dancing' would never get tens unless they made it appear to look that way too. I can remember what I took to be lascivious looks on some of the panel's faces after certain performances where the dance extolled the sensuality of the contestants.

I had a few dancing lessons in my youth, and was taught that one should be able to hold a sheet of paper between you and your partner. I remember distinctly on one occasion after I had danced with a lady, I overheard her say to another lady when she thought I was out of earshot, that she had nearly had a hole drilled in her. I should have had the courage to go over and tell her that it was only the keys that I always carried in my pocket. That cured me of dancing too closely on future occasions. It is not likely ever to happen again because I am not likely to dance again, but I now always have a chunky wooden cross in my pocket. It is the last thing Barbie ever grasped, and much more bulky than a bunch of keys.

I always felt safe in the knowledge that I could never make the first move anyway, because I had a very real fear of being rejected, and I had also the fear that any advances on my part could become the talking point in all the ladies' circles. I do not deny any thoughts I had on the subject however, and could always admire an attractive lady.

Government employees tended to keep themselves to themselves, and because they tended to be younger than we were, they had not had any time to save much, hence teachers were generally considered to be tight with their money. Barbie and I were more mature, and because we played a lot of sport, danced and played bridge, we were rather unique among the education set in that we tended to mix more with the commercial elements, who unfortunately fit more into the 'happy valley' category. They had more money and the women particularly had more free time.

Because we had never been with anyone else, I am sure that in the back of our minds was always the question of what it would be like, especially because it was always brought into the conversation at some point or other. We certainly enjoyed all the jokes that were circulated.

I have said that I could never make the first move, but I didn't have to. We had become very friendly with a couple and often kept company with them. The wife was rather curvaceous, like Marilyn Monroe, although some said that she more resembled Jayne Mansfield. She did what some ladies do when they have designs on a man, they become extremely friendly with his wife, and in my case his children, who thought she was lovely and cuddly. Maybe we hadn't cuddled them enough in their late primary stages.

She certainly did that. I have to admit that I was somewhat flattered that she should fancy me, and this time it obviously did go to my head, that this gorgeous creature should be attracted to little me. It seemed inevitable that one day we would find ourselves alone, which we did. I can't say that it was entirely satisfactory. There was no flash of lightning or ringing of bells, in fact I felt as if I had failed miserably, but she promised that it would be better the next time.

I sensed that there was something wrong in their marriage. I remember, too, my mother instilling into us to be always fair and never to use physical strength to resolve differences. Being stronger does not mean being right, hence I abhor any form of abuse, and it makes me sympathetic towards the victim. It is sad to think that so much more than I had guessed happens these days. How arrogant of some people who think that sexual pleasure is only for the males, and how sad that some females are brainwashed into subjugating themselves to become virtual slaves to men.

I wonder if everyone feels like I felt afterwards? Surely they can't, but for like-minded men finding themselves in my position, beware, because, incredible though it may sound, I now had the feeling that I owed her something and that she owned part of me. I now understand what the saying 'getting her claws into him' means, although that might seem unfairly to put all the blame on her, which wasn't the case. As I write this, I understand the situation better than I did then, because of a remark by a friend. She said that sex was now considered more of a recreational activity, though again, I do not wish to give the impression that it was merely recreational on her part. I feel sure that she was serious.

It wasn't a sudden flash of inspiration, but it did gradually occur to me that the story of Adam and Eve in the bible, which is full of symbolism, was less to do with the apple and more to do with the fig leaves. What Adam discovered, which was to cause more grief than anything else in this world, apart from religion itself, was 'sex for pleasure'.

To my old fashioned way of thinking however, sex is to do with love, marriage, and commitment, so now I had a problem. I had a family whom I loved, and a wife who, on some photographs, bore a striking resemblance to Audrey Hepburn, and I had allowed myself to become infatuated with someone else. Having taken that one fatal step, which seemed harmless at the time, could only end in anguish for one of the parties. I cannot ever remember comparing them at the time because they were completely different types, but they were both lovely people. It would have made it easier for me if one of them hadn't been. No wonder that I still feel guilty. Looking back, I realise that Barbie had a super figure that was allied to athleticism which I admired, being P.E. trained. The other lady was an archetypal sex symbol and I couldn't believe that she wanted me. She was also the cuddly type, which certainly made an impression on Ros in particular. I guess Barbie and I were more reserved except when we were alone. I don't know if it had affected my character, but although I had six brothers, I spent most of my childhood with just my three sisters. I still feel more at home in female company.

I don't know how it was managed, but somehow a wife swapping evening was arranged. I am absolutely sure that Barbie only went along for the ride, and agreed very reluctantly, but she must have been inquisitive as well and thought that everyone seemed to be doing it, so why shouldn't we?

Again, the expectation was greater than the realisation (that was one of my mother's favourite sayings). It wasn't 'us', and it never came up in conversation again. We had drifted out of the habit of going to church regularly while we were in Jinja. I am not sure that it would have made any difference, but I am quite sure that the pain and stress that I experienced afterwards because of my Christian upbringing, was a punishment that I deserved.

There is a saying that 'forbidden fruits always taste sweeter', but the silly thing is that they never did. I guess it would sound hypocritical of me if I said that I had too much of a conscience, because I was a willing participant. When we went to the same functions, the lady in question would often mouth 'I love you' across the room when no one else was looking, and so what could I do without hurting someone? I suppose also that there was always the fear in the back of my mind of what she might do if I broke it off. In my late thirties, I felt like a crazy mixed up kid.

We socialised a lot with the couple, going to the same parties and dances, but then the lady in question returned to the UK weeks before our departure from Jinja during the Christmas holidays in 1970. We never did understand the reason for this, but there was the thought in the back of our minds that she might have been pregnant which proved to be unfounded, or most likely it was what had happened at our last meeting. We had invited them to dinner and the husband and I must have gone to the separate loos at the same time. I heard a commotion and came back into the lounge to find Barbie on the floor with her arm around the lady in a headlock. I believe that she had said to Barbie that she would love to have a baby with me, which must have tripped Barbie over the edge. I quickly lifted each of them off the floor, and incredibly the evening progressed as though nothing had happened. It is indicative of our closeness that she could even say such a thing, but that obviously proved to be a bit too near the bone for Barbie.

We did keep in touch in the UK, in fact we met as a family and visited each other. We went to their home in Cheshire, and they came to Bakewell and to Ivy House where we stayed while on holiday during term time. Mum had got to know them well from her time on holiday with us in Africa. They were such a genuinely nice couple. I also saw her alone once or twice, but never in a situation where intimacy could take place. My mind felt divided all the while, and I still had that feeling of being in debt to her, while still loving my family.

When I was appointed as tutor/warden at Walworth, Barbie and I were forced to live apart because I was way down on the London council housing list, and she had a teaching post within travelling distance from Bakewell, which she couldn't resign from until I was given or found accommodation in London. I naively expected to be given preferential treatment, and meanwhile stayed with my sister who had an apartment on Wimpole Street. Barbie and I acted normally when we were together, but I wasn't such a good actor that she didn't realise what was wrong with me. Then, when we went to Nigeria at the beginning of 1972 the situation should have resolved itself, and it did while we were there, but it returned to haunt me once again when we came back on leave.

Throughout all my turmoil, Barbie remained her normal self. Maybe she knew me better than I knew myself. When we came home on our first annual leave from Kano, I even kidded myself that I wanted to get back on the promotion ladder in the UK and applied for the deputy headship of a primary school in London. I must have thought maybe that would resolve the issue for me. I was asked to attend an interview for the post on the same day that we were due to fly back to Nigeria. Barbie said that she was committed to going back in order to continue her teaching responsibilities there. I suspect that she knew that this was the final crunch time, and I can imagine that she had resigned herself to the inevitable, accepting the fact that I didn't appear to love her enough. I said that I ought to at least see what the outcome of the interview would be, so she flew back and I stayed at Ivy House with mum. The interview went well and I was offered the post.

The ensuing picture is forever etched in my memory. I was alone in the little kitchen when mum came in and I told her. She simply said 'Ken, what about the children?' and before I could stop myself, I blurted out 'But what about me?'

I felt at that moment that I had been struck by lightning. I realised in a flash the enormity of what I had just said, and to sound so selfish in front of my mother, after all that she had done for me, was a shame that was almost impossible for me to bear, and from which I have never recovered. I still feel ashamed when remembering that utterance. In that same moment I realised what a fool I had been. I had been a fool to carry on blindly thinking that the situation would somehow resolve itself. I finally realised that there was no solution except a decision that could only be made by me, and I had been wrong to all parties concerned by not making that decision earlier. There was only one possible outcome, and I should have made that clear from the start.

I cannot recall any further conversation in that little kitchen, but I hope my mum understood my feelings, because I packed my bags immediately and jumped on the first plane back to Kano, with a letter of apology to the school in London. What I cannot remember is whether I ever apologised to the mum whom I respected above all others. I know that I did wrong, but like Marilyn Monroe, or Lady Di, was the other lady the villain or was she badly wronged? Those debates still go on, but they only add more fuel for me to feel guilty about.

Gentlemen, it is never worth it. That is if you have old-fashioned ideals like me. I guess if you are of the type who views sex as a recreational activity, it is different. I was lucky because I had a wife who loved me and who may not have known all that was going on, but was wise enough to know that I would come back down to earth one day. She knew that there was that special something between us which would always be there. We not only had a guardian angel looking over us, but I realised that I had obviously married an angel as well.

Did I learn from my mistake though? Can a leopard change its spots? I wish that I could say so, and this is where I really do try to make excuses.

Homo sapiens are the highest order of the animal kingdom, but we are still all animals, although we do differ from other animals in some respects. In humans, some females become more attracted to the possession of money, and some females admire power in a mate. The prime motive is security and the quality of a material life. Having watched animals in the wild, as well as having learned about them on the television, female wild animals select on purely physical attributes. They wait for males to fight it out and accept the winner. We too cannot escape from our basic animal instincts, and being deprived of the physical side, and having married for security, some cannot avoid the urge to seek the physical aspect elsewhere. I do not mean to put all the blame on women, for things happen the other way round, and it takes two to make a bargain. I blame our modern social setup, and the influence of money and power on our lives, which provides incentives for promiscuity.

I possess neither money nor power, but without being big-headed, I have been blessed with a reasonable body. Not skinny, nor like a bodybuilder, but one with lots of energy and athleticism. I swam, played football, golf, tennis, cricket, badminton and squash, all to a reasonable standard, and for that reason, because I certainly have no film star looks, I have often had ladies 'make a play' for me and I am talking about the wives of bankers, high executives and a judge among others. I am not proud of this, in fact it turns out to be a curse. It reminds me of a story a friend told me. He was talking to a famous Australian sportsman, who told him he always asked a 'groupie' if she would outright. 'Don't you get slapped in the face?' asked my friend. 'Occasionally' the sportsman replied, 'but I also have great times!'

Occasionally, I have almost given way to my basic instincts too, but those occasions never amounted to anything. The fact that I even had a coffee with someone without Barbie knowing gave me feelings of guilt. It isn't the act in itself, which might be trivial, but it is the implied deception which causes that feeling.

Remember that this chapter was inserted as a separate entity, so I must now go back nearly two years to my ten months at Walworth, and close that episode of my life in the book, if not in my mind. Yet another move was coming, but this time it was of my doing.

WALWORTH AND THE END OF TEACHING IN THE UK

As soon as we arrived home from Uganda at the end of 1970, I had applied to Walworth, as I have explained, because I wanted to get on the promotion ladder and this was a graded post. If successful, it would do my career no harm. I also had the thought that there was scope to make a mark with the youth of London.

There were drawbacks. I had expected to live with my sister, Sarah, for only a short while until Barbara got a post down here, or until I was allocated a house or a flat. One would have thought that the London authorities would have made a special effort to accommodate us, but neither happened. I was then given some Science to teach which I hadn't done before and as I have explained, I was not particularly comfortable with teaching classroom subjects other than Maths.

The youth work was also a disappointment because not many turned up. I had an assistant who was a local teacher, but even he didn't seem able to attract many of the local youth. What the school needed was someone who lived and was known in the district. What influence could I have when I lived in the north and lodged on the other side of London? It was both naive and a mistake on both the London authority and me to think that my appointment was sensible. It needed someone who could walk the streets and meet the youth outside as well as inside school.

How different from teaching in Africa. I have to admit that this was not my finest hour. The pupils were unruly and the level of industry very low. I would have loved to get my teeth into some Maths but it seemed I was being used to fill in wherever they were short of staff in a subject.

Barbie, meanwhile, had secured a post near Sheffield and as usual she had fit in very well and was enjoying teaching. She too was finding it strange in the new system where two teachers shared a larger class, but I am quite sure that she had adapted to new ideas much better than I.

I was walking down the school corridor with one of the young lady teachers, and went to open the door at the end, as a gentleman would. 'I am quite capable of opening a door myself, thank you,' she said. I was flabbergasted. I realised that I had just had my first experience of 'Women's Lib'. What on earth was the world coming to? The daft thing is that I am a great believer in equality. One doesn't have to be a sexist if one is courteous.

The crunch came for me during a science lesson where we were using Bunsen burners. One of the boys picked his up and pretended to burn his partner, at which I spoke to him rather sharply. I couldn't believe it, he actually answered me back. He said 'Well you can't do anything to me, Sir.' That was the first time in my life that any pupil had ever answered me back, let alone challenged my authority.

I quickly retorted that I could do anything to him that a responsible parent could do. Thank goodness it calmed him down because had he thought about it, a parent cannot touch a child either.

What on earth did Labour do to our education system when they insisted on comprehensive education? There is virtually no practical work taught to fit the majority of children for the outside world and instead they are forced into academic studies to which they are not suited. It seems that they are ashamed of their own roots. No wonder the majority of children are bored and don't try. How many foreigners are making a good living in the UK because we can't find a British plumber, electrician, woodworker, or craftsman of any kind?

What the Labour Party does not get, is that everyone is NOT born equal. Everyone has a unique DNA so how can we all be the same? We might have the same genes, but they certainly don't all work to the same efficiency. What credence has a party when the Deputy Prime Minister thought that ALL children CAN be above average?

We all know that farmers breed with their best bull and they have proved that it works in improving the quality of the herd. The same can be said for horses, sheep, pigs or even wild animals. That is why the female animals wait until the males fight over them. Why then do people have a problem with inbred intelligence? Of course it isn't 100% accurate, because genetics is the product of not only parents, but of all the other ancestors who have gone before. Mendel taught us this, but it should be obvious that clever people are more likely to have clever children, and the reverse must also be true. I know because I guess that I was fortunate to be one of the exceptions to the rule. Yes, I know about the sonnenkinder project in Nazi Germany, and am not advocating anything like that, because that was taking an idea to its extremes, and for the wrong reasons.

Equal opportunity, as an objective, is good, but that isn't achieved by sticking every child into the same class. The equal opportunity was already given in primary schools. The ones who have displayed the most talents should be put in an environment to extend those talents. Those who demonstrated fewer talents should be helped in a more suitable environment for their learning capabilities. Late developers can be transferred, as they were in Dinnington, from secondary modern to grammar schools. It would appear that the Labour party are ashamed of their roots, and are afraid to educate children in the manual skills of which they are capable, and which the country needs. I cannot see that comprehensive schools provide an optimum learning environment for any child. Not for the more intelligent, not for the average, and certainly not for the less able. Headmasters overcome this by 'setting' subjects, but can you imagine the feelings of a child in the bottom, which might be the eighth set?

Where were the psychologists when this monumental change in

education was introduced? Did no one in government understand children? It is natural for some children to be jealous of others showing skills with which they themselves haven't been blessed. Unfortunately some of these will try to equalise matters and respond by disrupting classes and even resort to bullying. With the advent of modern technology, one doesn't have to be physically strong to accomplish this. Bullying no longer has to be physical, and can now be perpetrated by any child over the internet and can be much more damaging. Even at a grammar school, I remember Nikky didn't want to be considered a 'swat' because she was at the top of the class. She was afraid of becoming unpopular. What more so for children at comprehensive schools?

After the plundering of the Elizabethan era, where has our wealth come from? I maintain it has come from the top 1% of our society who became the inventers and innovators of our industries and sciences. We should celebrate and encourage these few. It is these students who need help as well, because they will contribute most to the future wealth of the country, with their new ideas and inventions. Encouraging them will help all of society, especially the poor, because there will be more money to distribute, and without them we will become just another second rate country playing catchup and follow-my-leader. What we should have are special schools for the most gifted children. Barbie and I saw them in China. We need an education system to produce excellence because of the system, not in spite of the system. How perverse can we get when we don't help the genius because it might upset the educationally backward.

I know that I have said this before, but I can't emphasise it enough. What have we done wrong in the UK? Anyone who has taught overseas knows that the Chinese, Asian and Africans have a different attitude towards education. They never need encouraging or disciplining. It seems that the majority of our children are brought up to think only of themselves and that a good living can only be achieved in a white collar job. They should be taught to compete in school, as they will surely have to do when they leave school. They should be taught the parable of the talents, as it applies to society. One is rewarded by how well one uses the talents that one has been given.

This applies to behaviour too. Yes, everyone's child is special to parents, but when we were young one never saw misbehaviour going unchecked; especially when it inconvenienced others. It is normal and accepted now, so no wonder we are in a me, me, me society. Respect for other people is generally not taught or appreciated as it used to be.

Only a healthy country can provide a high standard of living. The country must come first, and it doesn't work the other way round. Unless the country is solvent, everyone suffers, and unfortunately the poor in an insolvent country would seem to suffer most. A country running on a culture of debt hurts the very people for whom those in charge purport to be governing for, and the very people who put that government into power. It is strange that people idolise and promote footballers and football clubs and so called celebrities and entertainers who blatantly exploit them, yet entrepreneurs who create jobs and wealth are deemed unworthy of similar accolades. Remember Industry must be allowed to earn sufficient to pay enough in taxes and to employees, to pay for Government, Civil Servants, Education, the N.H.S, and all non-producers, including indirectly sportsmen and entertainers who depend on their fans having money to watch them.

While on the subject of teaching, I must comment on teachers themselves, for whom I have some sympathy. Teaching is an art form, just like any other branch of art. Teachers are born, not bred. Barbie was a genius when it came to teaching. One had only to watch her in front of a class and see the results, whereas I am not and never will be a born teacher. I consider that I am a decent lecturer, but good in only two areas of teaching, Maths and P.E. plus, I suppose, maybe a few organisational skills. Professionally I have a great deal of sympathy for teachers therefore, but politically they puzzle me. They all have above average intelligence in order to qualify, yet they don't understand that there existence depends entirely upon the income from industry and commerce in order to pay them. They then vote for a government which has little sympathy for the companies who create that wealth with which to pay them.

The country, unfortunately, needs thousands of teachers to satisfy its educational needs. That is like asking the country to produce thousands of Rembrandts or Picassos. I'm sorry, it just cannot be done. We must therefore be satisfied with the ones we have, who, like me, are not so gifted, but are willing to devote their lives, for whatever reason, to teaching the young. Like me, however, they will be put off if the social conditions are not made reasonable for them. The problem with education is not with the teachers, nor with the buildings, knowing those in which I taught in Africa. The problems lie in the attitude of many parents and children, who, because they are given something for nothing, fail to appreciate it. I even wonder if people should pay for education to make them appreciate it. Certainly I believe if children have time off from school, they should reimburse the government for the cost of their days off which they have wasted, and which the government has already paid for.

I have just watched an advertisement on the BBC news about a book recently published about why some children do better than their parents. No wonder that almost every child we know whom Barbie taught overseas progressed to top jobs. It is the sense of ambition, desire and encouragement instilled by parents and their lifestyle that children experience and grasp. The very fact that their parents had the ambition and courage to go overseas went a long way to instil that feeling.

I revert back to talk about Walworth. This is not what I was trained for, and I was no longer prepared to teach under these conditions. I set out to be a teacher, not a baby-minder. I even have issues about the new methods imposed in the teaching of Maths, which to my mind makes it more confusing than ever for the children, so I submitted my notice, and vowed never to teach in England again.

We had a good long talk over the Christmas holidays. Nikky and Ros were in favour of going back to Africa, and so were Barbie and I. It was just a matter of where and when. We wanted to be together as a family again, and it seemed that our guardian angel had once again manipulated events to this end. Barbie had not given in her notice, so should I wait, or go on my own for half a term? We decided that if I could get a job I should go. Double contracts were never offered in any case, and we knew that Barbie would have no problems getting a post when she joined me.

PART SIX

Life in Nigeria

I APPLIED THROUGH THE MINISTRY OF OVERSEAS DEVELOPMENT (M.O.D.) and as there was nothing on offer in Uganda, I was offered a post in Nigeria. These were annual contracts, so that we would get leave every summer holiday. Apart from that, the terms were similar to those of Uganda, so the girls got their wish to travel out to Africa every Christmas and Easter. They had moved back home for the past year, but would automatically be given a place back in the boarding house when we were both in Nigeria. How convenient was that? It only meant moving to live in the boarding house, just round the corner.

I flew out to Kano at the beginning of February 1972 and after going through all the formalities of registration in Kano I was posted to the small town of Gumel, an hour's ride to the North.

When I arrived in Gumel, I was taken to my bungalow which was remarkably similar to the ones in Uganda. The furniture was the same too, so I felt quite at home. It was not so inviting when I awoke on the next morning however because when I lifted back the mosquito net I could not put my feet on the floor. It was covered in earwigs.

I was surprised more than anything because I had not met this type of infestation before. I could have understood if it had been cockroaches, but this had me baffled. It wasn't a good start, having to greet the headmaster with that at our first meeting, but I tried not to make it sound as though I was complaining.

My recollections of Gumel are pretty vague. There was only a month to go before Easter, and although I did not know at the time, I would be leaving then anyway. I do remember teaching Maths there and the interest the boys showed. I was only there a short time, but it was clear that I was making an impression. I never understand why teachers don't like teaching Maths. I hadn't experienced any difficulties in England, and certainly the African children loved the subject.

After being there a week I began to look for mail. After two weeks I was asking at the office every day and I was beginning to get worried. After three weeks I said that there must be something wrong, knowing that Barbie would write daily as well as letters that I knew I should be getting from home, and so I went personally to the Post Office.

I was met by a puzzled official who said he couldn't understand why the school had not collected their mail, because they had been allocated a postbag and it had never been collected. Problem solved. When I took the postbag back to school I kept my twenty-five letters to take with me to read. What a lovely evening I had going through all the mail from Barbie, the girls, and Ivy House, and then sitting down to answer them all.

I needed a car. All expatriates need a car to get around with, because there is no reliable public transport. There are buses if you don't mind sharing three or four to a seat and at times sharing with market produce or livestock. The alternative in those days, was a 'mammy' wagon, which is an open backed lorry where everyone just piles on. In both you might be lucky to arrive within an hour of the scheduled time, hence very few Europeans used public transport.

A 'Mammy Wagon' in the Harmattan

With the best will in the world I could not see us staying in Gumel for more than one tour. The small town was isolated with very few expatriates. I could not see Nikky and Ros being able to enjoy holidays here, so I bought an 'ugly duckling', the cheapest car on the market. I wrote home to tell them that I had bought a Citroen, but forgot to tell them what model.

I had to go to Kano regularly to check up on money matters and matters relating to my contract, and called at Kano Club because I knew that was where I could enjoy a quiet beer and I would meet all the other expatriates. It doesn't take long to strike up conversations because everyone is interested in new faces and what they do for a living. I went to the bar, which was a rondavel which overlooked the first tee and twelfth green – it turned out to be a twelve holes golf course – and ordered a much needed drink. Kano is in a large depression and can get extremely hot. With the dry atmosphere, it was far more uncomfortable than anything I had experienced in Uganda, where the entire country was over 4000 feet above sea level.

Kano Golf Bar – (2nd Rumfa from the left)

I knew that my guardian angel was back with me again, because the person who came to sit next to me turned out to be the headmaster of G.T.T.S., the Government Technical Training School. He quickly found out who I was and where I was, and when I said that my wife would be joining me with Nikky and Ros I could see the cogs ticking round in his head.

'You know that you will be quite isolated up there, don't you?' he said, 'And I doubt if your children will enjoy their holidays up there with no other expatriates within miles.' He let this sink in for a while, then said 'As a matter of fact, I am desperate for a Maths teacher at G.T.T.S. and you tick all the boxes. How would you like to come down here and teach for me?'

I thought that this was too good to be true, but I could not see how he could arrange it at all. Of course I liked the idea and I said so, but with no great hopes of it materialising. He told me to leave it with him and we arranged to meet the following evening.

Whatever he did, or whatever he said to the ministry, I will never know, but when I met him the next day it had all been settled. I was transferred at the end of the term to Kano.

Nikky poses by the Indigo Dye Pits, outside the gates to Kano City

What is more, he told me that he was going on leave and he would be obliged if I could house-sit for him until a house became available for me from the housing pool. I began to wonder which reason for wanting me in Kano was uppermost in his mind.

Nicky and Ros must have stayed with Grandma Pidcock that Easter. They were not yet eligible to fly out until Barbie joined me. I know that when I met Barbie off the plane we went straight into the bungalow which we were to house-sit, and the girls never came to that particular house.

I have to admit that Barbie was hardly impressed when she saw the 'deux chevaux'. The girls were equally unimpressed too when the news was relayed to them. I think all three had visions of an ID19 or similar. We had the Volvo in Uganda, and they had got used to us having a big car.

The houseboy had agreed to stay on during the headmaster's leave, so we didn't have to worry about that for a while. That is what we thought at first, but it was to cost us dearly, because we had only been there for a week when we heard a crash in the night and got up to discover that our tape recorder and best camera had been stolen. We hadn't had time to take out any insurance, either, with all the dashing around we had been doing.

We informed the police, but nothing ever materialised. It was the first time we had ever been burgled because it was relatively unknown in Uganda. The crash we heard would be when they broke the glass on the way out. It was broken to pretend that it was an outside job. If it wasn't the houseboy then it is hard to believe that he wasn't an accomplice, otherwise how did the thief get in, or get the information about what was valuable and where it would be? Those were the only things stolen and unfortunately, that wasn't to be the last time we would be burgled in Nigeria.

Then there was the parrot. We had agreed to look after it, and we were told that it should be let out in the house during the daytime. The houseboy fed and watered it so at least we didn't have that chore. It became quite used to us, well, at least to me. It had the habit of perching on my shoulder during meals and trying to drink whatever I was drinking.

Aku followed me everywhere and shared what she could!

What we were not aware of at first was that it was female and didn't particularly like other females, including the human kind. I heard Barbie shout for me one night. She was in the bathroom, and when I went in, there was Barbie, sitting at one end of the bath, while the parrot was sitting on the other end facing her with its wings spread out. Poor Barbie, half immersed in bubbles, was afraid to move an inch. It did look menacing, but we had to laugh about it afterwards.

Then it started to lose its feathers. We didn't know whether parrots moulted or not, but we wondered what on earth the headmaster and his wife would say when they returned to find their pet parrot was completely bald.

In the end we were quite relieved when the headmaster came back and we moved into the bungalow which was going to be our home for the next seven and a half years. It was in the school compound and at the end of the line. It backed onto another bungalow and had a long drive up to a turning circle by the front door.

The turning circle was round a huge mature flame tree, which really set the bungalow alight. To the right of the drive was a lawn and then there was a garage which backed onto the boy's quarters. To the left of the drive was a reasonably sized garden. So all in all it was as good as anything we had occupied in Uganda. Now we could settle down and unpack and once more feel at home.

The roundabout around the Flame tree outside our veranda at G.T.T.S.

Nigeria was different from Uganda in many ways. Kampala was similar to an English town, but Kano was definitely African. It seemed to be more crowded with more hustle and bustle.

We had seen the occasional amulanki in Uganda, but here they used them everywhere. They were made from the chassis of a flat-bed lorry without the cab or engine, and were loaded with produce and pushed around by up to twenty straining, black bodies. I used to tease Barbie that seeing these glistening black bodies turned her on. This was obviously the cheapest way to transport goods, but it didn't say much for their wages, and fortunately for them Kano was very flat.

I would also describe it as a more working class city, and one didn't have to go far from the centre to get to Saban Gari, which was supposedly the largest permanent open-air market in the world. It seemed to be open 24/7, but more will be said about that later. Another thing missing were so many smiling faces, but that isn't to say that they weren't friendly people.

We also noticed that there were beggars everywhere. We had seen a few in Uganda, but not on this scale. We were told later that this was a business, and an Alhaji, in a flash car, would go round each day to collect the takings, leaving the poor beggar with a small amount as his or her wage. Beggars were usually lepers or cripples, because they invoked more sympathy. It was also rumoured that some had actually been deliberately crippled at birth in order to make them into a good beggar. One was left with the dilemma of whether to give to the beggar at all, knowing that most of it would be taken by a rich Alhaji who rented out the pitch.

The most depressing picture we retained, regarding beggars, was of a lady leper who could only move on her hands and knees, which were protected by sections of car tyres. She crawled around with a small baby strapped onto her back.

My mind was drawn back to Kampala and the ID. 19s of OXFAM, and of the Executives of Charities who award themselves six figure wages. Are they a lot different from the Alhajis? Don't reject this thought too hastily. Think about it. They all depict people living an exceptionally good life on the backs of the poor people for whom the charities are meant. Someone once cynically remarked that if you wanted a good lifestyle, set up a good charity, then you can pay yourself whatever you wished. Of course the majority of charities I am sure are run by well intentioned people who do not seek personal gain.

I can't let footballers and their like escape scrutiny either. When they step onto the pitch, with their million pounds wages, do they think of the thousands of fans watching them, many of whom have gone into poverty in order to pay the extortionate amounts charged for entrance and for the numerous array of shirts and memorabilia that they sell? They must understand that the parents know that their child must have the latest shirt because his friend has one, so what do the clubs do? They change the shirts regularly in order to sell two or three instead of one each year. I wonder how they can look up at the fans without feeling ashamed. If nothing else, they are guilty of exploiting the fans. Isn't it fair, therefore, to compare them with the Alhajis in their slick cars? I was a footballer and love football, and I admire them for their skills that I never possessed, but somehow the whole industry seems to have got completely out of hand, bordering on the farcical. Is a footballer, or indeed any 'personality', really worth more than a researcher working on curing cancer, or a brain surgeon? I would be happier if footballers projected sportsmanship and set a good example to children, but unfortunately they spend 90 minutes shirt tugging, pretending to be injured and openly committing fouls which they try to pretend were accidental. Surely a deliberate foul, which shirt tugging must be, is a sending off offence? F.A., for goodness sake get your act together. Players who pretend to be injured should be given ten minutes to recover on the touchline.

We joined Kano Club and met other expatriates and got in touch with the headmistress of the capital school where Barbie was offered a teaching post, so we were both set up for the term to commence.

Kano Club had a large swimming pool which was surrounded by a high wall for security reasons. It also had two tennis courts and a gate which led out onto the golf course. The golf section had its own bar in a converted rondavel overlooking the twelfth 'brown'. There was also a cricket field. I thought that I must have come to heaven.

You will have noticed that I said the twelfth 'brown' there were no greens on the golf course because it was unrealistic to be able to keep them watered sufficiently for the grass to grow. Instead there were 'browns' which were flat areas covered by a mixture of sand and light oil to hold it firm and prevent it from blowing away in the wind. Browns had to be swept between each putt because they left a slight groove indicating the line, which the next person to putt would have loved to be able to use when lining up his putt.

What we could hardly miss whenever we left the compound were the huge pyramids being constructed. No they weren't of stone, but of groundnuts (peanuts)! Thousands of tons of them for export, and to feed the factories making groundnut oil which we all used for cooking.

Pyramids of sacks of groundnuts in Kano.   (Try counting the sacks!)

From the first moment I stood in front of a class and saw the rows of eager faces, it was obvious that I was going to enjoy teaching at G.T.T.S. The students were taught English and Maths, but the major part of their timetable was taken up in the workshops doing practical work.

In the vehicle mechanics section the senior students had actual cars to work on, and took cars in for servicing as would a normal garage. The money they raised was then put into a fund to buy other needed equipment. The same scheme applied in the woodwork department and fitting shops. The students were keen to do well and had to perform to outside commercial standards. This carried over into the classroom, and though the standards were not very high on entry, they all had an incentive to improve and were a joy to teach.

We were understaffed when I joined the school, but after the first term I was joined by Taffy, a Welshman, to teach English, and three C.U.S.O. members who were the Canadian equivalent of the American Peace Corps. The Canadians were mature teachers and in fact they were all older than I was.

It was a surprise to us all when our headmaster suddenly left, because he had only recently been home to the UK on leave. His place was taken by an Alhaji, who was Nigerian.

I was soon to learn that this must have been a political move. The new principal did not take much part in the actual organisation of the school, and I was gradually put in charge, though nothing was written down officially. I was responsible for the timetables and the virtual running of the school except for finance and discipline. This suited me down to the ground. There may have been no rise in salary involved, but it meant a rise in status within the school, and there was never any trouble with discipline in the classroom.

Political decisions were being taken everywhere. I learned about the manager of a major motor showroom who was overheard to say jokingly that the Nigerians couldn't do without us. It was obviously heard in the wrong quarters and he was put on the next plane home.

Nicky and Ros now travelled together which was less worrying for us. They had their first taste of Nigeria during that summer holiday. I guess there would be differences from the Uganda holidays, but they would still enjoy their circle of friends in similar positions, and they had a large swimming pool to enjoy.

The pool was not without its tragedies though. There was a high wall around, but unfortunately there were one or two trees adjacent to it on the outside. Apparently, the local African children used to climb up and watch all the happy play that went on in the pool during the day. One night, two children must have climbed onto the wall, seen that there was no one around and jumped down inside. They obviously thought that it was easy to swim, and must have jumped in, as they had seen other children do. Their bodies were found by the cleaners when they opened up the pool on the following morning.

There were very few game parks in Nigeria, and the reports were that there was not much to see in them when one got there. Game had not survived as it had in East Africa. We only went once to Yankari Game Reserve. I don't remember seeing any game at all, but it has been developed as a tourist resort since we were there. Fortunately Yankari is also the site of the Wikki warm springs, which made the journey well worthwhile. It was a spa area where warm water bubbled to the surface forming a natural swimming pool. Anywhere in Africa where one can swim and relax is heaven.

Holidays for Nikky and Ros revolved around the club swimming pool and the new friends they met there. They were fifteen and thriteen years old now and were trying to throw off their young girl image. They were well into the latest music of Elvis and The Stones, but they shared our preference for The Beatles. This was what they went to boarding school for anyway, so that they could have these holidays in Africa, and they and their new friends all made sure that they had a good time.

A couple with whom we had become friendly had a badminton court and it became a regular badminton party every Friday night. I had played before, but never in a club. One of the other guests had played at county level and taught me the tactics, and eventually I was able to give him a decent game. Of all the games I had played, badminton was the one where I think I might have progressed further than I had done in the others sports. I certainly enjoyed the physical aspect.

Not many people know that singles badminton is perhaps the fastest sport in the world, and one of the most exhausting. Play your shot and get back to the middle; play your shot and get back to the middle; time and time again. This happens without the delay of the rebounds that one gets in squash. I loved it. It didn't do my knee any good though and I began to have arthritic pains in my left knee as the bones began to wear away. There was no longer the medial cartilage to protect them.

Meanwhile Barbie was getting along well at the school and enjoying teaching as much as ever. I don't think that there was a single one of the schools where she had taught that she wanted to leave because of the teaching. Nearly every move that we had made had been instigated by my need to progress up the ladder. At the time it never seemed to be selfishness on my part, because we always talked about and agreed on every move and there was never any argument over it, but I wonder now, in fact, if there had not been an element of that involved. Neither of us was conscious of it because it was the done thing then to follow the man.

The only niggle in the back of Barbie's mind was the fact that there were several young teachers at her school who were on contract to the government. This meant that they not only got more than twice as much salary, but they also got the perks that went with it. Barbie was only entitled to a local salary because government policy decreed there could be only one government contract per family. I got the perks, but she must have felt that she was undervalued. The government were really getting two for the price of one and a half.

Normally this would not have bothered us, because we had accepted these terms when I was offered a contract. However, it came up in gossip round the pool, and at dinner parties, that there was a great need for a nursery or preschool group. We heard also that non-English speaking mothers were keen for their children to acquire sufficient English in order to be admitted to the capital school.

We began to discuss the possibility of opening one at home. The garage was large enough to house the children in the few days of wet weather during the year, and a lot of teaching could be done outside on the lawn. I could buy desks and chairs and a blackboard at cost from school, and the rest could be obtained from a stationers. The car was no problem, because it could stay outside on the drive. We decided to go ahead and Barbie put in her notice and we started advertising.

Medical matters intervened. Barbie had been having a few problems and had to have a hysterectomy. That coincided with the holidays, when she had the operation, and in her usual fashion Barbie recovered rapidly, defying doctors orders not to drive for so many weeks etc. She couldn't understand why the lady in the next bed had her family smuggle in salt to her when she knew she was on a salt-free diet. Some people are so silly.

Meanwhile I had organised the workshops at school to have the furniture made and, after a short recuperation period, Barbie opened what was to become one of the most sought after schools in Kano.

One of the perks of timetabling was that I could arrange things to suit myself. I won't apologise for doing this because no one else suffered. School began at 7 a.m. at G.T.T.S., so I arranged for my breakfast break to be just after 9 a.m. I used to nip home to see that Barbie had no problems, it was only 100 yds, and to have my breakfast.

This became such a routine that it prompted one child to go home and tell his parents that 'there is a Mr. Pidcock, but he doesn't live there, he just comes every morning to do odd jobs for Mrs. Pidcock and then goes back.' I thought to myself 'how right you are.'

I often ate breakfast on the veranda and sat in awe watching Barbie with the children, It was quite emotional for me to watch how enthralled the children were, completely engrossed, and following her every word.

By the time we left Nigeria, Barbie had helped so many children gain admission to the schools of their choice. Many African graduates had returned to Nigeria with a wife from the country where they had studied, so as well as the expatriate children, she had many of mixed parentage who started with her, hardly understanding any English at all.

The parents of many of the children were to become lifelong friends, often communicating from the other side of the world. They could never seem to thank Barbie sufficiently for the start in life that she had given their children, many of whom became barristers and lawyers or other high ranking executives or entrepreneurs.

I must mention Tara, our dog, in relation to the school. She was a boxer cross with Heinz varieties. They had docked her tail at birth, but she never developed the boxer snout. She was simply amazing with the children and used to lie among them during lessons. During breaks she let the children do almost anything to her without any concern.

Almost all the children were brought to school by car, and she lay apparently asleep when they arrived. Should any strange car enter the drive, however, she would jump up and begin to growl in warning until Barbie or I said it was OK. She obviously knew the sound of all the usual cars, and was the best guard dog one could possibly wish for.

We had one child whose father worked on the new concrete runway being built at the airport. He mentioned once that he had lots of half bricks of concrete left after his stress tests. Barbie thought what a good idea to use them to build a low partition wall round the part of the lawn which she used.

He duly brought a load, but we were out, which gave him the idea to play a joke on us. He built a wall with them across the veranda in front of the door.

When Barbie and I came home late that night we laughed and cursed him at the same time. I had eventually to build the wall where Barbie needed it, so I decided that I may as well move them only once, and I completed the task around midnight. We are still friends to this day, and he and his wife have just been transferred to the Christmas Islands to start a new tour there.

We have always been keen on dancing and because we had rarely danced with anyone else we had developed our own style and steps, particularly in the jive. I could never attempt to jive with a different partner. It was inevitable that we would be introduced to the French Club. This was the place to go to on Saturday nights to dance. It was open air, with a circular dance floor surrounded by tables and chairs. The D.J. overlooked the dance floor, playing all the latest records from the 'hit parade.' It was kept very select, so there were never any scenes or drunkenness, and though it was always full, it was never overcrowded. In fact it was the ideal place to go. I was honoured to be elected onto the committee after two years.

It was naughty of us, but it was customary at parties to tell each other the latest jokes. It was also inevitable that some were about the latest escapades of houseboys. The current one was about the new houseboy.

The Memsaab wasn't sure about him, so to play safe she asked him to serve dinner through the hatch. Sure enough dinner time came and when she rang the bell for service a big foot appeared climbing through the hatch. I may have laughed, but I never liked the houseboy jokes. Think of how stupid the boy must have thought his new Memsaab was.

One I did laugh at was the one about the wife who had a few too many before she went to bed. Her husband wasn't expected home until very late. She was awakened as he got into bed and they made exceptional love. She said 'Oh thank you darling, can we have it like that every night?' to which the reply came 'Ndio Memsaab.' (Yes Madam, in Swahili!)

We had seasons, but not like the ones in England. Not summer and winter etc. because there was very little difference between them. I refer to the football season and the cricket season. We did have two rainy seasons as well, one for the big rains and one for the small rains, which are self explanatory and varied very little from year to year and were well catered for in everyday life.

The only other season was the season of the Harmattan. This is a trade wind which blows from the Sahara Desert westwards across North Africa. It often carries various amounts of sand with it, and very occasionally it becomes so dense that it appears like a red fog which can be as bad as any smog in the UK and can, and often does, ground air traffic.

It was the start of the cricket season so I naturally joined the Cricket Club, a section of Kano Club. They sing 'mad dogs' and 'Englishmen go out in the midday sun' and we certainly qualified for that.

The cricket field was naturally devoid of grass and had a concrete strip at its centre upon which we placed a mat each time we played. Leather balls were much too expensive because we had to be self-sufficient and they wouldn't last more than one game. We managed to find a composition ball which was much more durable. It had the appearance of a leather ball and, when new, would move quite a bit in the air. To compensate for that though, the mat wouldn't take much spin. It did make the game very competitive and we had an enjoyable season, playing against nearby towns interspersed with games within the club.

One had to always be aware of pickpockets, but I was caught out once because I was not quick enough. We had gone shopping in Saban Gari and were strolling along between the stalls when I knocked into someone in the crush. I thought I was quick, but I was not quick enough. I felt ever such a soft touch in my shorts pocket, and I whipped my hand down to it but I was too late. My plastic folder containing my residence permit had gone.

They are very clever. As soon as it is taken, it is passed to an accomplice in the same movement. While the thief goes one way, the receiver goes the other. He then may pass it along a chain, so that it is impossible to follow. However it did have a happy ending. The resident permit was no good to them and there was no money with it, which was what they were after, so further along a staged attempt was made to catch a boy who was then allowed to escape, and a man came to me and said 'is this yours, Sir?' and handed the permit back to me. We all laughed. We all knew what had happened, and none of us wanted to take it any further, which we knew would be pointless.

The neighbour's maigadis (night-watchmen) collect outside for lunch

On my way to school one morning, as I left the house, I noticed something strange about the car. There was no reflection from the windscreen, because there wasn't one there. All I was left with were bits of the rubber surround which had been neatly cut away to allow the screen to be extracted. I went back to tell Barbie, and explain that I wouldn't be able to do anything about it as I had a busy day at school and wouldn't even have time for breakfast.

When I finally returned home at 2 p.m. Barbie said that she had already been to the police station. Bless her, she said that she had seen a very helpful policeman who had even taken her to Saban Gari to all the spare parts stalls there. Unfortunately there was no sign of a Ford Cortina windscreen.

What the thieves didn't know was that we had all the removable parts on the car engraved with the car's registration number, so if ever we saw it again, we would instantly recognise it.

After two weeks, with no signs of it turning up, we bought another one. True to form, according to sod's law, a couple of days after we had bought it, a policeman called with the windscreen to give back to us. They had apprehended a man carrying it, bearing the number of our car, on his way from Saban Gari. When we eventually sold the car we were able to make the unusual advertisement of a car for sale, plus a spare windscreen.

Time flew by and it was time for our annual leave once again. We were so well ensconced in life in Kano that we no longer had any thoughts of it being only temporary. Tours lasting only one year seemed to be over in a flash. It was lovely to be able to go back to our home in Bakewell once again. There can't be many better places to spend holidays.

We still had the teachers renting when we were away, of course, and the house needed a bit of T.L.C. but it could have been a lot worse. We had many friends on the estate and lots of social functions were organised.

We even went to the local once or twice with a group. We had never been in the habit of ever going to a pub before. One of the friends, who was always the last to buy a round, nearly fainted when Barbie said 'just a brandy and ginger please.' That comment was to cause much amusement forever afterwards when everyone prefixed their requests with 'just.'

My knee had been really troubling me for a while and I arranged to see a consultant in Sheffield. After I had explained my problem and my lifestyle he said that he could give me an 'upper tibial osteotomy.' This entailed taking a wedge out of the top of my shinbone to angle the knee in order to take the pressure away from the painful side.

I had just seen on television that a farmer, who had damaged his knee falling from a haystack, was given a knee replacement and was back working within three weeks. 'Ah Mr. Pidcock' he said, 'If I did the same to you I could only guarantee it lasting for one year, because we have only been doing that operation for one year. I could not take that risk with you, knowing your lifestyle. With my operation, however, I can guarantee it for at least seven years, and if you come back to me then I may be able to guarantee the replacement for eight years.' So I agreed to his plan.

I had to have a plaster from my toes to my hip, and walk on crutches, and was supposed to keep the plaster cast on for seven weeks. This would delay my return to G.T.T. S. so Barbie had to go back on her own because of her commitment to her preschool group.

Of course I shouldn't have driven the car at all, but I was staying with mum at Ivy House, Bakewell being rented out. It was just too inconvenient not to be mobile because Norton is miles from anywhere, so I devised a method of sitting propped up on cushions, and as it was my left leg, I only had to push down from the hip, instead of the ankle, to operate the clutch. Thank goodness I was never stopped by the police.

After Barbie had been gone for a week I asked the consultant if I could have the plaster removed in Nigeria. I convinced him that I would have adequate care there and could have physiotherapy treatment there as well. He was extremely reluctant, but could see that I was keen and understood the risks. I was therefore able to return to Nigeria and only be two weeks late.

What a surprise I got when I arrived at school. It was the day after I had arrived back and I was hopping along on my crutches. I could see nothing happening at all. When I saw a member of staff he said 'Thank goodness you are back. We have been waiting for you to come and prepare the timetable for us.'

I was shocked, to say the least. With a Headmaster and three mature C.U.S.O. teachers, as well as the African teachers, one would have thought that they could come up with something.

I went round them all with a book and made a note of their requirement and went home. I then turned up on the following morning with a timetable which worked perfectly for the rest of the year.

I am pleased to say that I did all the necessary exercises, and more, with the physiotherapist, and had the plaster removed at the right time, and it was not long before I was playing my sports again. The consultant had been quite right. His operation actually lasted for over twenty years before I needed the knee replacement operation. I was sensible and didn't play football that season but I was able to play golf.

The cricket captain left too and I was surprised to find myself elected to replace him. That was the start of one of the most pleasing positions I have held. Zaria was a university town an hour's drive away. They had an ex Lancashire League player as captain, and thus began a great Yorkshire-Lancashire rivalry. I don't think either of us could claim overall victory, but every game we had was very competitive and enjoyable. We both beat the other northern teams comfortably, so it always boiled down to them or us as to who were the overall winners. The joke among the spectators was to keep away from Barbie. She used to get so excited that once, when we scored the winning run, she slapped her hand down on a friend's knee next to her so hard that it left her hand mark imprinted on her knee for ages.

Sharpie, their captain, introduced Lancashire League six-a-side to us which added an extra competition to the season. Gosh, what exiting matches we had. What was a really satisfying legacy was that both of us had introduced the game to Africans and we both had several Africans playing in our sides. In fact one of the most spectacular catches I have ever seen in my lifetime was by an African fighter pilot fielding in our slips. The batsman snicked the ball and dived full length, just like a goalkeeper, and held on to the ball in his finger tips.

We took a combined team down to Lagos and just lost out to their national team, so we came away thinking we had done rather well. When Lagos came up to Kano however we beat them easily, but I can hardly claim a terrific victory because it was the weather that really defeated them. They were mostly African, and coming from the moist heat of Lagos to the intense dryness of Kano had them literally collapsing on the field.

Wherever we went, there were always bridge players, which added the occasional evening bridge parties to our agenda. I introduced the Chicago system of scoring to them which added interest to the evenings. Again I worked the system whereby none of us played with our partners, resulting in very gentlemanly parties.

It was general knowledge that there was a group, or clique, among the commercial expatriates called 'The port of call.' This was a group of the commercial people and originally set it up to help each other if and when needed. I suppose that the name came from the understanding that each in turn would have an open house day, so that there was always a 'Port of call.' One had to be vetted and then attend a meeting before being accepted. No one other than members knew who was in it and who wasn't, but everyone had a fairly good idea. Barbie and I were never invited to join, but in retrospect we should not have been surprised because, being government, we had nothing to contribute commercially.

There was also a suggestion that it was more than a commercial arrangement, but we must have been blackballed by someone, because we exchanged dinner parties with most of those who were thought to be members, and on at least two of those occasions there was a subtle suggestion of swapping, but word must have got around that we didn't respond, hence we never knew for certain whether it did or it did not happen. We still remained friendly with all in the supposed group though, and played bridge with most of them, which was ideal because we did not want to join on closer terms.

I was also invited to join a poker school, and hadn't played much real poker before. Barbie raised no objections as she had such faith in my prowess at cards, so I thought that I would give it a try. The players took it in rotation to host the games and mostly the wives would go along to chat in another room.

It became a regular weekly event, and playing host one evening, I went around asking if the guests wanted their coffee white or black. Fats Asuni, the sales manager for Double Crown breweries and one of my golfing buddies, replied 'I like mine black please, like my women!' Fats was a good friend to have. We never ran out of beer when there was a shortage.

We had played golf one evening and were having a cooling drink at the rondavel bar. I was talking to one of the poker players when another player came up and slipped him a bundle of Naira, the Nigerian currency. Hawk-eye Barbie turned to me and asked what that was all about? I had to say that it was what he owed him from the poker game on the previous evening. I could see Barbie visibly blanch. She realised that I must also play for stakes like that.

When we got home I could see that she was still thinking about it, so I said 'Look love, I also won 95 Naira (£47) and there is a 20 Naira limit on bets. I can't stop while I am winning, but I will keep a book and record every game, and if I ever go into the red I will promise not to play again.'

I stuck faithfully to my promise but never had to give up playing, in fact the balance went a long way towards paying for our 'round the world trip' when we finally left Nigeria. I was the only player who knew to one Naira how much he had won or lost.

I knew that there were two of us who were constant winners. Funnily enough David thought that I had won the most and I thought that he had. When asked, I always said, quite openly, that I was a winner because I didn't gamble, and all the others did. I played the odds, and that is probably where my maths came in useful.

Poker is an addiction, and a very powerful one, and I would never get involved in playing for real money. We used to refer to the Naira as 'Mickey Mouse' money. My family have often asked me to teach them, but poker is something you can't teach and I always put them off. I have yet to meet a poker player who admits to losing heavily. I know for a fact that the rest of the group were losers, but if you asked them how they stood, the stock answer would be 'well I lost last night, but overall I think I am about even.'

Machines in a casino often guarantee to pay over 80% back in winnings. Forget that because it is misleading. What they really mean is that they guarantee to take up to 20% of your money. What is more, if they think that you have a system to beat them, they ban you from the casino, like they ban 'counters' at Blackjack.

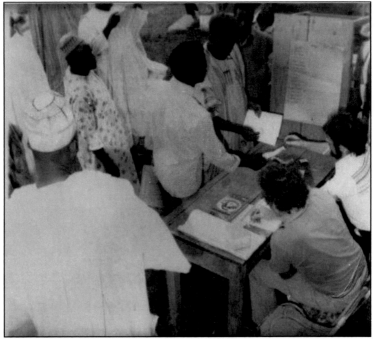

Queuing at the bookies

Do you gamble on the horses? Let me tell you of my experiences. One of the poker players came to me one day and said 'You're a maths teacher aren't you Ken?' When I confirmed that, he said 'Good, I want you to help me out.' I asked him 'How?' He then went on to say that he went to the races as a bookmaker and his partner had gone back to the UK and he wanted me to help him to run the book.

I simply laughed out loud and told him that I knew nothing about horses, or running a book, in fact I had only ever been to a race meeting once, and that was to watch the St Leger in Doncaster. Because of the crowd, neither Barbie nor I saw any of the horses as they raced by. 'That doesn't matter' he said. He knew the horses and he set the odds and all I had to do was add up the total bets taken and the liability on each horse. If the amount in any of the second columns exceeded the amount in the first, then he shortens the odds on that horse for future punters. 'Just come and try it once' he said, so I did. Money was paid out only on winners in those days because no one in Nigeria was sophisticated enough to work out place betting. That made it very simple arithmetic.

It was amazing. We turned up with a little table and blackboard and two stools and my book and David's slips, a pen, and some chalk, very advanced technology. We got the runners for the first race. David put them on the blackboard with the odds, and off we went. I recorded the total amount of the bets, and the running total of the liability on each horse, telling David whenever one in the second column exceeded the first.

Bookies just set up and ready to go. Note the latest technology

There were only three places to bet. The course ran a tote, but for some reason the punters didn't like to put money on with them, insisting that it was rigged. There were also a couple of Lebanese guys who had a similar setup to us, and there was us.

We had to smile. The Lebanese couple used to come to look at our odds and go back and offer better odds. We would take one or two bets until the Lebanese realised that they were in trouble. They would then have to slash their odds and come and lay off some of their bets with us. We then had their punters coming to us and so we ended up with the majority of the money on the course bet with us. This went on for season after season and the Lebanese guys never twigged what was happening.

We could have made lots of money, but we were doing it for the fun of it and the thrill of the battle of the punters versus the bookies. All we set out to do was to pay for our petrol money, a meal, and an overnight stay if we were in another town. In any case, if we had been too greedy, I'm sure that we would have lost the punters. As it was we had great fun and banter with the regular punters. There was always a long queue to pay out, and they always thought that they had 'beaten us this time.'

Let me emphasise this point. It wasn't difficult to make sure that we didn't lose. We could also, to some extent, determine how much we wanted to win. The maximum bet we allowed was 20 Naira (£10), and we could alter the odds after each bet, so it wasn't rocket science. This we managed with an exercise book and a pencil, so what can be done with the aid of modern computers now? Look at the modern bookie's car, and ask yourself if you have ever known a bookie to go bankrupt? I'm not advocating that you shouldn't back horses. All I can say is 'do not kid yourselves that they may lose.'

We became quite friendly with the regular punters and we only realised how much so when on one particular race, a rank outsider won. Realising that for once they knew for certain that we had done well, several came up to us and shook hands with us and congratulated us. When I look back, even though during each race we may have been holding several hundreds of pounds worth of cash, we never felt threatened, and never had any confrontations with anyone.

Were we popular? Make your own mind up after hearing this little story of what happened one weekend. The race meeting was at a place called Jos which was a small town up in the hills to the east, and a regular place to go for a cooler holiday at altitude. It was David's turn to take his car, and half way there we had a puncture. True to form there was no spare tyre, or at least there was one, but it was flat.

We waited ages before David could get a lift to the next garage and have it repaired. When he finally returned we debated as to whether it was worth going on for just one day, but eventually we made up our mind that we ought to go, and knowing that we would be at least an hour late, we drove on.

We arrived at the racecourse to find it unusually quiet, and, as we drove through the gates, there was a sudden roar and everyone started cheering. When we asked what was happening, we were told that they had DELAYED THE RACES until we arrived. No one wanted to bet with anyone else. To be fair, we think someone had passed us and said that we were on our way, but nevertheless, they had actually delayed the races for us, two *Msungu* teachers/part-time amateur bookies. To cap it all, they were all either Christian or Muslim and neither are supposed to gamble or drink yet the only two queues on the course were at the beer tent and at the bookies. Religions have their similarities after all.

The owners of the horses had a problem. They did not understand the first thing about doping. There were no such things as doping tests, so we knew that most of the horses were drugged. Even if they knew that they had the best horse, they always wanted to 'make sure.' What they didn't realise was that the drugs they used would only be effective for a short while, and eventually had an adverse effect on the horse. This worked in our favour because what was once the best horse never won again after a month or so.

The owners tried all the tricks too. On one particular race there were only four runners. They set off and we were waiting for the horses to reappear but they were taking ages. I usually had a job to finalise the bookwork before the race had finished, but this time I had finalised my calculations and still no horses had appeared so we looked over to the far side of the course to see what was happening. We couldn't believe what we saw. All four horses were virtually at a stand still, and one horse was actually eating grass. It was obvious that every jockey had been instructed not to win, and they dare not disobey the owners (it happens in the UK when jockeys are accused of 'pulling' their horse). That race was declared null and void, so this time it was a queue of punters, not to collect their winnings, but to get their money back.

I hope that when I left Kano, David found someone else to help him, otherwise the punters were genuinely going to be very disappointed.

Taffy left G.T.T.S. to return to Wales and as the school got bigger he was replaced by three Filipinos to teach English. I kept quiet over the new policy, and kept quiet when they walked about and taught in vests. The headmaster didn't say anything to them, and I had learned sufficient tact not to rock the boat. I did the best that I could and consoled myself by thinking that at least the students' trade courses were not affected. I did feel sorry for the students though.

Life on the compound was always interesting in some way, for example one of the Canadians in the bungalow opposite us began to build a 50ft Cape Ann Dory. When asked, he told us that he intended to sail it back to the Americas. We watched it grow day by day for the best part of two years, but we all wondered how he was going to transport it the 500 miles down to the coast.

Kirk's Cape Ann Dory under construction next door.
G.T.T.S, 500 miles from launching at Lagos.

After we returned from leave one year it had gone. Apparently he had somehow managed to put it on a train down to Lagos. It was damaged when it arrived in Lagos because one of the bridges had been a shade too narrow for it to pass through, or more likely it had moved on its moorings on the train. It must have been adequately repaired though because the last we heard, it had been wrecked in a storm off the coast of South America when it had broken away from its mooring.

We had bought a 12ft pool to put on the lawn. It was very simple. Just a corrugated sheet of metal rolled out into an upright circle, with a huge plastic liner which fit inside. It was 3ft high, and the pressure of the water from inside kept the whole thing stable. We then bought a large sheet of black plastic to cover it, and to prevent dust and leaves getting in. Two large tractor inner tubes were given to us. One we cut into a continuous strip and tied it round the pool to hold the cover on, just like a jam pot cover. The other we inflated and had fun with it in the pool.

Barbie nearly scalded herself on the first day she tried it. She took the cover off and put her hand in, as you would, only to find that the top inch or two was almost at boiling point. The black plastic had absorbed so much heat from the sun.

From then onwards it was James's daily ritual to take off the cover and stir the water, because the bottom of the pool was still cool. It did help to leave the inner tube in the pool to keep a space between the cover and the water, but it could still be dangerous.

The black cover was very effective in another way. We hardly ever had to put chemicals in because without the sun's rays, there was no photosynthesis possible, therefore algae could not grow. It was surprising how such a simple little thing could bring so much pleasure for family and guests alike, and make such a difference to our daily life. I passed this information on to a pool manufacturer in the UK, but I have yet to see a black cover for an outdoor pool. I wonder if it is because they also sell anti algae products?

I had also been elected onto the club committee, so it was natural for someone to come running to me in the clubhouse to tell me that there had been an accident outside involving a European. I rushed out onto the road to find a car with its engine wrapped round a tree. The driver was inside and unconscious and obviously in trouble. The driver's door was all twisted and couldn't be used, so I got help to take out all the other seats, and was somehow able to use the back seat as a stretcher and carefully ease him onto it and then slide it out through the passenger door.

I did all this knowing that there was no ambulance service or paramedics to call upon, but this would be the quickest way to get him treated. A bystander had a Land Rover and was kind enough to offer to take him to the hospital so we carefully lifted him into the back while still on the car seat and I cradled his head in my arm all the way to the hospital. He was still alive when we left him and I felt the satisfaction of having done my good deed for the day. All I could hear him say was 'Help me, help me.'

I was not to hear about him for over a week, so I called to see him in the hospital and was taken to his bedside. He did not seem at all pleased to see me and I left even more puzzled than before. His attitude did seem rather ungrateful to me. When I retold it to someone at the club however, he said 'Of course he wouldn't be pleased Ken you silly b. . . . . , he was trying to commit suicide.' So much for his unconscious pleas for help. My training in the SJAB and my first chance to use the skills learned to save someone's life, were all to no avail, and I never saw him again. I wonder if he did regret it finally?

It was thick Harmattan and Nikky and Ros were due to return to Lady Manners. The flight back had already been delayed for a day and we were given the news on reaching the airport for the second time, that no large aeroplanes could take off and land. Smaller planes, however, were going to be allowed to take off, and passengers to the UK were to board one flying down to Lagos and catch the London flight from there. Flights from Lagos could then fly over the Harmattan. It was with some relief that they could get back to school having missed only two days.

Unaccompanied minors were the responsibility of the airlines and would be looked after. We wish. That was certainly not what happened. The next letter from the girls told us their tale of woe. All the respectable hotels must have been full and they were taken to one which I dare not name. According to them it appeared more like a brothel. There were no sheets on the bed and no plug in the bath, nor was there any hot water. They went downstairs to get a drink and the only place open was what they described as a sleazy nightclub which they dare not enter. They also felt hostile stares from some of the 'ladies.' Maybe they thought that they had some new young competition. Poor Nikky and Ros hardly slept and were thankful when the airport bus arrived on the following morning. This was the second time that the airlines had let us down. When Nikky was only twelve, she flew unaccompanied back to the UK from Uganda. The flight stopped over in Rome and she was left on her own. She only reboarded the right plane because she recognised the coat of a lady whom she had seen on the plane and followed her. I wrote letters of complaint to various bodies but got nowhere.

Barbie was doing well at golf and was made Lady Captain. She also had a hole in one which I never ever achieved. I used to tease her that it must have rebounded off the sightscreen on the nearby cricket field. That was the year that we went to Kaduna, a town an hour's drive further than Zaria, for her to play in the Ladies' National Golf Championships.

No one before had ever been close to beating a certain lady from Lagos and once again she recorded the best score which was one better than

Barbie's. However this lady's playing partner reported that she had marked the 'browns' on almost every hole, flicking away bits which were on her line. This was quite illegal but the committee said that they could not disqualify 'such a great lady'. I afterwards wrote to the 'R & A' but they were in no way sympathetic and said that it was up to the local committee to enforce rules. I wonder if they would have said the same thing had it happened in one of their own competitions!

Barbie was to get her revenge though because the following year the tournament was held in Kano and Barbie won with strokes to spare. Barbie was now the official 'Nigerian Ladies Amateur Golf Champion' played off scratch. I couldn't be more proud, especially because all the tuition she had received was from me. My ten lessons during my third year at college had certainly paid off. When her handicap levelled off and she couldn't get it down any lower, I teased her and said that it was because she had stopped taking any notice of me. We were always teasing each other.

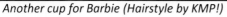

Another cup for Barbie (Hairstyle by KMP!)

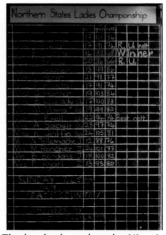

The leader board at the Nigerian Ladies' Open Championships. (Virtually The Nigerian Open)

At the same time I was having my most successful seasons of football. It was one of those times when everything fit together. Several good players had found work in Kano at the same time to form a solid team. I was in my preferred position of centre forward as usual, and, as at the Wireworks, we all blended as a team. It was just like being back in

Yorkshire all over again.

I had scored twenty-four goals in the first eight games in the league and it was satisfying (big head) to see the opposition pointing in my direction when we were grouped together before a game. Of course it was not because of my skill. I have always denied having any. I had an exceptional team around me and I just had to get into the right positions at the right times and the ball would appear in front of me.

The Nigerian National team Coach was one of the Hungarian team that trounced England 6-3 at Wembley. I think it was Koscis but I am not sure if my memory is correct. Anyway, because we were at the top of the league, he called on our captain and instructed us to play against the national team to give them some practice. We were all *Msungus*, so we thought that it was not such a good idea, but we couldn't get out of it so we decided to give it our best shot. We played in the National Stadium, and I would like to say that we beat them but of course we didn't. We lost 3–1 but I did manage to score the goal in the first half.

He had a tactical talk to both teams together at half-time and that was one of the proudest moments of my sporting life. He said a few things and then turned to his team and said 'I want you to take note of their centre forward. He hasn't half the skills of any of you, but watch him and learn from him. He is successful because he gets into the right place at the right time.' Unfortunately I wasn't allowed too much room in the second half.

I must mention the tennis soirees, if only for a couple of incidents. The owner of one of the textile factories in Kano had a floodlit tennis court with a rather posh raised gazebo overlooking it. When it was known that we played a fair game of tennis we were invited to attend.

Now members of the 'posh set' were all from the rich commercial world, so we felt doubly honoured that we, in education, had been invited to join the soiree. A judge, a lawyer, and a factory owner and their wives were among the guests. It was no secret that we had been invited because of our playing ability as opposed to our social status. There were constant drinks served, and at half time, snacks, canapés and cakes were brought out. We knew we were accepted because every Tuesday morning his 'boy' came round to deliver the next invitation. I have to say that we were always worried that one day he might not come round, and so every Tuesday we eagerly awaited the arrival of the coveted invitation.

We enjoyed some really very pleasant evenings with good games of tennis. One evening, however, Barbie had accepted too many drinks. It was very hard to refuse when one was offered champagne and one was thirsty. I had to help, or rather 'support', her back to the car. It was one of the very rare occasions when I can admit that I was 'not best pleased' with Barbie. I was sure that we would never be invited again, but no, his boy duly turned up on the following Tuesday with the invitation as usual. When we arrived, we discovered that she had become quite a star.

The second incident was not quite so funny. It was refreshment time, but the steward hadn't noticed that the veranda door was closed. He literally walked straight through the plate glass, still holding the cake trays. How he managed that is still a mystery. Why did the plate glass shatter? And how could he walk through without being injured and still holding onto the plates? It would have been funny except that Harry was furious. Apart from the vast cost, he had to wait three weeks to get a replacement from Pilkingtons in the UK.

Nikky was accepted at Manchester University to study Computer Science and Psychology. However when she arrived there she found that she was the only student taking that combination of options and felt lonely. She heard about a course in Agricultural Zoology, which seemed to be what she had been searching for in the first place, and was successful in securing a place and transferring to Leeds University to continue her studies there. She had excellent 'A' Level results and I am sure that she had been influenced in her choice by her experiences in Africa. She had done a thesis on grasshoppers for one holiday assignment, having had me up at 5 a.m. to catch samples in a grassy bush area using a large fishing net.

Nikky now had different holidays from Ros and often they were not able to travel together. Ros had flown back earlier from holidaying with us to start a Catering and Management course in Buxton. She didn't want to follow an academic career. We can't blame her, having suffered from the 'following a clever sister' syndrome. We had often wondered whether it would have been better to send them to different schools and had one in mind where her sporting prowess would have been fostered. We were to thank our lucky stars that we hadn't however, when we heard of the drugs scandal attached to that particular school. We felt, in retrospect, that once again we had been guided from above, and who can complain, considering where she is now? In our retirement, we can be justifiably proud of our two daughters.

It must have been the only time I was ill in Africa, but I had quite a severe attack of flu and was just at the recovery stage when we waved our farewells to Nikky. We suspected that Nikky was also showing signs of having contracted it from me.

We thought nothing more of it for three days until we were sitting in the dental surgery waiting to have our teeth inspected. A lady we knew came in and sat down and said 'I'm so sorry to hear about Nikky, how is she?' We looked at each other in shock and asked her if she meant our Nikky?

She then told us that her daughter had been travelling on the flight home with Nikky and they had all had to wait in London on the tarmac until men in what looked like space suits had come and carried Nikky off on a stretcher. They all had to give in their names and addresses and were then informed to report to their local G.P. immediately on arriving home. They were told that they had all been in contact with a Lassa fever suspect.

We were devastated, and spent a sleepless night wondering what on earth was wrong. We hadn't a telephone at that time and had no immediate means of communicating with anyone, but guessed that she had my flu and we could not believe that she had Lassa fever. Fortunately we received a very irate letter from Nikky the next day. She was in Coppice Wood Isolation Hospital, living in a tent with a specially sealed access vent. She had been allowed to write this letter as she was now over eighteen and was no longer treated as a child. This was the excuse I was given from my M.P., the hospital, and the airline, when I wrote strong letters to them.

She was very cross because she had insisted that she had only caught my flu, yet they were treating her as a Lassa fever suspect. She even told them that she had studied Lassa fever and probably knew more about it than they did, and was desperate not to miss any of her course work. I think that somehow the relationships in the hospital were not too convivial.

In retrospect I can see how the authorities have to be ultra careful, but I think that they should have gone out of their way to inform the next of kin, even though she was eighteen. If they had been concerned enough to instruct all the passengers to see their G.P. surely they should have made an effort to see if either of us or Rosalind had the disease? I wonder if they would have acted the same if it had been the Prime Minister's daughter. It resulted in Nikky losing over two weeks of her studies, and it was headline news in most of the British press during mid January, 1977.

I was chatting to friends after a game of golf when they mentioned some change in their National Insurance contributions. When I said that the government looked after that side for me they looked at me askance. They told me to check up on that quickly.

I wrote to the Ministry of Works and Pensions and found out the bad news. I hadn't contributed towards my old aged pension for the whole time that I had been in Africa.

I was both shocked and annoyed. I wrote back immediately to explain that at their request I had gone to Uganda without having the normal week's indoctrination course at Farnham Castle where all this would have been explained. Furthermore my government contracts while in the UK covered all pension contributions, so it was reasonable for me to expect government overseas contracts to include the same.

I got nowhere. I had done what they wished and gone at a minute's notice, yet it was I who had to suffer for their omission. I was only allowed to pay the maximum of five years back subscriptions, which left me many years short, resulting in me now only getting about three quarters of my full entitlement of old age pension.

One of my opening bowlers at cricket was also an area manager of one of the local chain stores. He invited us out for a Chinese meal at the Pink Peacock restaurant along with other guests. Everything was going fine, in fact it was going too well. We had one course after another, and still they kept coming. That was when we noticed that there were only Barbie and I eating. When I looked at our host he burst out laughing. 'While ever you empty your plate Ken, they will keep bringing more' he said. We hurriedly left a little, and that was another lesson learned. One can't win. We had been taught at home to eat everything up, and now we were being told that we had to leave something.

Meeting the girls from the plane also became quite an adventure. We never knew what the new fashions would be in the UK and wondered if we would recognise our own children in their new outfits. Our girls were always quite conservative in their dress, because they didn't have the money to be really extravagant, but one friend saw his daughter coming down the steps from the aeroplane and immediately disowned her until she got home and he had made her change into a different outfit. It must have been the time of the introduction of micro miniskirts.

CHANGING TIMES

The atmosphere in Nigeria was imperceptibly changing. There was tension in the air and people began remembering dead bodies in the street after the Biafra episode, which had occurred just before our time. No one had dared to touch them, afraid of being accused of sympathising with the wrong side.

We then experienced an attempted coup and the executions by firing squads of the culprits on Bar Beach. We used to play social bridge with Judge Jeffrey Jones – not the one of the same name in England – and he got an official gilt-edged invitation to witness the executions. It was an invitation that he would not have dared to refuse, so we had firsthand knowledge of the incident.

Burglaries were also becoming more common and we were not to escape from another one. We arrived home late from a New Years Eve party to find the veranda doors wide open and a pool on the floor. Our first thought was that it was blood, but as we got nearer it turned out to be a pile of my ties, some of which were red. When we went inside there was hardly anything left except the furniture. The robbers had even lifted the rails from the wardrobes and carried the lot to their vehicle, hence the ties outside which had obviously slipped off. We had to go back to the host of the party and ask for sheets to sleep in.

There was one piece of good fortune. I have said how the floors were polished to a dark brown gloss. Barbie had the same coloured handbag containing all her jewellery which we had pushed under the bed, and they had failed to see the brown handbag on the brown floor.

We were grossly underinsured of course, and as there were no European outfitters we had only what we stood up in to wear. Friends were very generous in giving and selling us clothes, and a child from Barbie's class said he would ask his mummy to look in the famine relief box.

One lady gave Barbie a tennis skirt. She said it was one she had in the WRENS during the war, and it was too, it was thick, white denim, and it still had her service number on it. Barbie bought a new sewing machine, and after I had redesigned the skirt and she had stitched some ricrac round the bottom, it looked quite presentable. I did get some size ten shoes from the famine relief box too, but when I went on leave in the summer I still had to borrow a blazer to wear on the journey. Africa does teach one to be quite resourceful. Long after we had been paid by the Insurance Co. we kept remembering things that had disappeared for which we hadn't claimed. The camel stool, which we had bought from the ship in Cairo, was one of them, and my very smart black bri nylon track suit with the permanent creases.

Teaching could not have been better for both Barbie and I. I had a wonderful relationship with the students and particularly with the African members of staff. The Filipinos kept very much to themselves and never attempted to socialise with the rest of us. What was about to happen, however, was not only going to affect me at the time, but I still think about it.

I had to go to the ministry to see the CEO to discuss policy for the next year. It was an impressive new building with floor to ceiling windows opposite the stairs leading to the upper floor. I often wish the window had not been there, because it looked directly over the car park.

I could not miss it. A circle of men were surrounding a lone man crouching in the middle. One of the men broke from the circle with a hedge stake and beat the man in the middle once. He then went back and passed it to the next man. When I say beat, it was from high over his head. When he started to go back to hand it over to the next man, I could not watch any more, and rushed up to the CEO's office. When he called me in he could see that I was as white as a sheet. I started explaining, but he told me to sit down and try to stay calm. He then said that the man had been caught red-handed stealing a briefcase from a car, but that the police had been notified. He advised me to go back to school and try to forget what I had seen. I realised that he had known what was happening, but I was in no position to discuss anything and sensed that I should not say anything more.

I went back to school in a daze and went up to see the headmaster, who excused me from school, and told me to go back home and try to forget about it. He had obviously been forewarned about the state that I was in, but why he had to tell me that the man ended up decapitated I don't know because it obviously made me feel worse. I did go home, but I have never forgotten. It was later suggested that the police might have not appeared deliberately until after it was all over. I never spoke of it again while I was in Nigeria.

It did make me think back to Kinyasano and what might have happened there if I had not left because of Ros's health. A lone European, probably having to argue his case against a Ugandan bursar, and his word against mine. Were the Ugandans different from the Nigerians? Surely they would not have held a kangaroo court over a white man? But then, what about the tribal war, the result of which we saw on the way back from Kilembe. Life was very cheap to some of the tribes, and the school was way out in the 'bush.'

I can understand a young ambitious African looking at us and comparing life. We come to Africa and are given a better dwelling. We are better paid. We appear happy and enjoy life, often playing a lot of sport. They must say to themselves 'what do they do that we can't do?' We don't look under stress, and the better we are at our jobs, the easier what we do looks to an outsider. They must think to themselves 'I'm sure I could do as well as that.' I can see that this outlook could lead to hatred, but I cannot condone the deliberate setting up of someone to make them appear to be a criminal, just because of jealousy. Or was it just opportunism?

I should stop thinking of what if this and what if that. This is why we firmly believe that we have had a guardian angel watching over us all the while and who was and still is prompting all our decisions.

Within a few days of witnessing this public lynching, I was driving back home on my own at teatime and stopped at traffic lights. A policeman came up to my open window and accused me of some traffic violation that I knew to be false. He said that I knew what I could do to prevent him from booking me. That meant that he wanted a 'dash'.

I was not in a good mood and I told him that I had done nothing wrong and that if he wished he could take me to his chief. After arguing a while he did escort me to the police station and to his senior officer to whom I explained the situation. The chief expressed his regrets, but he couldn't intervene as he hadn't been there, and that I would therefore have to do what his policeman had suggested. I said that I would go back to school and explain to my students what had happened, and I paid the sum requested which could only be called a bribe (the Nigerian expression is a 'dash'). It would appear that everything was conspiring to make us dissatisfied.

I did exactly that. After seeing Barbie, I told the whole school on the following day, and explained my disappointment that this was happening in their country.

It was rumoured that most of the robbers were wearing army or police boots and for the first time since going to Africa we were beginning to feel unsafe. We had another one of our discussions, and decided that I should hand in my notice and take our chances back in the UK. We had been in Nigeria for almost eight years and had some lovely times, but circumstances beyond our control suggested that it was time to call it a day.

It was my last game of golf in Kano, and the Chief Orthopaedic

Surgeon had joined Fats and I on our regular Friday game. I was having a final drink at the bar with them when the doctor suddenly said 'Of course Ken, it is all your fault.'

'What have I done wrong now?' I said.

'No, I don't mean you personally Ken, I mean your country, the UK.'

'OK, what have we done wrong then?' I replied.

'Well, you gave us independence too soon didn't you?'

I was very surprised at this revelation, especially to me, being a *Msungu*. I then tried to explain that we didn't give them independence because we thought they were ready for it, but that we were forced into it by the opinions expressed in the form of propaganda from America and the rest of the world, who were saying how we had exploited every country we had occupied. We were seen to be far too powerful a force with the whole of the Commonwealth behind us, and America in particular, didn't like that situation. This was more or less confirmed when I googled Uganda on the computer. I have always fiercely defended our position in Africa. As far as I could see we had done nothing but good, and certainly there was no evidence of exploitation where we were, and there must have been thousands of us out there trying to help them advance.

It is a good example of the local intelligentsia foreseeing why our former Colonies would all experience difficulties after independence. It is also interesting to observe that a friend had an almost identical conversation in Uganda, so it is reasonable to believe that the same view was held in all the Commonwealth countries. The problem was that no one could do anything about it. Once it had started it then carried on under its own steam. Unfortunately though, the politicians, as usual, got it all wrong and the intelligentsia have turned out to be correct.

Before flying back to the UK for good, we had to fly down to Lagos to finalise all our papers and our finances. Exchange Control allowed us only to take a percentage of our salary out of the country. We met old friends who had been transferred to Lagos, one of which was one of the managers of a chain of stores, and had been one of my opening bowlers back in Kano. They were kind enough to help us, particularly with transport.

There has always been a traffic problem in Lagos, and the latest attempt to solve it was to use the numbers on the car's number plates. They allowed odd numbered cars on the roads on odd dates, and even numbered cars on the roads on even dates. This must have been very good for car salesmen because most commercial people now had to have at least three cars and some had to have four, in order that husband and wife could be mobile every day.

The paperwork took several days, but eventually we got it all sorted out and thanked our friends, and left a little present for their hospitality. We said our fond goodbyes and flew back to Kano to say our goodbyes there.

We had one last task to perform. What could we do with our surplus cash in the bank? This was substantial because it had to include my winnings at poker, as well as some extra that Barbie had earned from selling her school. We could exchange it on the 'black market', but those who would exchange it charged commission resulting in us getting £1 for every £2 exchanged, and surely we could do better than that? I honestly don't know who came up with the idea first, but it must have been Barbie. I think that I would have remembered, had I thought of it.

'Why don't we buy a ticket to fly round the world and visit all our friends?' She said, 'You know, those who were silly enough to say 'If you're ever in our neck of the woods, please feel free to come and stay with us for a while.'

That is what we did. I still do not know how it worked, but we paid the overall cost of the journey in Nigeria and after confirming dates and times, we went to a travel agent in the UK who arranged the individual flights. All I do know is that it did work, and that, to us, was all that mattered.

We flew back to England with mixed feelings. We had certainly gained a lot of experience, we had seen lots of things that we would not otherwise have seen, and we had enjoyed our teaching tremendously. We had made wonderful friends from all over the world and we had also that feeling which everyone should strive to achieve, and that was job satisfaction.

I often said that we had played very hard, but we also had the satisfaction of having worked very hard too, and I am sure that our stay in Africa had contributed our little share to the education of the children whom we had been privileged to teach. It is a pity that we left Africa with a slight taste of bitterness in our mouths, and yet again we were moving, and this time with no obvious job to go to.

PART SEVEN

Back to Blighty

ROS HAD SUCCESSFULLY PASSED THROUGH CATERING COLLEGE and met and married Paul Higgins in 1977 and now lived in Buxton. Paul's dad had played for Bolton Wanderers and was a member of the team beaten by Blackpool in the epic game for which Stanley Matthews will always be remembered. His brother, Mark, had captained England Youth and was at that time captain of Everton. Victoria Louise was born the following year and Ryan Paul John in 1980.

Nikky gained her honours degree from Leeds and asked her professor for a reference. He asked her why she hadn't applied for the post as his assistant which he had just advertised, so she did. Her first period of work therefore, was helping the professor with his research work into cancer. Nikky now lived in digs in Leeds, so Barbie and I lived by ourselves in Bakewell.

We finalised our holiday plans, having made sure that our hosts were available on the appropriate dates. The travel agency in Matlock were very pleasant and helpful, but we were to find out that they were not so hot on efficiency.

Our first port of call was Vancouver which involved a flight over the North Pole, not that we saw much of it. We spent three nights with Guy and Gillian and it was virtually nonstop entertainment. We were to experience the same hospitality as this on all our stops, meeting old friends whom we had not seen, sometimes for years. We enjoyed the delights of the city and its food. We also saw a frozen waterfall which was hundreds of feet high, which gives you an indication of how cold it was.

We then experienced our first shock. Guy asked us if we had got our visa. We were making a stopover in Hawaii on the way to Western Samoa and Tonga, and Hawaii was part of the USA. We hadn't thought that a visa was necessary because it was only a stopover, and nor, apparently, had Matlock.

We were anxious all the way to the airport. Surely our holiday couldn't be jeopardised before it had hardly started? We went to the checkout, and were asked the inevitable question. 'Where is your visa?' I explained our situation and was then told that we must wait there and she would contact the pilot who would then make the decision. It was apparently entirely up to him. We hoped that he was in a good mood.

We sweated through the longest hour of our lives, waiting to see the check-in girl with the news. At last she came back to us. Yes we could travel on the plane, thank goodness, but the captain would retain our passports until we had left American territory. The walls bulged with our sighs of relief.

What a pity that we had not budgeted for a longer stay in Honolulu, but we did have time to tour the city before our early bed and early rise for the flight to Western Samoa. This was another long haul flight, and involved another overnight stay, before our flight to Tonga.

On our arrival at Western Samoa, we had been booked into an hotel at the airport, if one could call it an hotel. In fact it was a series of mixed dormitories for both sexes. We were glad to leave in the morning, after an anxious night holding on tightly to our valuables.

We did meet one interesting character. He was an ex-USA pilot who apparently lived there permanently. We were told that he was not the only ex-serviceman to go native after his experiences in Vietnam, and live a strange kind of hermit life.

When we saw our plane arrive we couldn't believe it. Surely it couldn't be that tiny twin-engined Otter? It was. And furthermore as we lined up to board we all had to be weighed. The Tongans are noted for their size which was a further worry. What if there were too many overweight passengers before it was our turn to board?

The pilot was finally satisfied and we were all safely on board as the plane trundled up the runway. We had no idea how near the limit the plane was. I was sitting next to a door and spent the whole flight leaning towards Barbie, afraid to touch the door handle.

What started as a hair-raising experience actually turned out to be one of the most exhilarating experiences of our lives. The plane flew at no more than a few hundred feet over the Pacific. The ocean was calm, and we could see the ocean bed in many places. We passed over numerous atolls which consisted of a few palm trees surrounded by sand and rings of ever deepening ocean greens. We landed on two tiny islands to drop passengers off and pick up new ones.

If there had been any fish as big as a dolphin we would surely have seen them, but in that we were not so fortunate. We really didn't want that flight to end, but too soon we saw an island ahead with a tiny gap in the trees. Surely we couldn't squeeze into that gap? We could, and we did. We had landed in Tonga.

Having passed through customs and collected our baggage we were mildly surprised because Pat had said he would be there to meet us. We found a telephone and Pat answered and was not too surprised when he knew we were at the airport. 'You were supposed to arrive tomorrow' he said. 'It's happened again, someone forgot to tell you that you had crossed the International Date Line.'

He was soon greeting us and driving us back to his home. Pat was the Deputy High Commissioner and he had met and married his lovely wife Stella who was Tongan. Unfortunately that meant his career in the Service had flatlined because apparently mixed marriages were frowned upon. I'm sure that it never bothered them as they are now happily retired in New Zealand. Both their two sons are now airline pilots.

What an idyllic little island Tonga is. We stayed there for a week, and could have stayed forever if we had accepted the teaching jobs which were offered to us. We were tempted, but the problem was the low salary, and we had been separated from our families for long enough. We were to be offered teaching posts almost everywhere we went. It seems that everywhere in the world is crying out for English teachers.

Stella's family were fishermen and they took us out in one of their boats for an 'Umu' on Fafa, a tiny deserted island in the middle of the Pacific. When we arrived and weighed anchor, we found that we could walk all the way round the island in a quarter of an hour.

An Umu is their version of a barbeque. A hole is dug in the sand, a fire is then lit in the bottom of the hole, and then the food is wrapped in banana leaves which they lay on the fire and cover up with sand for an hour. When they scraped the sand away and opened the parcels, the gorgeous smells wafted up to us, and the food tasted delicious.

As we waited, we couldn't resist having a dip in the ocean, but poor Barbie was touched by the long tendrils of a jellyfish and had an irritating rash for a day or two.

After such a wonderful day we were given the news that a storm was brewing and we had to make a dash for home. The waves seemed to be higher than the boat which was going up and down, up and down. Both Barbie and I were scared stiff, but the Tongans were laughing and were obviously used to such seas. We were still mighty relieved when we reached the shores of Tonga again.

We bought a turtle shell at the local market, only to be told that we would not be able to take it in our luggage to New Zealand. It was one of the protected species. We solved that by posting it home with excess clothing, not wanted on voyage.

There was to be a lot more hectic sightseeing, as it is such a beautiful island with lots of history attached to it, but too soon it was time to leave these lovely people. It is so happy meeting up with old friends, but it is so sad when one has to part again.

The next stop was New Zealand. We hadn't met any friends from there but we had to change flights there, so we made a long weekend of it anyway. We didn't want to miss the opportunity to see at least some of New Zealand.

Unfortunately we had to spend the whole of Friday afternoon and Saturday morning at the Australian Embassy in order to get another visa. That was the third error the Matlock Travel Agent had made. Who would have thought we would need a visa for Australia which was our next stop, and me a Yorkshireman. It was only through their good will that we were fast tracked to receive the visas in time. We did manage a tour of Auckland, Mount Victoria and Cockle Bay, and promised ourselves that some day we would have to come back and 'do' New Zealand properly. This was one of the promises that we were able to fulfil.

Barbie's Ladies Doubles partner in Uganda now lived in Sydney but was visiting relatives in Europe at the time. Julie did not tell us until after we had booked our flights, and insisted that we meet her parents in Melbourne who would entertain us, so that became the next stop.

What she had not told us until after we had finalised the arrangements, was that her parents were a Lord and Lady. Julie's father had been knighted for his services to plastic surgery. He pioneered the technique of reconstructing the faces of fighter pilots during the war. These were numerous because the cockpits were directly behind the engines, and if the engine caught fire there was only the Perspex windscreen between the fire and the pilot. This happened all too frequently during 'dogfights'.

We had known Tony and Julie for a few years and they had never breathed a word. Of course the parents had now retired, but were still young enough to give us a good game of golf and show us the sights of Melbourne. They were a delightful couple with absolutely no airs and graces. They were also heavily involved in fighting skin cancer, and would never allow us out of the house without headgear.

We also managed to meet Adrienne who had been Barbie's pen friend since 1948 in her sixth form days. We had only seen photographs of her, and it was nice to meet her in person. We were only with her for one night unfortunately, but Barbie and she had a lot to talk about. I never did much of the talking anyway in those days.

We then flew on to Sydney to stay with Julie's brother and his wife for two more hectic days of touring round, seeing the many sites such as the Opera House, the Harbour Bridge, and Bondi beach, and being treated to the warm and genuine Australian hospitality.

Of course we vowed to come again, for we had only scratched the surface of Australia on this visit. We could have stayed longer but our initial aim when we booked the holiday was not to outstay our welcome anywhere.

Port Moresby, our nest stop, was the capital of Papua New Guinea and that was where Tony had been posted with his wife, Connie. He met us at the airport and we collected our luggage – or thought we had, and he drove for half an hour to his home.

After greeting Connie I went to open a case and couldn't. Eventually we realised it wasn't our case, but was identical in make and colour. Who would have thought that anyone but us would buy purple cases. We jumped back into the car and fortunately there was our case still going round on the carrousel, with the other owner nearby, busy filling in forms. We apologised and all had a laugh about it. He didn't think anyone else would be daft enough to buy purple cases either.

Tony and Connie had been one of our best friends in Kampala. He was the one who took us fishing for Nile perch. He didn't look like an athlete but he generally beat me at squash. He was a fitness fanatic and to rub it in, he beat me again (well, I was unfit after all the travelling, wasn't I?).

Most of Papua New Guinea is forest and like the poorer parts of Africa. There is plenty to see though if anyone has the chance to go there. We were amused when we went out to dine. In all the good restaurants were signs saying 'No T-shirts after 6 p.m.' The place apparently attracted the down-and-outs from Australia.

The only downside to the whole trip happened here. I had given Connie an uncut ruby as a present, but when we were back in the UK they wrote and told us that their jeweller had told them it was a bit of glass. We had bought them from 'Gemstone' Gerry in Jos. He was a part-time prospector and he and Liz were among our best friends. We had bought other stones from him that we knew were positively genuine, and I tend to believe that it was the jeweller who was the rogue. We would have given anything though, for it not to have happened to Connie.

The flight over Papua New Guinea was easy to describe, perpetual forests. Then over the Philippines which were not much different. The arrival in Hong Kong, however, was spectacular. It seemed that if we had put our hand out, we could have touched the skyscrapers as we turned around them on the approach to the runway.

Everything about Hong Kong and the island is spectacular, and should be a must on everyone's holiday list. This book is not to describe holidays in detail but to whet your appetite to go yourselves. Anna and Roy met us and took us to their apartment near the top of one of the skyscrapers, all built using bamboo scaffolding. Anna taught for me in Jinja and left to become the first news presenter on Hong Kong television. Roy worked at the government Fisheries Dept.

The markets sell everything, including snakes, frogs and anything that can be described as a creepy-crawler. The ferry and the underground are so clean and cheap, and all the residents are addicted to the horseracing. Ocean Terminal is purported to be the best shopping place in the world and the nightlife satisfies every taste, not that we sampled any of it.

We must have chosen our friends well because they all turned out to be perfect hosts. Most of them had children whom Barbie had taught, and as such they went out of their way to give something back to her in appreciation. I didn't mind having a holiday on the back of their good will towards Barbie, but we did always leave them presents.

Edna and David met us in Bangkok. She also taught for me in Jinja and David had a factory manufacturing gardening implements. They left the next day on a prebooked holiday, and hadn't told us for fear that we would be put off visiting them. They gave us the free run of the house and left Sumchit, the housegirl, to cater for our needs. She did a very good job of it too.

If you are interested in Eastern architecture, religion, movement and art, floating markets, snake baiting and working elephants, then Bangkok is another must. I know that both Barbie and I enjoyed every minute. Beware at the markets though because the salespeople can be rather persistent. Bangkok has other attractions too, apparently, but we didn't sample any of those.

The travel agent must have been running short of money by the time we got to Thailand, because he had booked us on LOT, a Polish airline. It looked like a VC 10 on the outside but like the cheapest utility bus on the inside. The seats were canvas, and we hadn't the correct currency so couldn't get even a glass of water to drink as they only had water to buy in bottles. The captain never gave any announcements either, and we knew there would be a time change but had no idea by how much, so we had no idea what the time was.

When we landed in Bombay there wasn't a clock to be seen. The little three-wheeler taxi ride was the most hair-raising ride ever, and the taxi looked as if it would fall apart. Everywhere looked poor and shabby. Millions of people thronged the streets. How the driver missed them all I have no idea, but we did manage to dodge our way through to the Centaur, which turned out to be a very respectable hotel. At last we found out what time it was and we had a super meal and a restful night.

We had hoped to meet Barbie's cousin Marjorie who had seemingly caused disgrace in the family in 1949 by marrying an Indian. They also had a prebooked holiday so we were unable to meet up with them. We were able to make up for it though when we met them later in the UK at a cousin's birthday party.

We had booked an early flight from Mumbai to Aurangabad to see Ray and Jos whom we had met on the S.S. *Uganda* and again in Kenya. Ray had a most surprising job in India, the 'Land of the Sacred Cow'. He worked for Fray Bentos, and was there to build and open a corned beef factory. Not many moons ago this would have been impossible. They had a very fine house indeed but must have found life very different from their previous one in the 'Happy Valley' in Kenya. The local peasants looked poor and undernourished and must have welcomed some industry in their area.

One remarkable feature that they took us to see was the Ellora caves. These had been cut into the mountainside leaving a central column inside, from which a temple had been hewn from solid rock. How they could have done this work 1500 years ago with the tools they had then is beyond our comprehension. Succeeding dynasties then tried to outdo the first by creating even bigger and better cave temples. The caves had only been discovered recently, apparently by passing cavalry, who had seen something glinting among the trees and had gone to investigate.

Thank goodness there were no more taxi rides involved when we flew back to Bombay, and weren't we glad that it wasn't another 'utility' aeroplane on our flight to Abu Dhabi.

Irene was Barbie's tennis partner in the Sheffield league, and consequently she and her husband were the friends on the tour whom we had known the longest. We always enjoyed meeting friends, but Abu Dhabi left the least impression upon us. It was the capital of the Trucial

States, and I remember little, except that when we played golf we were allowed to use paper tees on the fairways because it was so barren.

What we were impressed with was the highway to El Ain, a university compound with a superb sports complex equal to anything at the time. The highway through the desert was lined with trees which had to be watered – no mean feat in the middle of a desert. The road was also littered with wrecks of cars, which indicated how dangerous it was to drive in such extreme heat.

We were driven on to Dubai too which was equally impressive. That was, however, before the building boom which has occurred since we were there. It is a very different city now from the one we saw. I still remember the crystal clear blue water as we strolled along the jetty with the yachts and dhows anchored up alongside.

Our final port of call was to Kuwait, to see Roger and Diana. We had met them in Uganda and it was they who advised us to board the children in Bakewell. The house we had purchased in Bakewell was only six doors away from theirs on the same estate. It was rather sad that this was going to be our final stopover before returning home.

Roger was the principal of the International School and they lived in a very impressive house. It had a courtyard with a fountain at its centre, and was so impressive that it was apparently borrowed by the high commissioner whenever he wished to entertain foreign dignitaries such as Margaret Thatcher.

After Roger had been there for a few years he considered that career wise it was time to go back to the UK. They doubled his salary in order to entice him to stay. The next occasion when he wanted to leave they gave him a Mercedes. It is nice to think that some countries value good teachers.

Everything here was on a grand scale. It was obvious that they were very well respected everywhere they took us. Our visit to the Gold Souk sticks in my memory and the feeling of opulence everywhere.

It was very sad that the year following our visit, Roger had a fatal stroke. From that second, Diana had absolutely no rights at all, in spite of what Roger's position had been. All Roger's possessions now belonged theoretically to the state. Women apparently could own nothing. It was very fortunate that one of their sheik friends helped her export all their possessions back to the UK, in spite of the prevailing law.

The flight home was accompanied by a feeling of sadness that it was all over, but we had enjoyed the most wonderful time and seen how the rest of the world ticks. The holiday had done one thing above all else. It had whet our appetite to see as much of the rest of the world as possible.

Our sadness soon changed when we arrived back in Bakewell and we walked through the door of our own home, and saw our own belongings and relaxed in our own bed.

Brother Arthur became ill. He had been working at the Coalite, in Askern, where coke was made through the destructive distillation of coal. He had been working on the burners, but had then been promoted on to the staff in the offices. When I heard that he had leukaemia, I immediately thought of all the by-products of the process of converting coal into coke. Some of these were extremely toxic, and the thought occurred that he might have been exposed to them at some time. He had several blood transfusions, but there was no cure, and after a few months he died. I was surprised that the possibility that he had been exposed to something toxic had not occurred to anyone else in the family, but that was before the age of litigation, and I was living out of the country and too out of touch to be of any help.

It has often occurred to me, after my experiences watching how Asian families, especially the Lebanese, work as a family, that had I been the oldest in the family instead of the youngest, surely I would have set up a family business to utilise all the skills for the good of the family. But that was just a pipe dream, and contrary to British traditions. We were brought up to be individuals, rather than to be family orientated.

MARKET TRADER

One would have thought that I could now bring this book to its conclusion, but events still kept taking place, and our varied life had still a long way to go. My grandson, Ryan, thought that we had been to every country in the world. We hadn't, because we had only completed half our travels. Ryan later served with the Irish Guards in Kosovo, and was in Macedonia at the time. We pointed out that we hadn't been to Macedonia, or anywhere in Eastern Europe, so he had actually been somewhere that we hadn't been.

I was faced with a problem. What was I going to do now for a living, because I certainly didn't want to teach in the UK. I had been spoiled in Africa. Barbie never had that problem. She loved teaching and with her curriculum vitae she was never turned down for any post for which she had applied.

I make no apology for the fact that I was willing to do anything to make money. We had been born into poverty and could still remember those days. It was a comforting thought that with Barbie's testimonials and references she would never be out of teaching, so I was on the lookout for something suitable.

Ros's father-in-law came up with a solution. He had a chain of market stalls selling seconds and offcuts from various national bakeries. It was not often possible to distinguish the seconds from the real thing, and they were at bargain prices. He wanted to retire and offered me 50% of the profits if I would manage them for him. Why not? I thought. It costs me nothing, and it was something to do until something else cropped up, for I was willing to try my hand at anything.

It meant early rising and lots of travel to nearby market towns. It also involved collecting the produce from various factories or bakeries in Stockport, Manchester, Warrington and Blackpool. I have to admit that I quite enjoyed the experience too. I had three regular men looking after the stalls on different markets.

Fred made me laugh. When anyone asked him if he had any change, he used to say 'Of course love, I can change any money but matrimony.' I watched him one day serving two women.

'How much are the Battenbergs?' they asked.

'20 pence each' he replied.

'Oh dear' they said.

'I'll tell you what love, I'll give you five for £1' he said to them.

'Go on then' one said.

'How about you Mabel?' he said to the other lady.

'OK, I'll have five as well' she said. So he had turned a dubious sale of one into a sale of ten at the same price. I walked behind the stall in disbelief.

The business was good and the money rolled in, but I have to admit that Barbie was not so keen. I don't think that she ever admitted to anyone that I was a market trader, even though I was buying a new Saab out of the business. For myself, I was quite happy. I enjoyed working hard and it wasn't just a job to make money. I had dozens of regular customers, who might not depend entirely on me, but would be very unhappy with us if we didn't turn up one day.

John, whose partner I had become, also owned a flourishing pub. He must have needed some ready cash, because after less than a year he asked me if I wanted to buy his share. That may sound to have been a good opportunity for me, but with him having played football for Bolton

Wanderers and having played in the famous F.A. Cup final against Blackpool and Stanley Matthews, I couldn't see the business surviving without Big John's influence and prestige. I couldn't expect to be given the same perks which had been bestowed on him by the bakeries, so I declined and we sold it on to one of his other acquaintances.

Again I was looking for employment and we were on the lookout for a Post Office to buy. We saw one advertised which we applied for, but we were too late. Thank goodness too, because some time later it was involved in an armed robbery. Once again our guardian angel was watching over us.

SHOPKEEPER

Then we saw The White Shop in Eyam had come up for sale. Eyam was famous, and known as the 'Plague Village' which attracted a lot of tourists. There were other shops in Eyam, but we bought it anyway and converted the area above the shop into our home.

We sold Castle Drive privately for £36,000, which we thought was good. An estate agent contacted us to say that he had a buyer who was willing to give us £35,000, but when I said we had sold it already for £36,000, he said that he would have to revise his estimates upwards. We later wished that we had continued to rent it out however because in 2004 it was on the market for £350,000.

The previous owner gave me a crash course in how to run a shop, as I was obviously a raw beginner. Once more it involved early mornings because we had to take delivery of the papers and distribute them out to the paperboys. I had then to make regular trips to the 'Cash-and-Carries' for all the produce, buying all the special offers when possible. I worked on the principle of selling ten for the price of a pack of a dozen, the other two being profit, and this undercut all the rivals. Bigger profits were made on the papers, sweets, icecream and souvenirs etc. and trade was very brisk. I had two part-time ladies to help me, and later that had to be increased to three.

Throughout this time, Barbie was teaching as a supply teacher and soon became a favourite of all the children and their mothers. On the occasions when she helped in the shop, she was often heard to say 'Of course, I'm a teacher really' It became quite a joke amongst us. She wasn't really a snob, but she did prefer to be known as a teacher.

We went on our first cruise. It was on the Ocean Village, which was one of the cheapest cruises going. It was during term time, hence there were not too many children on board. We sailed to the Caribbean and back, and of all the many cruises we were to take, that was one of the most enjoyable. We sat where we wished, when we wished and the food was buffet style but excellent. The day and night entertainment was superb and included trapeze artists performing outdoors in the middle of the Atlantic, which to us was amazing. Evening entertainment was also first class and we were never to better it for value for money. We regret that, when we last heard, it has been re-routed to cruising round Australia.

John, Ros's father-in-law, came to me with another proposition. Some land had come on the market in North Wales. It was extensive, natural woodland, but had been the site of slate mines and a stone quarry. It was on the mouth of an estuary and was situated opposite to where the gold for the royal rings had been mined. There were two ponds on the site which were well stocked with fish and there were fishing rights included on that stretch of river.

His idea was to create an aquatic sports centre there for canoeing and sailing. I could look after the sports side and John the catering side. There was another gentleman in the partnership and he would see to the landscaping and construction side of the business. With its subsidiary interests it sounded a very viable proposition.

There were already the foundations of a substantial building in an ideal position, and this was to be developed into the administrative building. It did, in fact, play an important part in later developments. I knew that Barbie wasn't keen on the shop, and that this was more in our line, so I provided the cash to put down as a deposit on an offer which, I made sure, was legally certified.

I ought to have known of course. When the time came to pay the balance, I was the only one with any cash. The owner, however, unwittingly saved us, because he tried to put up the price and change the agreement, causing a considerable delay. This boomeranged on him because in the meanwhile the bank forced him into bankruptcy, and it worked in my favour because I finally bought it from the bank at the bankruptcy price. I had to do this otherwise we most certainly would have lost our deposit.

I could not attempt to develop the site on my own. To do that I would need a great deal more professional advice. We had, however, acquired 90 acres of mixed woodland, with a partly constructed building and various quarries. We had bought it for a very reasonable price, so we thought that God was looking down on us once again.

It was not without its trauma however because then ensued a few years of anxiety wondering whether we would ever be able to get rid of it. I wanted to sell the land with planning permission for the house. I reckoned that to have built such substantial foundations there had to be plans somewhere, and with planning permission it was worth considerably more than we had paid for it.

I asked our solicitor to apply to the council for a copy of the deeds for the building, but then came the bombshell. The news came back to us that there was no planning permission. The council obviously no longer wanted a house to be built there.

I wasn't going to give up that easily, so I made the trip to north Wales to confront the council personally. If necessary I was prepared to take them to the site to show them the substantial foundations which had already been laid.

If you do not believe in God, or guardian angels, think on this. Could it be just by accident that the planning officer was not on duty when I arrived? I made my request to a junior official in charge and he said he would go to have a look. Imagine my complete amazement when he came with the plans in his hand and asked me if I would like a copy.

I left with the plans and the details of planning permission etc. inscribed on the top. I do not wish to accuse anyone, so I will leave it with you as to how the mistake or misunderstanding was made.

Once when we visited the site, we found a young man living in the woods in a caravan. He turned out to be a graduate who was living like a hermit, sculpting wood in order to make a living. He asked us kindly if we minded if he remained where he was, and in return he would keep the woods in order. His degree had been in Sylvan Culture.

Years later I heard that R.T.Z. (Rio Tinto Zinc) had accessed the land, illegally in my view because they had not had my permission, to drill for metals, presumably gold. Soon after that an offer was made by a neighbouring landowner, through my solicitor, which I refused.

When repeated offers were made which were substantially more that I had paid, and more than covered the loss of interest, it was the time of the very high interest rates I accepted and breathed a sigh of relief. Whether R.T.Z. ever had any more interest in it I will never know.

It seemed that every time I ventured into a new field, something would happen, and it did. I employed three ladies to help part-time in the White shop, and one of them said she suspected a customer of shoplifting. This was devastating news, because we were selling everything cut price and still someone was stealing from us. How naive we were. Other dealers told me that they always built in an extra 6% margin onto the selling price to cover thefts. It would seem that I had been lucky to make any profit at all.

We set a trap and watched the gentleman in question put things into his bag which he didn't then put on the counter to pay for. I got the signal and had to wait until he had exited the shop before I could apprehend him. I then made a citizen's arrest, which would not have been enforceable in the shop. I asked him to come back into the shop so that we could check the contents of his bag.

Of course he tried to bluster his way out of it. He had left the kettle on, or had to let the cat out, and various other excuses. I explained to him about my rights to use force if necessary, so eventually he came back into the shop with me. We confirmed that there were tins of cat food for which he hadn't paid, so I merely asked him politely never to enter the shop again.

We were in a tricky position. He was one of the village 'elders' and any announcement that he had been caught shoplifting would have split the village in two and ruined our trade. His daughter was our best customer and we took her aside to explain matters. She was very understanding, and asked if she could shop for him, to which we agreed.

For us, however, the whole atmosphere had changed. We had not been programmed to accept shoplifting as an acceptable hazard. After thinking long and hard, we decided that sooner or later the story would come out, so we put it on the market. It had acquired such a reputation that it was soon sold and we hadn't lost money, for which we were thankful. It ended with an unusual twist. The buyer was the lady whose father had done the shoplifting.

HOTELIERS

Ken was out of a job again, and all because he didn't want to teach in the UK. What was going to be our next move? Ros was into catering, but was really looking to run her own business, and this hatched the next idea. We thought 'what if we owned our own small hotel or guest house?' Ros could do the catering, Paul, her husband, could run the bar, Barbie could run the reception and I could manage overall and do all the buying etc. It all sounded fine, because when the time came for retirement, Barbie and I could retire gracefully, leaving Ros to take over, perfect.

We started looking around and saw an advertisement for the Club

House Hotel in Southport. It had thirteen en suite rooms, situated in a decent position, so we went to have a look, liked the look of it, and bought it.

On the surface everything looked to be working out well. We were getting to know the neighbours and people socially at the Bridge Club and the Conservative Club. Ros enrolled Vicky, her first-born, into a local school and Ryan was given a trial period in a nursery. They had the upstairs flat and Barbie and I used Room 13 to live in. That should have been an omen to us, but we never gave it a thought, after all, Ros had been born on Friday the 13th, so it should be a lucky number for us.

We bought an apartment in a nice block of flats on the corner of our road and the main shopping street, with a view to living there and freeing another room to let.

We targeted golfing parties as our main business, and organised games for them at the championship courses in the area. They could choose from The Royal Birkdale, the Royal Lytham and St Anne's, the S and A in Southport which many thought to be the best golf course, Formby G.C., West Lanc's G.C., and of course Liverpool's Aintree. Not many parts of the country could boast so many championship courses within such a short distance.

It is interesting to note that the gentleman from whom we had bought the flat, asked me to propose him to become a member of the club which we had joined. We had joined Hesketh Bank G.C. because we could afford it and I doubt if we could have got into those mentioned above in any case because of the long waiting lists. We duly proposed him, but didn't hear anything for a while. When I mentioned it to Paul, he laughed. 'He'll never get in, he hasn't a chance' he said. When I asked why not, he just said that he was Jewish. I had no idea that religion had any part to play in the membership of any British golf club. Apparently it was not uncommon.

Once again we had a business that was doing well and we had bookings for wedding receptions and a steady stream of regulars in the bar. I had been cautious about salaries, being the first year, for I wanted to see what we could afford. I decided to do a stocktake after the year was ended to really make a proper assessment.

After I had completed the stocktaking, I got an unpleasant shock. The takings over the bar did not even cover the cost price of the drinks. This included wine at the table which I knew made a healthy profit. Regrettably, the bar was running at a loss, even before any salary had been deducted from it.

When I mentioned it to Paul he casually said bars often ran at a loss. I knew the mark-up on drinks, and I didn't say anything then, although I thought that was a ridiculous thing to say. Once again Barbie and I had a discussion and had to make an unpleasant decision. We couldn't manage with a bar which made a loss, and we didn't want to cause a family row, I hate confrontation. I had hoped that if the allowance was not sufficient – after all, living, all bills and food was free – we could have discussed the situation, but I needed to be in control of the finances, so we applied for a teaching post in Spain.

We travelled down to London to attend our interview, which was to take place in the Spanish Embassy. We knew that we were on the right street, and stopped a passer-by to ask where the Embassy was. A very surprised and shocked Kenneth Williams looked up and pointed it out. He looked relieved not to have been mugged. I had forgotten that it is very unusual to actually stop anyone to speak to in London. I said to Barbie 'Did you realise that was Kenneth Williams, and he speaks with his normal voice on the telly?' We had always thought that it was a stage voice that he used.

The post was offered to us, and we accepted. We told Ros and Paul that we had changed our mind about being hoteliers and were going back to teaching.

Ros was naturally heartbroken, and so were we, because life had been good at the Club House, and we had been very happy. We did not feel too guilty because we knew that Paul had always a ready job to fall back on at his uncle's bakery in Buxton. As well as baking cakes and pastries, his uncle was a major supplier of the famous Derbyshire oatcakes. Paul had always been in and out of jobs, but we had given him his chance in spite of that.

We may have been influenced the other way if we had known that Ros was finding lipstick on his collar and earrings which weren't hers in his pockets. The marriage didn't last much longer after we left, and Ros became a single parent with two children, living in a council house in Buxton. As with the rest of our decisions however, life did turn out for the better for all of us, so in retrospect we wouldn't have changed anything. We still thought that our life was being guided from above.

Oh how we wished that they had parted earlier, because the three of us could have managed the hotel. As with the rest of our decisions however, life did turn out for the better for all of us, so in retrospect we wouldn't have changed anything. We still thought that our life was being guided from above and Ros obviously had a lot of her parents in her. She could hardly go into catering on her own with two small children, so she enrolled as a model. She soon became a victim of her own success, because she had demands on her for weekends and whole weekly sessions. She now had to make a big decision and choose between motherhood and her career, so of course she chose motherhood.

Quite undaunted, she embarked upon a course to become a chiropodist, and in due time passed the necessary examinations and set up her own business. Once again she became the victim of her own success. She shared property with a chiropractor, and was soon seemingly doing better than he was. For reasons best known to himself, he kept putting up her rent until it became ridiculous and she had no alternative but to leave his property and became peripatetic. He must have thought that it was his right to share in her success. In the meantime she met her true love and married Paddy, a financial advisor, and they bought a very old farmhouse with a few acres of land which they set about restoring. Ros was now too busy to work as well, but has recently set up as a potter in her spare time, and is already making a name for herself.

Nikky, meanwhile, had moved to London with the B.B.C. When she realised that she was in charge of contract workers who were paid twice as much as she was, she changed to contract work. It meant that she frequently had to change jobs when her contracts expired, but was never out of work long before starting another contract. The break until the next offer came along served as a holiday, and she was still well in pocket at the end of each year. She also met the love of her life when in her fifties and now lives happily with Tommy on Eel Pie Island, situated on the Thames in Twickenham.

I haven't mentioned that after leaving Africa and among my other attempts in business, I made a brief attempt at selling part-time. This resulted in us buying one of the luxury flats which the company was trying to sell. It was in Las Gondolas, a development on the beach in Almunecar, which is directly below Granada in Spain. We used it many times for holidays and we were to live in it for a while. I never thought that I was cut out to be a salesman however, and vowed that I would not enter the sales profession ever again, but that declaration was soon to come back and bite me.

It was September 1983 and we had been home for less than four years, yet we had already gone through three different businesses. I have had to double-check this several times because I seemed to have been in each occupation for years. Less than four years is correct though, and it goes to show how time seems to pass quickly when one is busy and enjoying the work. Yes I really did enjoy the work, in spite of the endings.

The saying had not been popularised then, but I am mindful of it being attributed to Lord Tebbit, when talking of unemployment. I realise that we had become the perfect disciples of his because whenever things were not quite right, instead of moaning about the situation, we certainly 'got on our bikes' and found something new.

This situation actually became implicit when I first decided to study to be a P.E. teacher, way back in college. I must have realised then that any change in school would mean moving districts. Positions in P.E. were always few and far between. Thinking of this prompted me to 'Google' Lord Tebbit. What a loss to the House of Commons. I can't help but agree with everything he has said. Yes, in spite of being from working class stock, or perhaps it was because we are able to do simple arithmetic, we will always be true Blues.

A country should be run as one huge business. I know that I have mentioned this before, but the expenditure of a business must always be covered by its income, otherwise it becomes bankrupt. The people to suffer then are the employees who are out of a job. Time and time again in my lifetime I have witnessed the Labour government run this country into debt. Where on earth did all our gold reserves go to? They were sold at cost by the 'prudent' Labour Chancellor. Long before that, our lead in the jet engine designs had been squandered by this 'prudent' government selling them to Russia and allowing them to be made under licence in the U.S.A. Then when the Conservatives gain power and rectify the situation, how are they rewarded? They are usually kicked out again.

Most people only think of the name when they vote, not the policy. 'I am a labourer so I must vote Labour' is the working class mentality, and it is so easy for their leaders to exploit this sentiment with their rhetoric. It was the left wing unions who further damaged our economy when they introduced demarcation. Plumbers couldn't fix a light switch, because that was an electrician's job. How daft is that. It ended our competitiveness and ruined shipbuilding as well as other industries. There is no such nonsense in other competing countries. Sorry, if an industry, nationalised or not, runs at a loss, then it has to close, which is what happened to the coal mines. If it is kept running, successful businesses have to be overtaxed to make up the shortfall making them less competitive. When members are on strike pay, I wonder if the Union leaders are also on a reduced salary, while they are driving around in their flash cars?

I have often thought that somehow wages should be tied to shares, so that workers have a vested interest in the business in which they are employed. Probably a basic wage plus bonuses is the answer. Surely there is someone with a better brain than mine who can work it out. Unfortunately this couldn't happen in the public sector, but it would be good if someone could work out a work related bonus scheme there too. I was brought up on 'piece work' in the pea field, and thus am a believer in getting paid only for what one earns.

PART EIGHT

Abroad we go again

WE DROVE TO MADRID to take up our new posts as the teachers in charge of the boarding section of Kings College. It was situated a few miles north of the capital and we were temporarily housed in a small primary school building at Pinosierra, a few miles from the actual college. The new state-of-the-art boarding house on the college premises was to be completed as soon as possible. As it turned out it took two terms.

We were given half of a normal timetable each, so Barbie taught in the primary section and I helped with the Maths at secondary level. It was a new type of teaching for me as the children were given assignments and the staff went around helping where it was needed. There was hardly any class teaching, which was strange to me, but I did what I was asked, and was prepared to reserve judgement. Barbie, of course, was in her element.

The boarding section we really liked. The boarders were from most of the embassies plus those children who had parents working or living outside Madrid, hence we had Japanese, Chinese, Vietnamese, Mexicans, Australians and Americans among others and from all the age groups. I organised a tuckshop for them and a private meeting time if they needed to see either of us privately.

One Sunday each month a bus was hired and we took them on an educational trip which we all adored because we got to visit places like Avila, Segovia, Toledo, Salamanca and Aranquez. We occasionally took them to the ski slopes, just north of Madrid, and arranged visits to the Prado and the Royal Palace. We even asked for suggestions where to go next, once we had exhausted the obvious places. The Alcazas (castles) and cathedrals at Toledo and Segovia are a must on any tourists list. Be sure to get a talking guide in Toledo if you don't mind shedding a tear or two.

This was as exciting for us as for the students, and in fact some of the time it was the senior students who were taking us around.

It was a lovely atmosphere, and the senior boys loved to try to beat me at badminton, which we were to miss when we transferred to the new building.

At the end of the first term, Barbie had the biggest surprise of her teaching career. Her class's reports were returned to her to rewrite. This had never happened to her before. What possibly could she have done wrong? Well, she had placed the children in positions in the class. Oh dear, they apparently shouldn't know who was the best and who was the worst. All rubbish of course. The children could have told the teacher where most of them were placed anyway.

During the school holidays we were introduced to 'Summer schools'. Those members of staff who wanted a bit of extra pocket money stayed on to teach and there was a queue of parents who were willing to pay for their children to stay at school for extra tuition during the holidays. The 'Summer school students' would all be boarders, but rather than use the new building, classrooms were equipped with beds and bedding, and converted into dormitories. I agreed to be the head of that year's intake and organised the timetables and staffing. The teaching and supervising had also to include night duties, but they must have all been so exhausted when they went to bed that we had no problems after lights-out.

The course was about 60% academic and 40% sporting activities to make it sufficiently attractive for the students, and we had no hitches at all. Everyone, staff and pupils alike, seemed to enjoy the experience, and this gave us a great deal of food for thought. Yes, my brain was ticking over and doing all the calculations. It was a VERY profit-making exercise.

The rest of the holiday was spent in our apartment in Almunecar, but we were invited on the way down to visit the parents of three brothers from the boarding section. They must have been reading our thoughts, because they had a proposition to make to us. The village of Mojacar desperately needed a primary school. They were prepared to build one if we would run it on a partnership basis.

This seemed too good to be true. It appeared that we were being directed once more from above. I could see it becoming very big once it built up, with the potential of generating a great deal of wealth when we introduced summer schools into the equation. We had plenty of time to think about it over the next couple of months and called in again on the way back to Madrid to look at the land and generally weigh up the prospects. Nothing was promised or agreed at that point.

Back at Kings College we found that another teacher had been appointed on the staff to 'help' us. We didn't think that we needed any help, and were not particularly impressed. The new teacher was a man who had qualified and taught in India. We had not long since spent years in Africa where Indian degrees were being advertised in the press on payment of an affordable amount of money, but our suspicions may have been completely unfounded.

When he struck up a close friendship with another male member of staff however, alarm bells began to ring in our heads. He altered the whole atmosphere among the boarders who were secretly saying that he was gay. This was in 1984 before it was an accepted practise. It was undoubtedly this that influenced us in our decision to hand in our notice and take our chances in Mojacar.

Of course, public opinion has taken a radical change since then, but in 1984 I was still under the influence of a strict Victorian upbringing.

Before we left King's College our coming enterprise was discussed and we were advised to be very careful, because it was hinted that our intended partner's family had been implicated in other questionable enterprises. Our spirits weren't enhanced either, after the reception we got in Mojacar, or lack of reception would be nearer the mark. What a change from the last time we were there and the royal welcome we were provided with then. Only a note was left for us, and the overnight accommodation provided for us left a lot to be desired.

If this was an example of how we would be treated in a new partnership, we were not impressed, and we were mindful of the warning we had been given. We just looked at each other and agreed. It was a gamble we were not prepared to take, so it was next stop Las Gondolas and our holiday apartment. We could always get a job on the Costa.

Yes, it was as simple as that. No crying over spilt milk, so move on. No we were not sorry to leave Kings College. We had never been consulted about having a 'helper', and because of my intolerance of anything resembling homosexuality at that time, it would have been wrong for me to stay.

There were plenty of adverts in the local papers. Barbie answered one for Aloha College in Marbella and was successful immediately. She could start in January after the holidays.

TIME SHARING EXPERIENCE

I answered an advert just asking for keen men or women. When I went for an interview and they told me it was selling property, I just laughed and said that I was the worst salesman in the world.

I was about to walk out when they called me back. They were willing to train me for a week, all expenses paid, and afterwards I could make up my mind whether to stay or not. Having nothing to lose, I agreed. We rented a lovely apartment in the Calahonda complex, because Almunecar would be too far from Marbella to travel daily for either of us.

I had not heard of time-share until then, and as it was explained to me, it seemed a very good idea, and something that I thought I was capable of selling. The idea that you could buy a week of your choice at the resort for about a thousand pounds and it was yours for ever sounded good. All you paid after that was a maintenance charge of thirty pounds or so, every year, to cover the upkeep. There was an exchange system whereby you could swap your week for one in another resort, and even in another country, at different times of the year, making it very flexible and an extremely practical proposition. One could holiday in most parts of the world for only the air-fare.

A team operated on the streets to persuade tourists to visit the resort, in exchange for a bribe of a bottle of wine or cheap brandy. They got paid a commission for everyone they sent. We at the resort took it in turns to welcome each prospect and try to sell spare weeks at the resort to them. Payment was commission only, so no sale, no pay.

I considered then, and I still do, that time-sharing is an excellent idea. In the light of its reputation at the moment, what went wrong was not the concept, but the administration. The fact that payment is made on performance is good for sales but bad for reputation. Salesmen on commission only have historically been known to bend the truth and in some cases mislead and tell deliberate lies. How prophetic was that going to turn out to be?

I decided to give it a go, and I actually surprised myself. I wasn't the best salesperson in the team but I was far from being the worst. Top salespersons sold to about 20% of the prospects, but a good living could be made selling anything over a 10% conversion rate. The more successful the team however, the quicker the resort was sold out hence the drawback was that a complex could be sold out in a matter of months, and this meant frequent moves to the next time-share development.

GRAN CANARIA

Christmas cards for 1985 had been sent and received and Barbie had enjoyed a whole year at Aloha. We had very good friends from there and Barbie had lots of kind words from the parents of children from her class.

Our New Years Eve dinner party was interrupted by the telephone ringing. Barbie, being the nearer, picked up the phone and motioned to me. 'It's a friend for you' she said above the rabble that was going on.

I took the phone into the next room so that I could at least hear him properly. We had met this friend in Kano, Nigeria, and played golf with him. He did a lot of work in the 'bush' but our families had met and entertained each other during the short periods he was in Kano. He started by thanking us for his Christmas card and the note that Barbie always put inside. Then he said 'You never told me that you were selling time-share Ken.'

That was the preview for him to tell me that he had a time-share setup on the south coast of Gran Canaria, and after quite a conversation explaining his setup he made me a proposition. Would I be willing to recruit a team of salespeople and take them over to G.C. and organise our method of selling for him. He had been using the old-fashioned way of holding seminars and speaking to groups of people, but this had proved to be no longer cost effective. He promised to fly me out with two salespeople and provide accommodation while we investigated the viability of his project. I asked him to give me a week in which to organise and recruit, and he could fly over and take us back.

It was too much to tell Barbie what the phone call was all about during the party, so she was in suspense all evening bless her. When I was able to tell her after the guests had all gone home, she had so many questions to ask me. I said that we had nothing to lose as I was being flown out and entertained at his expense and the worst thing that could happen would be that I had a holiday in G.C. for free.

I put it to the team the following day – sales people never have holidays – and it was not difficult to get two of them to offer to go with me. Our friend duly arrived and we had a night out at his expense before the flight back to G.C.

The flight to Gran Canaria and journey down to the south from Las Palmas, the capital, was unspectacular to say the least, like any airport and journey on a main road. However, when we rounded the headland and caught our first sight of the resort nestling round the bay, we were completely bowled over. From there on it just got better and better. There were apartments to time-share in an apartment complex right on the side of the marina, and other apartments in a complex commanding a lovely view overlooking the bay.

Of course my friend did his best to keep us entertained, but he didn't need to try very hard. The message that they took back to the team in Marbella was 'It is a license to print money.'

Gosh, when I look back on the decisions we made, it might appear that I was a dominating figure forcing my will on my poor wife. I assure you that it wasn't like that. Yes, Barbie was happy teaching at Aloha

College, as happy teaching there as she had been anywhere, but she was pragmatic enough to know that I was talking about an amount of money we couldn't even make between us as teachers. Barbie had the self confidence to know that she could teach anywhere, and she hadn't yet been in a school where she hadn't been happy. There was also the spirit of adventure that existed in both of us.

Generally, teachers from the UK sacrifice their UK salary and security for the pleasure of living in a warm climate, and by now we both knew that we could be happy and make lovely friends wherever we went. Barbie was a prodigious letter writer, and she always kept in touch with the special friends we had met and had to leave. Other friends had to leave us for personal reasons too. That is how it was when one lived abroad.

Two weeks later I flew back to G.C. with a team of six salespeople, a couple and four young men. There was a large balcony attached to the complex with a superb view overlooking the bay, which was ideal for selling to prospective buyers and we were given temporary accommodation in the unsold apartments.

I set up a sales area on the balcony where we saw the prospective buyers, which we called 'Ups'. I understood it to mean Unqualified Prospects. I had also to recruit a team to patrol the busy streets and induce Ups to visit us and find out what time-sharing was all about. Within a week we were up and running and waiting to make our first sales.

Barbie had to stay at Aloha in order to serve out her notice, so we had to be apart from each other for a few weeks. We never enjoyed being separated for long, but we were both very busy, so the time seemed to go quickly.

When the parents of Barbie's class heard that she had put in her notice, they held a meeting. Barbie then received a beautiful letter from them which must be unique. At least no one that I know had ever had an offer like that. The letter explained that they, the parents, were willing to rent an apartment, with all expenses paid, if Barbie would stay in Marbella to continue teaching their children. It was very touching, and very generous, but of course she declined. We could not bear to live apart for any longer than we had to.

I mentioned earlier that good salespeople could convert 20% of Ups (Unqualified Prospects) into sales. We were so successful, however, that the whole team average was well above that figure. I had plenty of organising to do, banking deposits and paying the team on the streets and the salespeople their commissions, that I had no time to do any selling myself at all. Instead I was paid a small commission on each of the sales that the team made.

Everyone was happy. The sales team, the team on the street, I was, and certainly the owner and his company were. It was a happy crew that greeted Barbie when she came to join us, but Barbie and I were the happiest of them all.

We had developed a good working relationship with an estate agent who had a 'front line' real estate office in the shopping complex. He allowed us to use his office telephone, typewriter and copying machine. I was always sure that he had ulterior motives, and had ideas for future sales of his own, however that was to be expected and we could not have operated efficiently without his help, hence we were extremely grateful.

We met another Englishman, a teacher from the UK, who had rented a little school in the next valley, (or *barranco* in Spanish,) a couple of miles away. Having learned about us, he asked Barbie to act as headmistress of the few children he had enrolled, to which she said that she would be delighted. It was an older version of her preschool business in Kano and just up her street. Things seemed to be working out well for us.

Word got around and Barbie soon had too many children for one class and an assistant had to be appointed to take another class. Barbie ought to have insisted on a salary proportional to the number of children she attracted, but to be fair, she got a reasonable salary.

As usual, our social life was secure, because most of the parents of the children Barbie taught wished to get to know Barbie and entertain us, but we always insisted on reciprocating, and so acquired many friends.

Meanwhile I and my team soon became victims of our own success, because we were quickly running out of apartments to sell. I had become the 'Golden boy' of the owner of the time-share company, and was taken to his home in Northern Ireland. He introduced me to his accountant brother and took me sailing on his yacht. There was even talk of me becoming a partner.

We agreed that he needed to buy any apartment in the two complexes which came on the market. He did, in fact, buy two, but when another came on the market he hadn't sufficient ready cash. He asked me if I was willing to go fifty-fifty in the purchase of one and we would split the profits from the sales and I agreed. It was done very legally in front of the notary, and this was to become a very important issue in future developments. I was so pleased with the generous offer, because for me it was a win-win situation, that I overlooked the fact that he must have been in real financial difficulties before we came if he was still short of cash after all our successes.

Not only did all the weeks to sell dwindle, but it was apparent that we urgently needed another complex to sell. In spite of all the money coming in, the bank account from which I paid the teams was often deficient, and I often made up the shortfall out of my personal account and didn't always take out my full earnings. I was careful of course to keep a record and have it verified by the brother who was the accountant.

Buying another complex was now the most urgent project, and I left that entirely to them to find one. I was very excited therefore, along with the rest of the 'crew', when they told us that they were going to a meeting to negotiate the purchase of a spectacular complex perched on a promontory overlooking the sea. I expected to go with them, for after all I had been in full charge of the costing and accounts and I was convinced that I knew the market better than they did, but they declined and said that it wouldn't be necessary. I sensed a bit of secrecy in their manner and began to get a strange feeling about what was happening because I had been at the forefront of all decisions up to that point, but maybe it was just in my imagination. I should have realised though that in their financial position they wouldn't be able to purchase it on their own.

The following day they came along with champagne and we all celebrated because they had bought it. I got round to asking the price, and was more than surprised at the figure. I didn't comment but I considered that they had paid far too much. The price of individual time-share weeks would have to go up considerably.

In retrospect I questioned the deal in my mind. I now believe, in the light of what happened later, that they must have indeed been so short of cash that they had to make a deal with another developer. That only confirmed the fact that they must have been more seriously in debt when I joined them than I had realised, because we had made them a lot of money. As things stood, I began to get vibes that something else was cooking. It wasn't usual for them to be so secretive. One of my salesmen even told me on the quiet to 'watch my back'. Why weren't they open with me and tell me that there was a third party involved? It may be that what transpired was at the insistence of this third party, but if so, surely they would have apologised to me and offered that as an excuse.

The bombshell was dropped the following morning in the office. The two brothers breezed in and announced that they had consulted so-called experts, who had said that they would now need a sales force four times as large as the one with which we were operating, and I fully agreed. They then said that the experts had acknowledged that I had done a fantastic job, but after all, I was only an ex-teacher, and a professional organisation would now be needed to sell the new complex. I was not to worry however as they would make me an executive director, working from the office. No salary or contract was mentioned of course.

I was naturally devastated, and I explained how I had controlled the teams. I had not allowed them to tell lies, either on the street or in the sales process. I had monitored all the expenses they claimed and kept a tight rein that didn't exist in other time-share setups. I warned him that there were many ways in which he could be defrauded, and who now was going to keep an eye on things for him? He had only experienced our clean operation, and didn't know what went on in other parts of the world. I had experienced several shady operations while on the Spanish Costa, and I genuinely didn't want him to fall foul of the unscrupulous elements which I knew existed. However it had no effect on him whatsoever. Something had influenced him and his mind was made up.

REAL ESTATE AGENT

The estate agent came up trumps. He said 'Join me in this business Ken and you can have one share to my two, but we will split profits fifty-fifty.' This was a fantastic offer, and once again underpinned the esteem which was attributed to me. I agreed immediately and it was properly notarised. I had a half share in the profits of a business once more without having to pay a penny. He lived in Las Palmas in the north, while we of course were in the south of the island so this meant that he need only come to work during the afternoons, or not at all on some days if he wished. This was because I had earned the reputation of being scrupulously fair and honest. I was well aware that I hadn't been so lucky with my other partners in businesses, but maybe I would be lucky this time.

No, I haven't forgotten. There was still a little matter outstanding of the loans and unpaid commissions owing to me. At first it was lack of cash flow given as an excuse. Then they made me a silly offer to settle for much less than they owed to me. It was given as an ultimatum, but they knew that I was now a partner of an ex-solicitor and I still refused to accept. I had it in black and white, and I submitted to them the amounts in detail, showing what each amount was for with dates, but I still heard nothing for a while.

My time came soon afterwards. My ex employers breezed into the office one afternoon as if we were best buddies and asked me if I was free. I said that I could be, but what for? He said that we needed to go to the notary in order to sign the final document on the apartment which we had bought between us. I then said 'Yes of course I will go with you, but only after I have been paid what I am owed.'

He physically went as white as a sheet. 'But it has to be done this week, or I will have to pay a fine and go to court' he stuttered. 'Well it is up to you, I'm only asking for what I am owed' I said. There must have been something else involved, because I was an equal partner, in the purchase of the apartment which we had bought between us, but whatever it was worked in my favour.

Somehow they suddenly found the cash. It goes to show that one should be very careful, and much more careful than I had been, when entering a business partnership. I had been very lucky to have been given this situation to use in order to recoup my money. The whole time-share operation had left a nasty taste in my mouth, but financially it had been much more rewarding than I could ever have earned from teaching, so once again we had to put it down to experience. We must have been a bit miffed at the time, but life was so good that we quickly got over it.

I never wished him ill, but I did hear rumours that he had, in fact, gone into partnership with someone else, and I heard later that he was still in financial difficulties. I believed it was the same man who had once milked me for information, in which case I could have warned him. I hope, therefore, that he too learned the lesson that honest partners are hard to come by.

We still had many friends around us and I now had an office job. Once again our guardian angel had guided us out of disaster.

We got on very well in the office, and we began to do well business wise. He was friendly with the local Spanish builders and had priority rights for selling what they built. We built up a reputation for honesty because all money handed over to us were done in front of a notary and properly documented. We were, I believe, the only ones to guarantee that the deeds were properly registered with the Land Registry.

This was very important in Spain. Without this final document many people had thought that they owned property, only to find that it hadn't been properly registered. In some cases the property had been sold twice in front of different notaries, so that it was the first to register at the Land Registry who actually owned it. My new partner thus spent a lot of his time obtaining the registration documents from the Land Registry which was conveniently situated in the north of the island for him, and an important reason for him not needing to come down south every day.

We were entertained in their fine house in Las Palmas and his wife served beetroot as a vegetable on one occasion, which was lovely, but we had to laugh afterwards because he went to see the doctor the following day with red urine. He thought that he had internal bleeding.

We weren't up to posh cuisine, so we took them to choice restaurants to reciprocate. We were also entertained on their boat, a 25ft cruiser, and they even made a special effort to take out our grandchildren. Ryan must have been about ten when he was given the wheel for a while, which absolutely made his day, and then we enjoyed diving over the sides into the Atlantic.

The one thing that the south coast lacked was a golf course, though we didn't seem to miss it at all. We did play tennis, in fact I still keep in touch with a couple who live near Perth, Australia, with whom we played regularly in Gran Canaria.

After we left the time-share business we bought an apartment in the next *barranco* looking towards the sea. Here there were more tennis courts close by, and it was in the bay below where we swam several times each week. The bay in the resort in which we used to swim was protected by almost touching piers leaving a narrow entrance, and was therefore sheltered and generally calm, but the beach below our new apartment was open to the Atlantic rollers and often much more fun.

It did frighten us on one occasion though when a particularly high roller broke over us and we were hurled through triple somersaults before we were dumped on the sand. I remember I nearly lost my swimming trunks which were dragged by the water to below my knees. After that episode we had a little more respect for the waves. It was not unusual after a particularly bad storm to find most of the sand on the beach had disappeared, but then it reappeared as quickly as it had gone after the next storm.

I had played golf once in Mas Palomas, a tourist resort further up the coast on the way to Las Palmas. A couple from there befriended us and they invited me to take their son round for a game. He was a promising junior, and we quite enjoyed the game. Their real objective however was to quiz me on the running of the time-share operation, with promises of course. I then learned that he was the man who became tied up with the brother's time-share setup, so I heard no more from them. It was fairly obvious that they had just used me. Yes, we have met some wonderful and unscrupulous people on our travels, but then, most people in tourist resorts are out to make a quick buck, so one more was no surprise to us. That accusation would seem to apply to us, but I genuinely believed when I started each new project that it would last until I retired, and I never resorted to deceptions or lies. I still believe that would inevitably lead to the downfall of any business.

Barbie and I were discussing the possibilities of what we would do when we retired. We both wanted nice weather, and we both wanted tennis and golf. We were also mindful of our desire to see the States, and possibly visit friends there. We had also heard about Sun City, and how fabulous it was supposed to be. It sounded the ideal spot to retire to. We decided to splash out on a big holiday across the pond in order to explore the possibilities. Barbie had written to Waldo, from Kinyasano, and Bob Kay, one of the C.U.S.O. team at G.T.T.S. to arrange meetings.

Virgin Air was probably the best airline we have ever travelled with, and what better place to start from than New York. We didn't stay long in the Big Apple, however, that would come later, but we hired a car and set off to Cape Cod where we had booked a week in a time-share complex.

If I tell you that Barbie filled a scrapbook which I can hardly lift, you will forgive me for not relating all the holiday in detail. A few highlights will suffice.

- Tanglewood, watching Bernstein conducting the Boston Symphony Orchestra.
- Hamilton meeting Bob Kay, and Connecticut meeting Waldo.
- Toronto meeting David and Maisie Brooks, who took us for a flight in his plane and fishing on Lake Ontario where we caught a salmon for supper.
- Dinner in the C.N. Tower, and watching the Blue Jays in the Sky dome.
- Watching Pancho Gonzales and Pancho Segura play Illi Nastase and Vic Seixas from courtside. They were the tennis idols of our childhood.
- Seeing Niagara Falls from the Canadian side which Barbie aptly described as 'A beautiful sight.'
- Dinner in the Skylon.
- Visiting the Mennonite's village and spending days visiting Gettysburg.

- And then to Somerset and back to New York.

After an apprehensive first few hours in New York, we finally took our hands away from guarding our purses and pockets and began to relax and enjoy ourselves. We took an eight-and-a-half-hour tour, seeing the Twin Towers, where Lennon was murdered, Macy's and Trump's. We then went to the top of the Empire State Building, walked in Central Park, and visited the Statue of Liberty. These may not be in chronological order, and I'm sure that I have missed some out, for it was one highlight after another. It had taken us nearly five weeks and we were exhausted, but gosh, it was worth it.

I mentioned Virgin going out, but coming back we were delayed for six hours and the flight was now due to leave at 3 a.m. We were whisked off to the Airport Hotel and booked into a room for the night. We were then awakened at 2 a.m., given a quick snack, and taxied back to catch the plane. We thought it was amazing to be booked into an hotel for such a short time. Other airlines would have left us sitting at the airport.

Our thoughts about a home in America hadn't got very far and had certainly not been answered on this trip. We would have to think of going to Florida at another time to find what we were looking for.

I heard that a group of Indians were trying to get a cricket club together, so I turned up for a practice session. They had managed to find a patch where they could lay a cricket mat on which to practise, but where they intended to find an area big enough for a cricket field I had no idea. The practise went well actually and we all took turns at batting and bowling, and most of them had obviously played before. It looked like a promising beginning.

It was during the second session when it came to an abrupt halt for me. Once again, as in football, my lack of preparation and training was to catch up with me. I wasn't even bowling fast, but was sending down my slow tweekers, when I put a bit of extra effort into one bowl and felt a sharp pain in my left groin. When I put my hand there I felt a lump and that was the end of the practice session for me.

I went to see a doctor on the following morning, who confirmed that it looked like a hernia and made an appointment for me to see a consultant on the Thursday. I thought that was pretty good. Accident on Sunday, doctor on Monday and consultant on Thursday, not bad.

I saw the consultant on time who confirmed that it was indeed a hernia, so I said 'What does that mean then?' He replied 'Oh, you will have to have a small operation, but you will only be in hospital for three or four days.'

I envisaged weeks of waiting and then recuperation. Bang goes my swimming and tennis for a while, so I very tentatively said 'Whe-when might I be able to have the operation, Sir?' He then casually reached into his back pocket and took out his diary and flicked through a few pages. 'Can you manage next Tuesday?' he said.

I don't know what my reaction was, but I was mighty pleased. Ten days from accident to hospital, beat that. I had the first of my epidural injections and the hernia repaired on the Wednesday in what was the old Naval Hospital in Las Palmas. He told me that he had inserted a net, so that it shouldn't ever happen again, at least not on that side.

Barbie booked into a hotel for a few days before I was discharged and she then drove me home. I didn't want her to have to travel all that way every day.

We wanted to visit Egypt, but every time we attempted to arrange a holiday there, something happened to deter us, and so we never did. Our only experience of Egypt had to remain with what we saw on our passage through Suez to East Africa.

Barbie always kept in touch with friends that we had made, so that it was no surprise that in 1991 we were invited to visit a teaching couple who had taught with Barbie at Aloha. They now lived in Argentina, and we started to plan a holiday there.

There were no direct flights to Argentina from Gran Canaria, so we had to fly to Madrid to get a connecting flight. It was strange that six hours after setting off from Las Palmas, the pilot announced that we were now flying over G.C. and Las Palmas was to our left.

Sue and Mick met us at the airport in Buenos Aires, and took us to their home in the northern outskirts. It was during the last few days before the school holidays, which fit in well with our itinerary, because while they were at school, we had time to tour round the city and get to know our way around. It reminded us very much of Madrid with its multilane highway bisecting it. Mick was the head of a primary school, and Sue was already making headway even higher up the education ladder. Their two children were completely bilingual, speaking English at home, and attending a Spanish speaking school.

For the second week we had booked a week's time-share at a beach resort. We saw for the first time what must be the largest bus station in the world. It was built in a huge circle on two levels, and had bays for almost every town or city in south and Central America.

The actual time-share resort would have been fine a few weeks later, but it was the first week of summer and we were about the only people there. That didn't deter us however, and we were on holiday and the weather was hot with wall-to-wall blue skies. One afternoon we watched a man digging up clams from the beach. What a good idea we thought, and we dug up our own clams out of the sand to supplement our dinner that evening.

We met up with Mick and Sue again, with their two children, on a prearranged holiday down to Chubut and Patagonia. It was a properly organised coach tour, but we had a job to follow the courier with our limited Spanish. Everyone was asked to introduce themselves in turn round the bus, and I felt embarrassed, and caused a laugh when I said, in my best Spanish, that I was on holiday with my husband. I had said *marido* instead of *esposa*. After an overnight stop we finally reached Trelew in the province of Chebut. The hotel was first class with a heated swimming pool, and was to act as our base from where we took our daily excursions.

The first excursion took us to Punta Tombo, a nature reserve for the penguins. We were completely fascinated by being able to walk among thousands of penguins, some of which were sitting on eggs in their rudimentary nests. They seemed quite unconcerned with the tourists walking almost within touching distance of them.

The bus then took us to Punta Norte, where we saw the huge sea wolves and even bigger elephant seals, basking on the rocks. They looked quite grotesque – except to their mates I suppose.

The main reason for the holiday of course, was to see the orcas, or killer whales. We had planned to hire a boat to sail among them, but unfortunately we had to be content with watching from the shore because on the day we had scheduled, it was too dangerous for the boats to venture out into the rough seas.

The Welsh village that we visited in Gaiman could have been in south Wales. The entire population was Welsh speaking. They had emigrated there *en masse* to escape the English invaders, about the time of the pilgrim fathers. They have been exacting revenge on us ever since, charging the English tourists extortionate prices for their Welch teas. We were certainly a bit miffed because we could not buy just a cup of tea, but had to have a full cream tea, each.

I remember that on the way back to Buenos Aires I got rather worried. The driver and conductor were passing a pot backwards and forward, drinking through a metal straw. I thought it was some sort of drug to keep them awake and for ages I felt quite alarmed. Sue had a laugh at my expense but allayed my fears, explaining that it was merely mate (pronounced matay), which was their form of fresh herbal tea. We then bought some mate pots to remind us of the incident.

We left Sue and Mick again to fly up to Iguacu, the largest series of waterfalls in area and volume in the world. The falls were at the junction of three countries. The actual hotel in which we stayed was in Brazil, and while we were there we went to a well-known market over another border into Paraguay. Apparently all tourists went to shop there. It was tax-free, and we saw fellow tourist carrying back televisions and all kinds of electrical gadgetry. We must have been the only couple not carrying anything because we had only gone to sightsee.

Back at Iguacu, we spent days going from one vantage point to another, and unlike Niagara, one wasn't held back by barriers. We found we were able to go really close to the waters, both looking down on them from above, and then we were supplied with capes to borrow to enable us to stand virtually underneath them, with the spray almost enveloping us. Whereas the other falls we had seen were concentrated in one or two areas, Iguacu extended over vast areas, covering miles. Murchison had been the most concentrated, Niagara probably had the most cubic metres per second concentrated in a limited area, and Iguacu the most widespread and the most volume overall.

It had been a most exciting trip and one we didn't want to end. After flying back to Buenos Aires, we then said a big thank you to Sue and Mick before the long flight home.

We enjoyed three years of heaven. We lived in a holiday resort, business was good, Barbie was enjoying her teaching as usual, and we had lots of friends. We didn't miss the dancing, or the golf, because we were so busy. Social life consisted of entertaining at home or going out for meals, and we made a habit of taking customers up into the centre of the island for a meal. It was an interesting ride through the mountain scenery, often with a very steep drop on one side which proved to be a bit scary for some of our guests. Finally, at the top, we came to this delightful restaurant.

'Restaurante Hao' was set amongst very tall palm trees. The tables were made from solid planks of wood of various sizes, but some were about 3m by 1m, and several cms thick. The trees must have been immense, and the tables must have been made from leftovers from the trees which were cut down to build the Spanish Armada. Those were the days when the islands were thickly forested, and were named after the dogs which roamed wild and could be heard by sailors as they sailed by. The name Canary Island comes from canine, the dogs, not the canary birds, which is the common misconception.

The food was home cooked and always delicious, but what was even more interesting was the museum of the owner's private collection. He had on display thousands of shells of all varieties from the ocean, and bones from the many caves found around the island. Included were hundreds of skulls, all having their individual history described underneath. I understand that he had been honoured by the previous King of Spain for his research.

We were thinking of this year's holiday, and we decided to use a couple of week's time-share in America. We thought it would be nice to take Ros and Paul and their two children, and arranged a convenient time and date. We flew to Orlando and hired a car and drove to the fantastic resort of Orange Lake, where we were given a massive, four-bedroom bungalow for the two weeks. The kitchen had a huge fridge with ice-dispenser and just about every gadget one can imagine.

We swam every day, and Barbie and I played tennis on a plastic court while Ros and family sunbathed. That was when I really learned about slow courts. On the slow plastic, it was virtually impossible to hit a passing shot.

Ros and Paul played a four-ball with us at golf. I remember playing one par three, with the green on a promontory in the lake. Barbie's ball was usually attracted to water, but not this time. We all landed safely on the green and collected our par threes.

Ryan spent his spare time retrieving balls from the lake by our bungalow, the one without the sign warning of alligators. I nearly put crocodiles, but crocodiles grow much bigger and don't exist in America, just as alligators don't exist in Africa. He then proceeded to try to sell them to the other holiday-makers.

The highlights for Vicky and Ryan were Disneyland and Sea World, but for Barbie and me it had to be the Epcot Centre. I was to learn a lesson at these centres. Always remember where you park your car. If it had been left to me I would have never found our car in these massive car parks. Thank goodness Paul remembered the row and number each time.

I am sure that we all enjoyed that holiday, but we still hadn't done anything about our retirement plans.

It was not often that we had a telephone call from England. When I heard Sylvia's voice on the line, I sensed that it would be bad news, and it was. Sadly mum had passed away in the night, without much warning. 'We will be home on the first available flight' I told her.

There was a very sad atmosphere around Ivy House when we arrived on the following night. Mum had been the matriarch of the family, and it felt like the end of an era. Marjory, Les's wife, filled us in with the details. Daisy had called her from across the road to come to see to mum, who was coughing up blood. Marjory told us that she was holding her and trying to clean up the mess at the same time. Mum always knew what was happening though, and true to fashion she said 'I'm going, Marjorie' and then she stopped breathing.

It was a big funeral. All the family were there, of course, including many of the relatives. Mum had been the real head of the family and was well known in the village. She was the one who was called out, both to deliver babies at birth, and to lay people out after their demise. Those were in the days before all that became commercialised. We all took it very badly, and I think that I had probably the most to ponder upon.

Sarah was working in London, and Sylvia was living in Dronfield on her own, so it was arranged for Daisy to live with Sylvia. It was a much cosier bungalow for her to live in than big, old, draughty Ivy House, and entailed much less work.

Sadly, the furniture had to be sent to auction, from whence most of it had come in the first place. As happened, when it was bought, it was sold for a pittance, lovely though some of it was. I was particularly sorry to see the large extending oak table go, but I had nowhere to put it. It had seated twenty-two for Walter's wedding, which was purely a family affair. The wood alone was worth ten times what was paid for it. At least Edwin had bought the house which the owner had put up for sale, so that stayed within the family.

The arrangements worked out well. Sylvia was no longer on her own, and Daisy kept the bungalow spotless. It was chicken feed to her, compared with the work needed at Ivy House. I imagined that the last year or so was the most comfortable Daisy had enjoyed during her whole life. She had outlived all our expectations, and it was very sad, but no surprise when it came to an end. It was after a very short illness and she fully deserved the peaceful ending. It is sad to note that family reunions now occurred only at funerals.

We still had unfinished business in America, It must have been me, because Barbie was never keen on living there. We still had lots to see over in the States however, and she was keen to go on holiday again, so we organised another trip and we landed once again on American soil less than a year later.

By now we were used to staying in motels, so we planned to hire a car and play it by ear. We landed in Orlando, picked up the car, and found a motel.

Cape Canaveral was only a day's outing away, and we made that our first port of call. We saw replicas of the various rockets and satellites, but except for the museum, we didn't feel as excited as we had expected. I suppose because most of the exhibits were replicas.

Our next destination was Tampa which involved an overnight stop on the way. We had left it a bit late and it was getting dark and we hadn't seen a motel for miles. Then we saw bright lights ahead. Hurrah, a motel at last. We pulled into the car park and were amazed at the size of the car park and the number of trucks parked up. I was interested in the sheer size of some of the juggernauts but I should have been looking more at the display of lights.

We were shown to a room. We had seen better, but hey, we had to take the rough with the smooth, and it was supposedly a no smoking room. We had a wash and freshened up and went down to dinner.

I think Barbie twigged where we had landed ourselves before I did. The clue being when she insisted on changing places with me so that I had my back to a raised floodlit dais. Our meal arrived and the music began. Believe what you will, but I was thankful to have changed places.

I honestly find public displays of that sort embarrassing, and Barbie did her best to try not to look disgusted. I was allowed to turn round to see the men stuffing notes under the lady's G-string, which I did find amusing. According to the amount of money tucked away, she must have been considered pretty entertaining.

When we drove away on the following morning we should have known. There it was in 6 foot lights. 'GO-GO Dancing 9 till 1.' We now knew what that meant, and what to avoid in future. No wonder there were hundreds of lorries parked up.

From Tampa we went down to Sarasota which reminded us of La Manga in Spain. The houses were built only a few metres above sea level, and water from the bay was channelled up to the front of the houses from where they could moor their boats.

We had called to see friends of friends who owned a small antiques shop. I can't say it was a great success because it was spoiled by a deliberately obnoxious eight-year-old girl of theirs, who resented any of the attention that was being paid to us. We were glad to say our farewells for once, and found an hotel nearby where we could sleep. For once we were thankful that we hadn't been invited to stay the night

Miami didn't appeal to us, probably because of its reputation on the television, so we avoided going there or the Keys. We travelled in that direction for a while in order to drive round Lake Okeechobee. This was disappointing because we could never actually see the lake from the road, nor were there any obvious roads leading to it where we might have stopped for a picnic.

By the time that we were half way round the lake, we suddenly began to feel a little apprehensive. We hadn't seen a white man for hours. To feel apprehensive was strange to us, after having lived in Africa for fifteen years, but the feeling was quite real in both of us.

Then a rather large, coloured sheriff stepped into the road with his hand held high and I stopped, wondering what could I possibly have done wrong? He was very polite, and asked us where we were going. When I said Orlando he told us that there had been an accident ahead, explained the directions of the diversion, and then waved us on, saying 'have a good day.' By now, of course, we were quite used to that expression, which was used by everyone on departure.

The journey continued to be uninspiring, but then, out of the blue, the reason why we had come to America materialised. We had seen quite a number of golf complexes and finally found one like a mini Sun City where we were able to rent a bungalow on the site in order to get the feel of the place.

We played golf on the golf course, tennis on the tennis courts and even went to a weekly dance. That was quite an experience. The popular dance was called shagging, an unfortunate name for us Brits. It was a kind of jiving, but to set patterns as in sequence dancing. The music they danced it to was lively, and we would actually have liked to become more proficient at it.

We found an estate agent on site and looked at one or two properties. Even Barbie was getting interested because there was no doubt that they were super houses and very inexpensive by UK standards.

The agent asked us where we came from. When we said Gran Canaria, he walked over to a wall map of the UK and said 'Where in the UK is that, I haven't heard of it?' We tried not to smile. We had heard that

American geography usually ends on their coastline, and that confirmed it.

When he said that he could get us a green card without any problems, he lost all credibility, and we abandoned the idea of buying. We had envisioned spending summers in the UK and winters in Florida, and in spite of what he promised, we could see problems over the letting during their off season, even had we been able to obtain a green card. We returned to Gran Canaria with thoughts of living part time in America well and truly buried.

Before the year was out I had another hernia. I was playing tennis with my grandson, Ryan, and normally kept a spare ball in my right hand pocket. I was about to serve, and put my hand in my pocket to get a ball, but the lump there wasn't a ball. It was a huge lump in my groin, but on the right-hand side this time.

Oh no, have I got to go through all that again? I thought. Still I knew the procedure this time and I knew it was a manageable hurt. I pushed the lump back and limped the short distance home. This time the consultant laughed and said that at least I couldn't have another one because now I would have both sides netted and stitched up. It was another epidural, so that once again I was awake during the whole procedure.

Selling property is such a fickle business. One week we would be selling daily, and the next week we would sell nothing, and the next week, and the next week. There was a recession in Europe and no one had any money, or if they had money, they didn't want to part with it. My partner was a Gran Canarian and should have known that historically this happened every decade or so. We depended solely on tourists to buy.

He had also ventured into property and had built a complex on the crest of a hill overlooking the resort on one side and the valley housing Barbie's school on the other. It was built on a raft covering three levels with one to two feet difference in height between each level. When half constructed, one of the levels broke away from the other two. It wasn't a big crack, but who was to know how it would develop? The building was completed and the cracks patched up.

The most important question which concerned me now was whether I could sell anything on that site? I was determined that my honesty was not going to be compromised, yet I daren't mention outright that I wouldn't sell them. I took people round to inspect it, but managed to get them to come back when I knew my partner would be around. I'm sure he sensed my reluctance, and was annoyed. I realised too late that I should have discussed the subject with him, but I guess the result would have been the same. He thought that they were OK to sell, but I didn't think it ethical to sell without explaining the history, which would, of course, kill any chance of a sale.

How people change. The atmosphere in the office got gradually worse and I didn't feel that I could do anything about it. With two shares to one he told me one day that he had decided to close the business down and share the outstanding assets. I say share, but that doesn't mean share fairly. I got all the bad debts, which were never paid to me, and he got the positive assets. I hadn't a leg to stand on because he had been a solicitor and the company solicitor was his relative. I am convinced that as soon as I went he would reopen the office, but I had earned more than a teacher's salary over the years so was satisfied in pocket if not in mind.

The commissions which we earned, as I said, were shared. On one property however he had asked me to put all the commission in my bank and then transfer his half to his wife's account in the UK. I wondered afterwards if that constituted money laundering, but it was too late, it had already been transferred. Had I realised, however, I maybe could have negotiated a better deal at the break-up, but in retrospect I'm glad I didn't bother to go through the hassle of doing battle with two solicitors. I was satisfied and opted for an easy life.

There was nothing to tempt us to stay in Gran Canaria now and we prepared to retire back in Spain. We had our apartment in Almunecar to fall back on until we had sorted out what to do next. We decided to retire to the mainland to our flat in Almunecar, and the amazing thing was that we were able to sell our apartment in Arguiniguin with a small profit, in spite of the recession.

As we now realised, we were both over sixty and it was about time that we retired. We had no serious intention of seeking work, and we both agreed that we wished to see as much of the world as possible, so why not?

We expected to drive to the UK from Spain, and vehicles were cheaper in Gran Canaria, so we bought a V.W. Transporter Van which had been converted into a camper. It was the modern version of the 'Dormobile', and served as both a car and a camper. It was ideal for the job because it had a diesel engine, and diesel was cheaper than petrol in Spain, and it did around 35mpg so was fairly economical.

Our Gran Canarian neighbour arranged a super party for us before we left and gave us a personally inscribed meat plate as a leaving present. They had always had difficulty over my nickname, so we smiled and thanked them profusely when it was inscribed Barbara and Kent. Barbie now had dozens more names in her address book to add to her list of pen friends, some of whom we were to see again in different parts of the world.

BACK TO MAINLAND SPAIN

We loaded the camper to capacity but still couldn't take everything at one go, so we stored the rest with a friend, and took the ferry to Cadiz. I would have to make a return journey for the rest of our possessions.

Cadiz is worth visiting. What we saw was very picturesque and it is steeped in history. We wanted to get to our apartment quickly however and settle down, but I wish we had spent more time there now. We couldn't sleep in the laden camper however, and we didn't fancy leaving it overnight in an hotel car park. 1992 had been our 'Annus horribilis', and we wanted to move on.

Our apartment in Almunecar was in decent shape, but the estate agent we left in charge said that it had hardly been let at all, hence we got very little rent. We tried to quiz our receptionist, but he was no help. When I saw them together I got the impression that there was something going on between them, but at least we weren't in debt.

We agreed that I may as well go back for the camper on my own while Barbie stayed to sort out the flat and enquire about property. We didn't want to stay in Almunecar where there was no golf or work.

I was gone for a week, and on the ferry back to Cadiz I was bored and lonely. I was queuing for a meal when I saw the men in front handing in vouchers, and being curious, I asked the server what the vouchers were for? She said 'Oh haven't you been issued with yours sir? Wait here and I will get you some.' She duly came back with a handful and I had free meals for the rest of the voyage. It dawned on me afterwards that she must have thought that I was a lorry driver. It was one of their perks to be given free meals. I didn't own up, as it would have been too complicated. Barbie had a good laugh when I told her the story, and said 'Trust you.' An old friend was advertising a bungalow beyond Marbella, and Barbie had a list of other properties to look at, so we set off to inspect them. Isn't it strange? The friend's place was not in a pleasant complex at all and needed a lot of work doing on it. We rejected it straight away, but when we told her that it wasn't quite what we were looking for, she was so upset that she didn't speak to us for years afterwards.

WE BEGIN RETIREMENT

We continued on our quest to look for somewhere nice and looked at one or two properties on the list but saw nothing suitable. We set off one day to drive along the coast to look for anything interesting to buy and had almost given up hope, but decided to keep driving west past Estepona just to enjoy the countryside. After five minutes we came upon a large sign that we recognised from our days in Africa. Four little men pulling on a rope could only mean Taylor Woodrow, so we pulled in to have a look.

When we found the office we also found a couple who were to become our lifelong friends. Tony took us around several complexes and told us which were empty and which were for sale.

We began to get excited with the last complex which he took us around. The houses were linked together, but staggered. Each one consisted of a garage accessed from the road with steps at the side leading up to the front door on the next level. This led into a large split-level lounge/dining room with a good kitchen, toilet and stairs leading off. There was a large balcony over the garage at the front, and at the back a fair-sized garden accessing onto the first fairway of the golf course.

Upstairs were two large bedrooms and a bathroom which included a bidet. Another flight of stairs led to a small room with a large patio area, designed, I suppose, for barbeques.

It appeared too good to be true, and we were very excited. Tony told us that actually he wasn't selling those particular properties, but guessed that they were what we might be looking for and he told us at which real estate office to enquire.

The offices were situated across the main road in Puerta de La Duquesa, an idyllic marina surrounded by shops, cafés and restaurants. We called in the office to ask the price but told them that we wanted to explore the complex first to decide which was in the best position because there were many to choose from.

Apparently the housing complex had been built before the recession hit Europe, and only one or two of the fifty that were built had been sold. The houses were now being sold at half the initial market price. Had we landed in paradise? It felt like it. Thank you once again our guardian angel.

We drove back across the main road to choose which number would be the most suitable before making our final decision, and were walking up and down, obviously trying to decide, when a man came out of one of the houses opposite. He introduced himself, and having ascertained what we were about, said that he could get No. 8 for three thousand pounds cheaper than we had been quoted, and on top of that it would include a golf share worth another three thousand.

It turned out that a man from Las Palmas had bought it and wanted priority in getting it off his hands. He took us to the office where he worked and we bought it. I was able to make sure that it was signed in front of a notary and eventually registered at the Land Registry, so my experience in Gran Canaria had at least confirmed that it was done legally. We were now the proud owners of No. 8, Jardines del Golf, Golf de la Duquesa, Manilva, and it was right opposite the Marina Puerto de la Duquesa.

This was our first retirement home. We had given up any ideas about earning any more money, although Barbie often said that she wouldn't mind teaching again, she was loathe to give up teaching which she loved. I admit that I was relieved that there were no schools in La Duquesa or even anywhere near us that had a European element. Though her Spanish was quite good, it was not so good that she could teach in that language. Anyway, I told her that she deserved a rest. We soon became so involved in the social life of the community however that Barbie realised that she would have had to give up an awful lot to teach as well.

We truly were legally retired, because, since Barbie was over sixty, I was also treated as a pensioner. In Spain, if one of the partners is a pensioner then the other partner is also treated as one. I didn't receive a pension of course, but pensioners in Spain have many perks bestowed upon them which English pensioners do not get in the UK. One such perk was a government-subsidised holiday every year, which we were to take advantage of several times.

An advert came through the post promoting a holiday in China. Normally we throw them away without a second glance, but not this time. We had more or less agreed to have a big holiday each year in our quest to travel as much as possible, and we had never been to China. It seemed an interesting package, and what appealed more to us was the reasonable price quoted. We decided to strike while the iron was hot, and go.

It must have been the longest single flight we ever made, because I don't think we made one stop. I only remember a very modern and very comfortable aeroplane.

From the moment we landed in Beijing, we called it our 'outward bound holiday for geriatrics.' We seemed to be on the go from early breakfast every day, to late dinner. The only breaks we had during the day were when we were flying from one place of interest to another, or on a bus when the destination was within or near Beijing.

Everything about China is on a grand scale. We couldn't have started the tour any grander. It was a flight to the Great Wall, and of all the things I remember about that day was my embarrassment. I was taking a photo of Barbie when a kind Japanese tourist offered to take one of both of us together. He had half a dozen cameras and telescopic lenses strung round his neck, and I handed him my little camera. It had been dropped on our travels, and I had put sellotape round it to hold it together. Surprisingly it still took good photos, but he must have been thinking 'these poor English.'

We did walk a considerable distance along the wall until we were surprised to see steps confronting us. We shouldn't have been so surprised because the wall does run in more or less a straight line, and has to go up and down with the contours of the land. No wonder it can be seen from space, because the sheer size of it is remarkable, and much taller and wider than we imagined. It was designed large enough along which to march regiments of troops. Barbie decided to rest while I tackled the steps and walked up to the first tower and back.

Then we flew to Xian, where we were greeted by dignitaries giving us all the 'Freedom of the city', in the shape of a large medallion on a red ribbon which they hung around our necks. Of course the Terracotta Warriors continued with the grand scale of everything, but it was a pity that exposure to air had faded the colours completely. It must have been truly spectacular to the first viewers, to see it in technicolour, but it didn't really diminish the spectacle for us.

Beijing continued the theme in spades. We did travel by bus now, but we were still up early and back late. The meal times were interesting. We were seated on tables for ten, and hardly ever knew what we were eating. It always tasted good to Barbie and me, but if we asked what it was, the waiter would usually play safe and say 'tofu.'

The Summer Palace and Gardens, Ming Tombs, Tian an'men Square (Chinese spelling), and the People's Gardens were so interesting, and the acrobatic displays more than rivalled the Russian state circus. We were also taken to specialist schools for gifted children, not only in intelligence, but in music, art and drama. This is something I have always advocated that we should do more to promote within our education system in the UK.

On our return, I can only say that Travelsphere had done us proud and it had more than fulfilled our expectations.

Back in La Duquesa we made full use of the golf section with Barbie more often than not being involved with the competition winners. She served separate terms as golf captain, and when not filling that office she was the automatic choice as secretary, if only for her calligraphy. No one was ever able to match her immaculate scoreboards or impeccably written minute books. I was a midweek bandit again, playing below handicap during the week but unable to replicate that in the weekend competitions. In all the eleven years that we were there, I only featured three or four times on the top of the leaderboard.

We were about the only ones to make use of the tennis courts which were ideally situated between us and the clubhouse. It was unfortunate that there was never a tennis section formed.

On two evenings each week we attended Whist drives. We also took our turn in running the whist in order to give the regular organisers a rest. It wasn't the running on the night that was the problem, but the running around involved in buying different prizes each week which took up so much time.

The Wintertons (Tony had shown us round our house prior to us buying it) were keen on playing bowls, and encouraged us to join the bowls club at Benavista. We both soon got hooked on the game too, playing twice a week, and particularly enjoyed playing against the English teams that toured Spain during the winter. We even entered the Spanish championships on the Costa Blanca, more for a holiday there rather than thoughts of success. I was lucky to have been chosen to play lead to our best player in the doubles competition. We got through a few rounds, but then were put on the end lane on which there was quite a camber, making it very difficult for him, being left handed, to bowl down his forehand. We lost that round, but it had been good fun, and I hadn't expected to progress as far as I did.

Bridge parties, dinner parties and dining out again constituted our social entertainment in the evenings, and this was enhanced with Sky television when it became available, though if I remember correctly, most people on the Costa received it illegally.

There were two Chinese restaurants in the port. People usually favoured one or the other but we always went to the Cheng Du. They seemed to use less monosodium glutamate. The two young waitresses there were delightful and had been victims of the one child policy in China. To keep them both, the mother had to emigrate. We did dine in other venues, but that was only when we were being entertained, or when our guests fancied a steak or Italian food.

Saturday nights were spent at the Jolly Sailor on the second storey overlooking the marina. It was only tiny, but a super trio played our kind of music, and Barbie and I liked to dance close together anyway. That was where I first heard George Harrison's 'While my guitar gently weeps' and where Barbie heard her favourite, 'Fields of Gold'.

At least once a year we would drive to the UK. We would make one stopover in France, using the chain of Shell garages which specialised in all night stops for the long distance lorry drivers. They were usually excellent, with good food and showers if needed. Then we would drive to Dunkerque to board the Norfolk line ferry to Folkestone. This was a commercial ferry which also took private passengers, and, true to the Pidcocks, it was the cheapest way to cross the channel, in spite of the extra distance we had to travel.

Depending on the time of arrival, we would usually park overnight in a lay-by with other lorries, make a meal, and try to sleep, then travel up to Derbyshire in daylight on the following day.

I can't remember how we met up with Mary and Humberto, it must have been on one of our government-subsidised Spanish holidays. She was born in Gibraltar and he was Spanish and had retired from being an orthopaedic surgeon. We became very good friends, and although they were staunch Catholics, they told us of spare places on the bus taking them to Rome for the week, and suggested that we applied. We jumped at the chance, because it was somewhere we had never visited. There was such a demand for places, however, that the organisers eventually had to hire two buses and unfortunately we were to be seated in a different bus from our friends.

It was a long drive through southern France to get there, but what a beautiful city we saw when we arrived. We had a bus tour round the city and marvelled at all the sculptures and ancient monuments. The allied forces did well during the war, because it was said that they deliberately tried to avoid damaging these national treasures.

Further excursions took us on a day trip to Naples and having made a detour, it was particularly poignant for me to gaze over the sands of Salerno where the bus stayed for a while. I imagined the spot where my brother Edwin was left for dead, and subsequently rescued. Although we didn't visit it, the scene of the Battle for Monte Casino was also pointed out to us on a distant hill during the drive back.

On our free day we took a trip to Pompeii, and judging by the number of brothels, the inhabitants must have lived a life of debauchery. It brought to mind what I was told at school, that both the Greek and the Roman empires collapsed because of the debauchery and loose living which became prevalent. I wonder if our modern society is going to end up in the same manner? It seems to me that it is heading in that direction. I am thinking particularly of almost every advert on television and of videos of the latest songs. They are mostly sexually suggestive and would not have passed censorship fifty years ago.

One week was not sufficient for us to see as much as we would have wished, but we were still very grateful to have been given the chance to go.

I mentioned government-subsidised holidays. Of the ones we accepted, the most striking one was the week we spent visiting Santiago de Compostela in the northern province of Galicia. The cathedral there is dedicated to St James, to which thousands of Christians still make their pilgrimage as they have done since the ninth century. The complete holiday was full board all the way, and cost us very little.

I can now say that I have played cricket at the 'Oval.' No, not the London Kensington Oval, unfortunately I wasn't that good. This was at the 'Oval' at La Manga, on the east coast of Spain. We had gone as a party with the cricket team from Marbella. La Manga is a popular holiday resort, situated on a peninsula. The inhabitants there must all pray that global warming does not raise the sea level substantially because the whole of the peninsula is only a matter of feet above sea level.

I learned two things on that pitch. Firstly, I realised that I was too old to play at silly mid on any more, after a ball brushed my hair when I was too slow to get my hand up to catch it. Secondly, I wasn't so hot with the bat anymore either, because while trying to hook a simple ball to leg, I must have taken my eyes off the ball, and it flew off the edge of the bat and split my chin open. I was not out nine (Or should I say knocked out nine) and had to have three stitches in it.

Back in Duquesa, another phone call came from Sylvia. She was ill, and wanted me to help her make her will. We flew home again, but this time we stayed in Dronfield with Sylvia. Sarah was also there when we arrived. We were told that Sylvia had leukaemia, or a type of cancer of the blood, and had to have periodic transfusions. I asked her how that had happened, because there was no history of cancer in the family, and she looked at me and I will always remember her reply – 'Don't be silly Ken, when we were young nurses we used to supervise x-rays with only a rubber apron on to protect us.'

Between blood changes, Sylvia was well, but gradually became weaker as each transfusion became due. Sarah had not enjoyed the best experiences in London and had decided, very generously, to sell her lease in Wimpole Street and come up to live with, and look after, Sylvia.

Sylvia had no dependants, and had the idea of splitting what she had to leave in her will between all our seventeen nieces and nephews. By now, after mum had died, the family had become divided and some siblings had not been in contact for years. I asked her if she was sure that is what she wanted to do, and she said 'Well, what else can I do?'

I thought for a while, and then suggested that as far as I could see, there was only one person who deserved her money, and that was Sarah who had given up her life in London to come and look after her. That made her happy, and we made the will out to that effect. I was aware that I had just deprived Nikky and Ros of a reasonable sum, but because of that, none of my brothers could complain afterwards about me having influenced the decision and depriving their children of anything.

One thing that made me wild, but nothing could be done about it, was her bank account. She had many thousands of pounds in a current account, and it had been there for years without accruing any interest of course. Surely the bank manager should at least have advised her to put it into a savings account.

I am pleased to say that the arrangement worked well for both of my sisters. They got on very well together with their pet dog, and Sarah made friends with the neighbours. One of them was later to become a joint executor of the will, but that was long after I had flown from Spain to advise Sylvia what to do. Having been a nurse, I knew that Sylvia recognised that there was no cure for her, but they spent a comfortable year together.

The inevitable happened however, and Sarah rang us to say that Sylvia had been kept in hospital. We knew that this signalled the end, and once again we flew back to the UK. That was before peripatetic care was given at home which I was to learn about much later on in life. It was decided that we should take it in turns to stay in the hospital with Sylvia overnight. By now she was on oxygen and a constant morphine drip, and it was once again my turn to sit with her. She had asked after me during the day, and I think that she recognised my voice when I sat beside her. The nurse came periodically to check the drip and the oxygen supply, but on the third round she turned to me and said that she was very sorry, but she had gone. I wasn't aware of this because of the noises which were made by the apparatus. Thankfully, although she had needed the morphine, it had given her a peaceful ending.

At the meal after the cremation, I made the contents of the will known, and my involvement in the making of the will at Sylvia's bequest. I half expected the announcement to cause criticism from some quarters, but fortunately everyone seemed to be in agreement with the outcome.

During the following year, we had to be grateful to Mary and Umberto once again. The Catholics had organised a *peregrinacion* (Spanish spelling) or pilgrimage, to the Holy Land which certainly turned out to be the most moving of all our holidays. We flew to Haifa and from there we were driven everywhere by bus.

Mention a place in the Holy Land which appears in the Bible and we visited it. We looked down on the amphitheatre in Caesarea and also had a swim in the Dead Sea. No, we didn't have a paper to read, lying on our backs in the water motionless, which some of the party had remembered to organise. Was it easy to swim you might ask? Actually it was quite difficult after being used to being submerged in the water. Swimming on top of the water was peculiar to say the least.

We went on excursions to Bethlehem and Nazareth and walked the 'Path of the Cross' in procession through the streets of Jerusalem. We were also taken to view the site of the caves where the Dead Sea Scrolls were discovered. We could not get close to the caves because that was the only time when we were not waved through one of the frequent roadblocks.

One of the most significant acts in our life took place in Canaan of Galilee. Barbie and I, although we were Church of England, were invited to join in with the Roman Catholics, and take communion when we wished, so on alternate days we attended Mass with the rest of the party. After Mass on this particular day, the Father asked if there were any married couples in the congregation. Almost everyone raised their hands, so he explained that he was going to stay behind and go through the marriage ceremony if any of us wished to renew our vows. Again we all raised our hands. The Father proceeded to conduct the service, and we all renewed our vows in a very moving ceremony.

Another thing of note happened when we were in groups being shown around the Basilica of St Francis of Assisi. We were with our group who were being lectured in Spanish. When we passed a group with an English speaking guide, we transferred from our group to theirs, but their Father who was guiding them stopped and asked us who we were. When we explained, he insisted that we should go back and join our own group. I remember thinking at the time that if St Francis was indeed looking down on us, he might not be feeling too pleased with the Father who deprived us of understanding the history of the Basilica.

Soon after we arrived back home we had two parcels delivered by post. We couldn't think what they might be, but when we opened them, they contained a certificate each for having attended the *peregrinacion*, and a separate one which was a record of the renewal of our vows. All three were illustrated and written in beautiful illuminated script, and they have always been prominently displayed since then, in a place of honour on our wall.

In 1998, two couples invited us to visit them in Australia. We had already seen Sydney, but now we were to be entertained by Tony and Julie themselves. The other couple were in Perth on the western coast. We decided to see as much as possible on the trip, with stopovers in Bali on the way out, and Singapore on the return journey. We also remembered our promise to revisit New Zealand. Australia could be organised when we got there.

Bali was just paradise. Our hotel was in the centre of the island, a heavenly site set amongst the palm trees, so we never saw the coastal resorts. I hope they weren't copies of all other resorts one sees around the world, which would have spoiled the image. We did travel to a nearby town to shop, but our gold watches turned out to be plated, I understand, and we have never known the grandchildren to wear their presents.

We had hoped to see a couple in New Zealand from whom we had bought Batiks in Kano. We had been very friendly with them and admired their artwork. It is sad that after arriving in New Zealand, the wife was diagnosed with cancer and became very ill. We had written many times about our exploits, emphasising what an interesting life we led. Little did we realise how distressing it was for Peter, who at the same time was caring for his very sick wife. It was no wonder that he didn't really want us to visit them.

We had prearranged a guided tour of both the north and south islands with Guthrie Tours, and from the point of view of organisation, Guthries must be ranked No. 1. The driver, acting as tour guide, described every tree, flower, bird and animal that we saw, and kept up a running commentary of all the features of the landscape and its history. He made travelling so interesting that we were sometimes sorry when we stopped, except that it would usually be to see something even more interesting.

New Zealand was turning out to be a fascinating place. He took us to Auckland, Taranaki, Rotorua with its hot springs and geysers, and Wellington on the North Island. Then we crossed by ferry over to the South Island to travel to Christchurch and Dunedin. We walked on glaciers, watched dolphins on the Milford Sound and saw demonstrations of some of the 59 million sheep in the country.

Perhaps the most spectacular event was visiting the actual bridge where 'bungee jumping' originated. We were both unable to make the attempt. At our age they wouldn't let us. Would we have done so had we been allowed? I can't speak for Barbie, but from me that would be an emphatic no! Especially after I had watched one or two.

What an inspired choice it was when we decided to travel with Guthries. We left New Zealand filled with satisfaction, having enjoyed every minute.

This time we had a visa to enter Australia. The flight arrived very late at night, so we had arranged to stay overnight in an hotel and meet Tony and Julie. We were up early and checked in the telephone directory in case there was a local dialling code. I confirmed A Phillips and then Barbie said 'Turn over the page and see if there are any Pidcocks'. We were amazed to see several columns of them. That set us thinking of course under what circumstances they had arrived there. Had they got a free ride at His Majesty's pleasure? We often joke about it.

Incredibly, it must have been nearly twenty years since we had seen Tony and Julie back in Mbarara, and it is always the same when meeting old friends after a long time. We inevitably began with reminiscing and saying 'I wonder what happened to old so-and-so' etc. It is always 'old' so-and-so isn't it, even if they were younger than us? It's not possible to have had better hosts though, and they did us proud, as usual, and showed us all the parts of Sydney and the interior that we hadn't already seen.

Tony asked us if we had sailed before, and when we said that we had, he asked us if we would like to go for a sail in his yacht. Of course we said 'Yes', but we were surprised when Julie stayed behind to prepare dinner. When we arrived down by the river he said, as if in passing, 'Oh by the way, this is a race.' The gun went off and away we sailed. He then told us that he was going to gamble, and start on a different tack from the rest, which could turn out to be a good move or a bad one.

We hardly saw any of the other yachts throughout the race, and sailed along merrily with Tony telling us what to do next. In fact, it was almost as if we had forgotten that we were in a race. When we clocked in at the finish, we wouldn't know the results until the next day because the handicaps had to be worked out, everyone having a different class of yacht. It was actually several days before he said 'Oh, by the way, we won that race' as though it was no big deal. It was to us though, when it finally dawned on us what he was talking about. I think he knew secretly just how competitive we were over everything.

Their house backed on to a wood at the bottom of the garden, where they had placed food trays, so we spent lots of time watching the exotic birds and little forest animals come to feed, most of which we had never seen before. I remember being fascinated at the time, but I hate to say that I have little visual memories of what we saw.

We met their relatives again, and the next week flew by. It is only *au revoir* though with Tony and Julie, not goodbye, because they fly over to visit his relatives regularly who live just south of us. Leaving is still a sad occasion though.

We flew north and spent two nights touring through the impenetrable forest in Army 'Ducks' and Land Rovers, before going to Cairns in Queensland. Here we booked a week exploring the Great Barrier Reef. You will have seen it all on television, but it was something else to be swimming with goggles and a snorkel, and experiencing it all live.

As a bonus I saw a giant manta ray glide gently past below me. I wished Barbie could have seen it but she was a short distance away from me. I'm sure she saw things that I didn't see, but she always talked of the manta ray that she had missed.

We did stopovers in Alice Springs, Ayers Rock and Kings Canyon. It must have been a bad day at Alice Springs, for we saw many Aborigines lying about as if they were drunk. Apparently they are given the equivalent of our social security, and with no work for them, they had little else to do.

Ayers Rock was impressive, but again we were unlucky because it was overcast all that day, and consequently we didn't see the 'glow' for which it is famous. Kings Canyon, however, was impressive, and was well worth the travelling.

One realises the size of Australia when one flies. The flight to Perth was a long-haul flight in itself. Vince and Glenys were the couple with whom we practised our tennis in Gran Canaria, and had a lovely home just north of Perth. As well as driving us sightseeing both north and south along the coastline, they actually managed to get tickets for the World Swimming Championships, which were conveniently held in Perth whilst we were there.

We were amazed when they cheered for the Aussies in preference to the British. When we were living overseas we always cheered for the country where we were, but never in preference to the Brits. They had become true Australians though, and we realised that it was a good thing really because, after all, they had emigrated.

There was a very inexpensive public transport system operating in the Perth area, and with a cheap one-day ticket one could go anywhere. After two days touring Perth on our own, we found that a day ticket would take us all the way to Freemantle. We couldn't miss an opportunity like that and spent a day there, exploring the museums dedicated to the convicts who had been transported there.

For fun we again looked in the telephone directory for Pidcocks, and oh dear – there were even more columns of them in Freemantle than there were in Sydney. Once again we wondered for what reason they were there. Had they gone to make a life in a new country, or had they had no say in the move?

We then took a ferry to Rottnest Island and saw their species of the Quokka, a weird animal which is only found in a few places in the world. That day out had been both interesting and extremely fruitful.

After a last day lounging in the sun and winding down, topped with an evening barbeque, we had to say goodbye to Vince and Glenys, and reluctantly to Australia.

On then to Singapore which is a very interesting island in many ways. We couldn't leave without visiting the cemetery and Changi Prison with all the history attached to them, and we simply had to go to Raffles to taste the famous Singapore Sling.

It was in Singapore where at certain times no one was allowed to drive into the city alone. One had to have a passenger with you in the car. I forgot what the penalty was, whether one was fined, or one had to turn around and was sent back. All this was in an effort to save traffic congestion, and is an idea that might be tried here in the UK.

It was while flying home, and passengers were invited to try to guess the exact time when we reached point of no return. Apparently my guess was the nearest and we were presented with a bottle of champagne. What a fitting end to another wonderful holiday.

Every year that we lived in Southern Spain, they held the Volvo

Masters Golf championships at Valderama, only a few miles west of La Duquesa. Nearby golf clubs were invited to provide Marshalls for the event. We applied and were accepted as part of the team from La Duquesa, who were asked to provide Marshalls for holes three, four and five. I'm pleased to say that we were among the six allocated to hole four, or *Las Cataratas* (the cataracts, in English).

I was particularly pleased when it was my turn, as one of a pair, to patrol the middle section and measure the lengths of all the drives. There were distances marked on each side of the fairway and my partner and I, whoever that happened to be on the day, just had to square them off with the ball. Not rocket science, but it made it very interesting, and relieved any boring intervals.

1997 was something special. It was the year of the Ryder Cup and Europe had to play host to the event. To our delight it was to be held at Valderama, and the same system for Marshalls applied. Barbie and I were allocated back to *Las Cataratas* and measuring. They needed to know the distance to the hole, but we were sure that for some, they were more interested in who was going to win the bet they had placed between themselves, on who had hit the longest drive.

The experience of the opening ceremony and the closing ceremony and just being there when the events unfolded was simply magic. Of course it was extra special and exciting when Europe won.

After every event, the Marshalls were given a free round of golf for their labours, usually in the form of a competition. I was proud to win the prize awarded on our first competition, having gone round exactly to my handicap. I have to admit though, that at my age, my handicap was not what it had once been. We played eight times altogether, which collectively would have cost over a thousand pounds for each of us.

Gosh, I nearly forgot another holiday to the States. This was a package tour to further west. Our priority was to see The Grand Canyon, where the sheer grandeur is difficult to describe. This was where we first realised that Barbie suffered from vertigo, after looking down on the spectacular views below. It didn't affect her at the time, allowing her to enjoy the moment, but it was as if it had a delayed action effect and she was very ill during the night.

Having travelled all that way, it was natural to visit Yosemite National Park and to travel onwards to Las Vegas, San Francisco and Los Angeles. In every hotel, as well as the casinos, there were rows and rows of gaming machines. I cannot see the sense in putting money in a machine which is programmed to pay out only a percentage of the money it gobbles up and we must have been the only tourist not to waste a dime on them. I'm afraid I only gamble with my skills in a fair contest, and never when it is all weighted in favour of the house.

One year later I could hardly complete a round of golf. My knee had been getting progressively worse, and when I visited the consultant he decided immediately to give me a complete knee replacement. The prognosis got worse. After my pre-operation checkup he asked me why I hadn't told him of my heart problem.

I was flabbergasted, and said 'As far as I know, I haven't got a heart problem, how could I have one because I swim regularly, play golf, and can play a long game of tennis without any trouble.' He said 'Nevertheless, you have a problem with a leaking aortic valve which is regurgitating some of the blood instead of pumping it all round the body. You will eventually have to have an operation, but meanwhile we will try to keep it under control with drugs.'

I tell people that the knee operation was more like being in a carpenters shop than an operating theatre. I was given an epidural (my third) and could hear sawing, drilling, and hammering, just as if I was indeed in a carpenter's shop. In a way he must have been like a carpenter at work. I knew how quickly muscles can deteriorate, so I had spent hours building up my knee muscles before the operation, and it paid off. The consultant said that I recovered the use of my leg more quickly than most of his younger patients, and it wasn't long before I was able to forget that I had ever had a problem. This is not bragging, but given as advice to other patients.

We often played bridge at Soto Grande where Tony Jacklin had set up his golf course. Two of the couples with whom we played bridge were going to Morocco and asked us if we wished to accompany them. They both had very large campervans and we thought that it was a good opportunity for us to join them as we were in our little V.W. In the event we never had to call on their resources. We had no shower facilities in our little camper, but all the camp sites were good, and the shower facilities there were kept clean.

It was only a short drive to Algeciras, and a short ferry ride to Tangier. We then took two days before reaching and exploring Rabat, after which we headed south to Casablanca. Each place held lots of historic interest, but of all the places we visited, I would have to say that the market in Marrakech was the most spectacular, with its snake charmers, water carriers, tattooists and other entertainers. There were even dentists practising in the open. Storks were everywhere, in chimneys, on telegraph poles and any tall structure they could find.

Christmas and the New Year were celebrated in style. We combined to make a traditional Christmas Dinner, and had a super barbeque on New Year's Day which included a fish course of fresh whole fish caught on the day.

Everything we saw was worth the journey. We were fascinated by the amazing wood carving centre in Essaouiri, where all the carvers worked on tiny adjoining work benches, and we couldn't resist buying handmade dominoes. We arrived in Tiznit and then Tan Tan Plage, and that was as far south as we were able to go, because the border with the Spanish Sahara was only a few miles further. Many Land Rovers passed us which had just crossed the desert, driving northwards. They had all travelled caravan style, because no one would risk the crossing alone.

The next idea was to go up the Anti Atlas Mountains, but it was soon evident that it was too dangerous in the strong winds for the big campers. We decided to separate and meet them back in Taroudant, while we drove up to Tafrout.

The scenery was simply spectacular and parts of the country were surprisingly fertile. It was here that I was introduced to chips with a mustard sauce. You might like to try it sometimes.

When we returned to Taroudant it started raining, and it simply poured down. The campers were nowhere to be seen so we assumed that the weather had forced them to move on so we set off to Ceuta via Volubilis, the site of the best preserved Roman remains in the world before a recent earthquake destroyed most of them. However there are still some wonderful relics to be seen there and the mosaic floors were truly amazing.

From there we saw very little of Fez because of the rain, which by now was absolutely sheeting down. We vowed to return, but unfortunately we never did.

On the way to Chefchouen we had a narrow escape. The river was in flood and the water actually came over the long bridge. We saw a bus drive through, and thought that if a bus was able to get through then so could we. We followed it across sending spray as high as the windows, and made our way to Chefchouen. We were to learn there that a section of the bridge had collapsed shortly after we had driven over. Whew.

It was now raining so hard that we dare not even get out of the camper and decided to motor up to Ceuta and go home. We were so lucky. The ferry was ready to depart but actually waited a few seconds to allow us to drive on. It was then on the move before we had even parked properly. I would say that our guardian angel certainly looked after us during those last two days and we breathed a sigh of relief.

We arrived back in Duquesa in less than an hour, where we learned that it had rained nonstop since 20 December and it was now 22 January. We had enjoyed the best of the weather right up to the last two or three days. What a relief to settle down at home again, even though it had been an amazing holiday.

Gibraltar was always on the agenda. It was only 20 minutes away, provided that we didn't have to queue too long to cross the border. They often held 'Go slows' there as a reprisal to something that Britain had done or said, but it always rebounded on them because half the Spanish work force had to cross the border as well as the tourists. It was so convenient that we could go to Safeways (later to become Morrisons) and buy any English products which were not readily available in Spain. We could always do without that of course, but what we didn't want to do without was the diesel. It was always significantly cheaper in Gibraltar, and more than offset the travelling costs.

Once I tried to fill up a large can to take back into Spain, but the customs stopped me. At least they let me take it back into Gibraltar, so I left it with a V.W. mechanic whom I used when the vehicle needed servicing and with whom I played golf. I called at his garage to fill up with it on the next trip, so it only cost me a drink for storing it.

We would be hard pushed to say which of our holidays we enjoyed the most. They were all spectacular to us for different reasons. Our trip to Russia was certainly up with the best. All these holidays took place during the twelve year period of our stay on the Costa, so we were not always on holiday. I promise that this is the last one I describe, because it is worth it.

We flew to Moscow in the Russian copy of our VC 10, and we saw little difference from the ones in which we made our early flights to East Africa.

As soon as we had gone through immigration we were whisked straight off to the river boat which was to be our home for the next three weeks. Our cabin on the MS *Sergei Yesenin* was superb, in fact a fellow passenger with her husband, who were to become our lifelong friends, remarked that they had paid more for their cabin upstairs, and it wasn't half as nice. The weather remained good anyway, so we never had to spend much time inside.

For three days we did a whistle-stop tour of Moscow, which kept us enthralled full time. I had always pictured from spy books that the Kremlin was a dark foreboding building, but I couldn't have been more wrong. Inside the high, red-bricked walls were magnificent buildings, including the Palaces of the Tsars and their churches and a cathedral. I counted over fifteen minarets, most of which were painted in blues and gold, and together with the famous St Basil's next door, it was a very spectacular sight. We were able to wander round at our will, or we had the option of going with the tour guide who could explain its history. I remember that there was a 200 ton broken bell, and the broken piece weighed eleven and a half tons on its own. It had fallen when they were trying to install it into the belfry, and they had left it where it fell as a tourist attraction.

How we packed in everything that we saw I don't know. We were taken to see the Bolshoi Ballet, the Moscow State Circus, Red Square and Lenin's tomb, the Church of the Patriarchs, and G.U.M., the equivalent of Harrods G.U.M., however, was only for designated customers, such as government officials. Oh and so much more. Wow, I nearly forgot the Metro which has to be seen to be really appreciated. We saw the BBC TV programme on it which hardly did it justice.

Meals on board were very good, but often consisted of traditional Russian food. We enjoyed everything, but of course there were always the moaners, grumbling about beetroot being served as a vegetable etc.

We didn't really want to leave Moscow, but we had only just started the holiday, so at the same time we were eager to set sail for the rest of the adventure.

Sailing up the rivers was interesting when we were near enough to the banks to see the countryside and sometimes the people working there, but often in the lakes or reservoirs the shores were out of sight in every direction.

Full provision was made, however, and every day there would be Russian language classes. I say classes because we split into three sections, and from thence it became a competition as to who would put on the best show at the end of tour concert. Our group learned *Katyusha* and *Dark eyes*. Incredibly by then we could not only sing it in Russian, but we could read it in Russian as well.

During these times were scheduled the most popular lectures of the tour. There were only a dozen at the first lecture, but it was standing room only for all the lectures after that. Both Barbie and I thought that professor Inna was small, but one of the most beautiful ladies we had ever seen. She explained that in education at that time, one had to have two jobs in order to survive, three if one wanted extras, and this was her third job, lecturing during the holidays.

We were amazed by the headings of the lectures. 'The Russian Monarchy and its Tragedy', 'The Communist experiment in Russia', 'Russia's road to Market', 'Democracy in Russia' and on the last day we were invited to her 'Question and Answers' session. Believe me some people asked very political questions, and they got truthful answers from her heart. She didn't pull any punches about the politicians either. We were all amazed that she could get away with it, if, in fact, she did.

We were fully occupied, with a pending talent show and lectures on Art etc., plus blini parties and vodka tasting. On the way we stopped at towns and islands of interest, including Uglich, Yaroslavl, Goritsy, Kizhi, and Svirstroy. The churches, monasteries and museums were as opulent as anything we had seen in Europe.

In one monastery we were entertained by a choir singing Gregorian chants. We still play one of the tapes we bought. Probably the most interesting was the island on which there was no metal allowed. In its centre was a magnificent cathedral, constructed without even a nail or screw being used. It was interesting to see how the wooden joints were either pegged or interlocked in some way.

St Petersburg was the icing on the cake. We saw the Opera Giselle at the Hermitage Theatre, but I can't adequately describe the Hermitage (museum) itself. It is worth a trip from the UK, even if that is all you go for, because we could have spent days there. For me there is nothing to compare with it, anywhere. Remember 'Voyagers Jules Verne', our tour operators.

That was it. We travelled home Aeroflot with all our memories. WOW.

One day I couldn't find my *residencia*, or Spanish Residents permit, so I called into a police station to report its loss. When I gave my particulars, the policeman looked up something on the computer, looked up at me, and said. 'We have a warrant for your arrest.' I thought he must be joking, but they took me a short ride to another office for questioning.

He first verified that I knew my partner in the estate agency, to which I answered

'Yes, of course'.

'Did you know a certain builder?'

I said that I did but only by sight as he couldn't speak English.

'Did you have any dealings with money?'

I explained that we split profits, but I was concerned only with sales. I never touched money or do any negotiations with the builders, nor had I any dealings with the banks.

'OK you can go then.'

I thought that my ex partner must be under investigation about possible connivance with one of the construction firms, and they wanted to see me merely on a fact finding mission. However, I never heard anything else about that episode, but it shook me up for a while. I still wonder what I should say if I was asked if I had ever been arrested. I still do not think that it was a genuine arrest. No restraints were ever put on me, but was this divine justice coming to another of my ex partners?

My other knee started playing up, which affected my golf, tennis and swimming, especially the breast stroke. By now the consultant and I were almost buddies, because he had also been monitoring my heart all that time. He was very sympathetic because he knew that I was very active, so I soon had all the pre-op tests and he agreed to operate and give me another replacement knee in February '02.

I had to submit to epidural number four and went into the carpenter's shop again. I was awake through the whole procedure once more, but this time I saw and heard the rattle of about half a hundredweight of ice cubes which they packed round my leg. I hadn't noticed that the first time round. There was still no video to watch, and it became boring waiting until they had completed the replacement.

I made the usual quick recovery, exercising by going up and down our three flights of stairs several times a day. I wanted to be active once more as quickly as possible.

It must have happened during the first Sunday golf competition which I had entered after my operation. We had a draw for the starting times, and Barbie and I happened to be at opposite ends of the golf course, when one of the officials came hurrying to me on his buggy and said that Barbie had broken her ankle.

The course had been hollow tined and not swept clean, and Barbie, stepping off her buggy, had slipped and twisted her ankle. It was much more than twisted, because her foot was pointing the wrong way.

When I arrived at the entrance, she was already in the ambulance, but was refusing to allow it to set off until she had seen me. I expected to see her screaming in agony, but she appeared quite calm. This lack of the normal pain one could expect, after such an accident, was to have unfortunate consequences in her later life. Barbie had sustained a fracture, where the ankle bone had twisted in the joint under pressure, and had caused a vertical split up the bottom of the Tibia. I think it is known as a Potts fracture. It should have been excruciatingly painful until it had been stabilised and set in a plaster. The fact that she wasn't in agony seemed good at the time, but it should have been noted in her records, and recorded as a warning.

I dashed back to No. 8 and jumped into the car to chase after the ambulance, but by the time I reached the hospital she was already in the theatre. It was an anxious wait before she eventually reappeared with a welcome smile together with a large pristine white plaster on her foot. She had to learn to use elbow crutches for a while, which wasn't easy for her, but she recovered well. I have always had tremendous admiration for her because throughout all her traumas she never complained, and she always took her illnesses in her stride.

Our daughters

PART NINE

Great-grandchildren calling

THERE WAS TROUBLE AT THE GOLF CLUB. It was to be taken over by a commercially minded firm and prices were going to go up and every round, instead of being free to members, would have to be paid for.

Much more important in our decision making was that by now our grandchildren had children of their own. We were Great Grandparents. We were over seventy by now, but we never felt that age. Our family did come out to see us, but not often enough for Nana, as Barbie preferred to be called by them. We decided to go back to the UK and that meant that we had to put our house on the market.

Things happened quickly from that moment. No sooner had we announced that it was for sale, than we had a couple round to see us with an offer which we could not refuse. This happened just before the start of another recession in Europe, hence we were extremely lucky once again. We had bought at the bottom, and sold at the top of the market. More than ten years later, no one on that development had sold for more than the amount that we had received. Once again our guardian angel had shined down on us. The golf share and golf buggy went with the house and we managed to sell all our possessions that we did not need in the UK.

Things went like clockwork, and at the same time Ros and Paddy told us of a house for sale in Peak Forest where they live. It is only a tiny village so we were very lucky once again. Paddy negotiated for me and we now had the cash from the sale of our property, and we bought it.

We were not quite finished in Spain, because I went to see my consultant for a last checkup. He said that it was now time for the aortic valve to be replaced. I had to tell him we were going back to the UK later in the month, and he became rather concerned. He gave me all my medical records and told to report to my G.P. immediately on arrival back in the UK.

If I had stayed in Spain I would have been operated upon that summer, but as it was, in spite of the first consultant I saw telling me that I was sitting on a time bomb, it took fourteen months before a surgeon was free to perform the operation in England. Thank goodness the time bomb didn't go off.

Hernstone Lea in Peak Forest was a house built in the 1970s by the man from whom we bought it, hence it was purpose built to live in. It had a garage and laundry room, a large kitchen with an AGA range, plus conventional hob and microwave. It also had a large dining room and lounge. Stairs led from the front door and hallway, up to a master bedroom with en suite and three other generous bedrooms, two with converted en suite facilities. It takes no guessing to realise that it was built with B & B in mind. It was far too big for us, but in fact on occasions we did have guests to fill them, but we never attempted B & B.

To us, one of the most important features of the house was the fact that it already had a bidet installed, saving us the bother of rearranging the bathroom.

No one on the continent, or even in Africa, understands how the British can manage without bidets. Everyone in the UK emphasises the importance of washing hands after using the toilet, but think that paper will do for their bottoms. If that was sufficient, surely paper would do for the hands too, or do people think that underwear insulates them from any bacteria or viruses that may be around? Then we go and sit in public areas. Do the same people then take a bath? Ugh. Imagine washing your face in the bath in which you are sitting.

Is this why Barbie and I have hardly ever had any bacterial infections? I am convinced that many infections are caused by inadequate cleansing after using the toilet, and I wish someone would do an investigation into the potential saving for the N.H.S. if everyone was taught how to use bidets. Our great-grandsons think it is a child's urinal. Even Nikky and Ros did not carry on this practice.

Ros lived half a mile away overlooking the village in a converted farmhouse. The grandchildren lived in Buxton, six miles away, leaving Nikky and Tommy the only ones to whom we needed to travel some distance to visit, Twickenham, in London, being about 170 miles away.

We were at last surrounded by our family, and though we may seem to have lived away from them most of their lives, and they had all gone through their own trials and tribulations, we have always been, and still are, a very close-knit family.

Settling down into the community was no problem, and we were pleased to be regular church goers once again. We had neglected our spiritual life, or at least the attending church part of it.

Buxton is a whist-playing area, so we had several venues to go to and history societies and museum memberships to join. We joined the Swimming 'Over-50s' Club, which was not as good as swimming in the sea, but very sociable and it helped us to keep fit.

We realised that we knew more about the rest of the world than we did about the British Isles, so we embarked on five day holidays, visiting places where we had never been to before.

We had one holiday in Bournemouth and tried to find our honeymoon hotel in vain. Our hotel staff couldn't even remember a hotel of that name. We guessed that its position must have made it a prime location on which a supermarket chain could build yet another one of its stores, but in that we were wrong. No one could remember it because its name had been changed from The Hawthorns to the Wessex Hotel in 1960, five years after we had stayed there.

We did include Scotland, Ireland and Wales in these trips and we tried to arrange it so that we were able, at the same time, to meet up with friends whom we had met on our travels.

Cruising was next on the agenda, and again it was to see places we had never visited before. Cruises had to start and finish in the UK. We were fed up with the protocol and waiting about at airports.

Over the next few years we had visited most of the islands in the Caribbean and had twice cruised in the Med., to different ports each time. We sailed up the Bosporus, and Egypt was always on our agenda, but as I have said, we were destined never to go there.

What was to be the last crossing of the Atlantic for us was to cruise through the other great canal, the Panama. This was not as we expected, being so unlike the Suez Canal. It would be true to say, however, that it would be admired more by the engineer rather than the common man, because it was a succession of joined up rivers and lakes with a few locks in between. It was still spectacular in its own way, and obviously had been a massive and costly engineering feat.

After very interesting visits to the Central American countries, we docked and flew back to the UK from Acapulco. This was the straw that broke the camel's back for us, as far as air travel was concerned. The waiting, queuing, walking, and general palaver was crowned when I discovered that customs had broken the locks on my cases, all because of the two loose batteries that I had taken out of my travelling alarm clock. To add insult to injury, they kept the batteries too. We had enjoyed the cruise, but vowed in future never to involve air travel in our itinerary.

We were visiting Lichfield regularly to see Van and Marcia with whom we had become friendly on the Russian holiday. They told us that they had the ideal place for us to live, and they took us round to see Beacon Park, an ExtraCare Village in Lichfield where their aunt was staying. It was for retired people and we immediately fell in love with the concept, and agreed to apply for any vacancies that might arise.

We were unsuccessful in Lichfield, and unlucky too when we applied to the newly built one in Sheffield. The city council had control of the sales, and they had more than sufficient numbers to rehouse from the city. While attending that interview, we became friendly with a couple who actually lived in Sheffield, with a child who needed care, and even they were unsuccessful.

We were advised to apply to Lark Hill Village in Nottingham, which was the latest and largest of the ExtraCare villages to be constructed. Here, sales would be in the hands of ExtraCare rather than the local council, giving us a better chance of selection. We took a trip to Nottingham, liked what we saw, filled in the forms, and sat back to await the outcome.

PART TEN

Lark Hill Village, and the last ordeal

BARBIE WAS UNDRESSING AND PREPARING FOR BED, when I glanced across at her and did a double take.

'Stand up straight love' I said.

'I am standing up straight.' she replied.

'But you have scoliosis' I said, 'I've never noticed that before. We must go to the doctor's tomorrow, to get that checked.'

When the Dr examined Barbie, he asked if she had any pain, and she said 'No.' Should that have sparked off alarm bells ringing in my head? I could hardly have expected the doctor to relate it to her not getting the expected amount of pain with her ankle injury. He wasn't aware of that, but should I have mentioned it?

He then asked if she had suffered any trauma recently and we told him about the broken ankle. 'That must be it' he said, 'One leg must be shorter than the other.' He said that he would arrange for Barbie to see a consultant. I asked if she should have an x-ray, but was given a lecture on why x-rays were not taken when the cause was apparent.

The consultant duly arranged for Barbie to wear a platform on one shoe, in spite of me trying to point out that it appeared to be the wrong leg that was supposedly short. It did, however, slightly straighten the scoliosis, and I reluctantly gave way to expert opinion. Should I have insisted? Would it have made any difference in the end? Those are just two of the questions that I was later to become plagued with, but at the time I don't remember consciously linking this situation with her pain threshold.

Barbie wore the raised shoe for the best part of two years, and as she was in no apparent discomfort we thought nothing more of it. We led a normal life, except Barbie began to tire easily and could not walk far without having to rest.

The next holiday on our wish list was to go to Norway and Iceland on a cruise. It wasn't like us to go to colder parts, but we thought that at least the ship would be warm and we took plenty of extra clothing. It had not been advertised, but we thought that we might be lucky and see the Northern Lights.

For some reason this was the least exciting of all our cruises. We didn't relish the cold, and we had seen mountains and snow before. What we saw did not compare with the South Island of New Zealand, and coming from Derbyshire, we regularly saw plenty of hills. There was nothing at all about Iceland to enthuse about as far as we could see, and we were pleased when it was time to be on the homeward lap. Thinking back, it could have been that Barbie was already beginning to feel the effects of what was later to be diagnosed, and any subtle change in either of us was always reflected subconsciously in the other. We had been inseparable for so long.

The highlights of the cruise were the mealtimes, which we shared with two lovely and interesting couples. It is always true that whom one dines with is one of the most important factors on a cruise.

It was shortly before the cruise was scheduled to end when Barbie complained of backache. When I asked her which part ached, she told me it was the area around the scoliosis. There was only one day to go so there was no point in seeing the ship's doctor at that stage, but I was determined that we would see one as soon as we got home. We disembarked the following day and I made an appointment immediately to see our G.P.

Our regular doctor was on holiday so we saw another member of the practice. He asked us when Barbie had her last mammogram, which was about seven years previously in Spain. Our age group was not included in the advertisements programming the ages for attention in the UK, hence we thought that we were out of danger. He asked if she minded him palpating under her arms, and after a quick examination he tried not to show his concern, but arranged an immediate consultation with an oncologist. Within the next two or three weeks, Barbie had a mammogram, a biopsy and an M.R.I. body scan.

When we then saw the oncologist for the results, we were given the news that we had both been dreading. We knew by then that she had a lump in her left breast, but were still hopeful that it wasn't serious. He confirmed that Barbie had breast cancer, and that it had spread to the lungs, the liver, and yes, you guessed it, the spine in the area of the scoliosis.

Chemotherapy did not start off very well. After only three doses, the oncologist said that it was doing her general health more harm than good, and they would have to discontinue with that line of attack, and try a different approach.

It had got to the stage where I had to hire a wheelchair, and poor

Barbie had already started to lose her hair. She was given wigs but never liked wearing them. The good news, however, was that Barbie was one of the 20% of ladies who were receptive to treatment with herceptin, a new drug on the market which was proving to be successful with other patients.

What a scare we had after the first administration of the drug. Treatment had started, as usual, with a double dose. This produced some sort of reaction in Barbie, resulting in three doctors and three nurses huddling around her bedside at the same time. They did manage to stabilise her eventually, but decided to keep her in overnight to monitor her condition.

I did not know much about driving home that night, except that I got a photograph from the police showing my car driving through red traffic lights. In my defence, I did go through the lights, but I stopped within yards when I saw traffic coming across in front of me, and there was never any risk of a collision. They ignored my excuse of course.

Fortunately, subsequent treatments with the herceptin produced no further side effects, and her hair did grow back, even more luxuriant than before, and amazingly without any grey ones showing.

Things always tended to happen at the same time, and once again they did. After weeks of haggling we had an offer on the house, which meant that even in the falling market, we didn't lose any money. We then told Lark Hill that we had sold our house and had cash, and we were offered a bungalow to buy by return post. Initially the people in Nottingham were reluctant to commit to what they considered as another 'Old Peoples' Home'. We were the lucky ones because now there is a long waiting list of people waiting for the next available property here to become available.

We realised that we had a problem about Barbie's treatment, for we were loathe to leave the care and expertise of the Christie Hospital because of its international reputation. I asked if we could travel from Nottingham for the treatment sessions, but was told that it wasn't possible because it was a completely separate N.H.S. district. We were assured by the oncologist at Christie's however that Nottingham had an excellent record, and we would be guaranteed the same treatment there. It appears that our guardian angel had not forsaken us after all.

On 4 October 2009 we moved into Lark Hill Village, near Clifton, south of Nottingham. We had bought a large, two bedroom bungalow with a conservatory. It was the first bungalow on the right after coming through the gates, but with a wide area of grass around, it was probably the quietest and most private of all of the eighty-two in the village. We had chosen a bungalow rather than one of the two hundred and fifty plus apartments available in the main village block. We had to wait a while for the en suite to be installed, together with the bidet, but at last we were able to move in.

Two days after we had moved in we visited our new G.P. in Clifton, and were amazed that he already knew Barbie's medical history, and had already set up an appointment with the oncologist here in Nottingham. There was hardly a break in her treatment therefore, which they had arranged for her to have at home.

Every three weeks, a nurse would turn up with a mobile drip, and administer the herceptin. Apparently it was cheaper and more convenient for the hospital to do it this way. It freed up hospital beds and apparently saved on V.A.T. for some reason.

The most important thing about herceptin, in Barbie's case, was that she had virtually no side effects whatsoever, and early results were very promising, with monthly visits to see the oncologist and occasional scans revealing decreasing tumours.

Barbie was mobile again, and we even went and played a few holes of golf on a small municipal course nearby. Barbie wasn't really up to it though, but insisted she came with me to walk, so that I could play. This too proved pointless and we decided to sell our clubs. Correction – we tried to sell our clubs, but no one wanted my cheap set. I don't know why, because my clubs would hit the ball as far as the expensively branded ones others were using. We did manage to continue our five day holiday however, by courtesy of John, one of the residents, who was the organiser.

Life in the village was very good. We used the gymnasium regularly and we joined the Drama Club. I loved to act on the stage, and Barbie filled in with the piano music when necessary. I wanted to run a Bridge Club, but a lady who had joined the village before us had already started one, so I started a Whist Club instead which we both naturally attended weekly.

A better description of the village can be found by going into 'Google' and finding ExtraCare villages, and follow the links to Lark Hill. We could have been occupied every minute of the day, because there were probably forty activities to choose from throughout the week. Barbie particularly liked the Monday quiz night, and Friday evening film shows. We were sad not to be able to dance anymore because any turns on the dance floor would make Barbie dizzy. When we did something we always wanted to do it well, and though we loved dance music, it was too heartbreaking not to be able to perform as we used to.

Lark Hill is such a friendly place. Everyone makes an effort to speak to everyone else as they pass by. We soon had a circle of friends, and Barbie had her 80th Birthday Party in the restaurant for about thirty of us. My birthday fell during Easter the following year and so we organised a family party in Peak Forest.

As with all new establishments, the village did have its teething problems. We had trouble with the macerator in the en suite. They were reluctant to change it for a new one, but eventually had to replace it. It then took fourteen weeks from it being installed to making the en suite usable again. In desperation I had written to head office complaining, and the job was then finished off. I had upset the management though, and they changed their mind and allowed my next door neighbour to put her water butt within 6 feet of my front door. Oh they had some silly excuses to offer, but it looked mighty vindictive to us, and other neighbours agreed with us. One thing it didn't do, and that was to put us off Lark Hill. This place was more important to us than any manager.

We made monthly visits to the oncologist and Barbie had regular scans which kept showing slight improvements. The cancer in the breast, lungs, and lymph glands had been virtually eliminated by radiotherapy and the herceptin, and for the next three years we were as happy as we could be under the circumstances.

With cancer, things can happen so slowly that it is hard to recognise change. Barbie began to write everything down, because her impeccable memory started to let her down. Once, when I had gone to Drama on my own, I returned to find her in quite an agitated state, or confused might be a better way to describe it. It happened again when I had been to play a weekly game of bridge. I ended both commitments.

I asked the oncologist if memory loss or confusion could be associated with her condition, but he always said no. Whichever oncologist saw Barbie, they always asked if she had any pain or headaches. Her reply was always 'No', and she often said that she didn't even know what a headache was. Should we have associated this with her pain threshold?

We were never told any statistics, probably because we never asked for any. We didn't know whether the length of time that herceptin was effective in Barbie's case, was more or less than expected. She had been treated with it for nearly three years when they told us that it was no longer completely effective, because one of the tumours in the liver had begun to increase in size. Before we could begin to worry though, they assured us that there were two drugs, lapatinib and capecitobine given in tablet form, which had proved effective when taken in conjunction with each other. Five tablets taken three times per day was the prescribed dose. Poor Barbie, she wasn't very good at swallowing and the lapatinib tablets were quite large, so it became a constant problem for her to swallow them.

Barbie suddenly began to talk about teddy bears. I treated it as a joke at first, and even teased her a little. She did bring it up several times, and even told a friend that she had never had one as a child. I asked her if she would really like one, and she said that it would be nice to have one to cuddle. I began to feel just a little bit inadequate. The problem was solved within days though, because we went across to the village street to find a second hand sale in progress, and there stood a teddy for sale. I said 'Do you want it love?' and she said she did, so I bought it for her. It looked almost new, and I think I paid just £3 for it, not that the price mattered. I didn't see her hug it much, but she did have it on the settee beside her always. This was the first indication of something going on in her head, though I didn't recognise it as such at the time.

I was careful to check everything Barbie ate, and in particular she must never eat or drink any grapefruit products. Invariably when we went on holiday she would choose grapefruit with her breakfast, being her favourite, and always I had to take it from her and remind her. Imagine my horror when I saw grapefruit displayed on the carton of her favourite tropical fruit drink. I know it was not listed on the older type of carton that I had been buying. I still wonder and worry over whether I had ever bought any of the new cartons containing the dreaded stuff, or whether the old ones contained it. How could I have been stupid enough to think that there would be no grapefruit in tropical fruit? Had I unwittingly contributed to jeopardising her recovery?

Her physical condition was not improving though, and I frequently suggested buying mobility aids for her but she would not entertain them, even though walking more than a few yards became very tiring for her. We went on walks most days for the exercise because it had become difficult for Barbie to cope with the apparatus in the gym, but Barbie had to stop to rest more and more frequently. She loved to go and sit by the pond to watch the ducks and see the fish. Occasionally she managed to walk up to the wooden 'lookout' which the residents had built, from which to watch the birds feeding.

Barbie had been receiving treatment for over three years when she asked me one day what a headache felt like. When I quizzed her over this, she said that she had just experienced a funny feeling in her head. I made a mental note for her next appointment.

The following week we saw the oncologist. He asked her the usual questions, any pains or headaches etc. – and when she said 'No.' I reminded her of the 'funny feeling' that she had experienced. The oncologist, sensing my concern, said that they would include a head scan, as well as the body scan which was now due. I had always questioned in my own mind why they had never included a head scan, and I had a feeling of relief because I expected it to allay my fears.

Twice in the three years of treatment after a scan, the nurse had taken us to one side and said that they wanted to admit Barbie for further checks. The first time was early in 2012 when the scan had showed up a pulmonary embolism which they treated successfully with drugs and she was only kept in the hospital overnight.

This time however, in October 2012, my alarm bells began to ring loudly, though the significance did not seem to register with Barbie at first. We were taken to a ward on a trolley and Barbie was allocated a bed in the corner to wait for the doctor.

When he came he told us that he had good news and bad news. The good news was that all the past cancers were significantly reduced. The bad news was devastating. They had found multiple lesions in the brain.

We were to await the result of a meeting of the oncologists, which came on the following Monday. Barbie was to have a course of five doses of radiotherapy on her head.

I was actually invited to watch them mould a perforated plastic sheet which they softened in hot water and stretched over her head until it dried. This became a firm mask to hold her head rigidly in place during the administration of the radiotherapy. I was then allowed to see the controls operating the treatment. The technology involved was fascinating for me, but was allowed, I believe, in order not to frighten Barbie throughout the procedure.

I sensed that this time it was serious, and from scribbled notes which I discovered later, Barbie was not only worried but frightened.

I was always waiting at the door prior to visiting hours, and I was always the last to leave afterwards. We were soon named 'The devoted ones', but I thought that it didn't say much for the relationships of the other partnerships in the ward. I didn't realise at the time how unusual we were.

The day following the five treatments of radiotherapy, Barbie was discharged. A lady from the team of oncologists came to explain to us that Barbie would be given palliative care at home, and I was given lots of tablets for her to take, including the chemotherapy pills.

I have to admit that I had not heard the term palliative care before, and didn't understand what it meant. We both thought that this was just another stage in the healing process, especially because she had been given more of the chemotherapy pills. We just thought that recovery would now take a little longer.

I didn't realise it, but Barbie was getting confused. She began to question me about what happened in Uganda with the other woman. I must admit that at first I thought that she was just nagging, and I was quite upset. I tried to explain that it happened over forty years ago, and we had surely got over all that. Thank goodness I hadn't got cross. After two days, she stopped mentioning it, and I began to feel guilty over having been upset. I realised then that she was becoming confused over many things, and her memories were going further and further into the past.

If, during my writing, I have implied any criticism of the N.H.S. it was not intentional. Medicine is not an exact science. If things had been done differently it would not necessarily have affected the eventual outcome. Even if it had, there is no guarantee that the outcome would have been for the better. Earlier treatment might have triggered off something else, causing it to become far worse.

One thing does strike me though on my many visits to hospitals. We had always been health conscious over smoking, drugs, and taking care of our bodies. We think, therefore, that it is incongruous to see a clinically obese person, especially in the medical profession. Obesity, drugs and alcohol abuse account for a good proportion of the National Health budget expenditure, yet N.H. insurance is the only insurance scheme I know that does not depend to some extent on the health or weight of the individual. The N.H.S. is desperately short of money, so shouldn't people have to pay somehow for their self-abuse as they do in other insurance schemes? To those who say that weight is controlled by their genetic make-up and they can't help it, I can only say that we never saw an obese person between 1940 and into the 1950s.

Our G.P. came to visit several times per week, and so did the district nurse. When they offered to provide carers for us, initially I said that I didn't need any carers because that was why I had married her. I was her

24-hour carer. It was only after her legs gave way returning from having a shower that I realised that perhaps I did need help.

The G.P. took me on one side and asked why I spoke so positively. He then gently explained to me exactly what palliative care meant. There was no more treatment that they could give her, and the chemotherapy tablets were not expected to cure the brain tumours. She was to have all the amenities at home, however, that she would get in hospital.

She was given an emergency pack, a hospital bed, air bed, commode, slipsheets and various walking aids. He also explained what the emergency pack contained. Included were injections in case of severe pain, convulsions, aggressive behaviour, breathing difficulties or vomiting. It was to be kept available should I ever have to phone for emergency help, when someone competent to administer them would attend immediately. I am eternally grateful that none ever had to be used.

It was arranged that two carers should attend to her four times per day, but I was adamant that Barbara should not be told that there was no more treatment they could give her. The G.P. said that he had to tell the truth, but I insisted that he need not tell her anything, as long as he didn't tell a lie to a direct question. I quoted my mother when she said that 'It is better to live in hope, than die in despair.'

I told Barbie that she was very ill, but that if we both fought together I was convinced that she would get better. I said that we would have to pray hard and believe implicitly that she would recover. I also said that faith had worked historically, and I was sure that our guardian angel would continue to look after us. I wasn't just saying this, I really believed it. We both firmly believed, even up to the last day, that she would win the battle.

There was, however, to be no miracle for us. Over the next four weeks, Barbie gradually grew weaker and began to lose mobility from the feet upwards. It is only in retrospect that I realised that this was happening, because it happened so imperceptibly.

Barbie then started counting. She would start at one, and slowly get up to the twenties or thirties, when something would distract her, and she would lose her place, and start counting again. I tried everything I could. I counted with her, I told her that was good and she needn't count any more. I tried distracting her by doing something else, which worked for a while, but then she would begin again. Only when she went to sleep did it stop, but then it would start in the middle of the night if she woke up.

The following day was Christmas Eve, and Nikky and Tommy had come to spend Christmas with us. I had established that Barbie thought that she was at school, but it was Tommy who asked her for whom she was counting. She said that the headmistress had come into the lesson and been cross with her and told her to practice. With my last shot at resolving the situation, I told her that she knew that I was a headmaster, and I was able to tell her that her counting was excellent now, so she needn't practise any more. We were all so relieved, because it seemed to have worked. The cancer was obviously slowly reawakening her past memories?

Ros and Paddy came on Christmas day to join us, and we had a lovely Christmas together. Barbie had recovered her lucidity and with the whole family together, we were laughing and joking over lunch around the bed. Even Barbie contributed with one or two saucy remarks. I really thought that we had got over all the crises, and once again my hopes were raised. We were all in a relatively happy state of mind therefore when it was time for them to leave us to go back home.

We spent a quiet week, and New Year's Eve came and went. I had bought her favourite flowers for her, and we just enjoyed a quiet day together. On the Thursday evening she ate a whole lasagne which I had prepared for both of us. I took that as a good sign, and prepared more for myself later.

We were looking into each other's eyes, and I blew her a kiss. I then gave her a kiss on her lips, and though she couldn't move, I could sense her straining to hold it. I wish now that I had never broken contact.

In the early hours of the morning of Friday 4 January, I called for the emergency staff because Barbie's breathing had become laboured. They came quickly and were preparing the injection.

I noticed that her breathing suddenly seemed normal. For a few seconds, my hopes were raised again. However, it then gradually became slower and slower as I held her head in my hands. I just didn't want to believe what I was witnessing and was speechless. I wanted to say something but couldn't, and I guessed what was happening, but I didn't want it to happen, and I couldn't do anything about it. The breathing got slower and slower, until it slowed down and eventually stopped. A nurse asked me which leg I would prefer them to inject, and all I could say, was 'I think you are too late nurse.'

When the carers came, they both gave me a big hug, and asked me if I knew that we were a unique couple. They said that they had never witnessed such deep devotion between two people. Two vicars and a reader who had visited us to administer Holy Communion during the preceding weeks had all remarked separately about the peace which they had felt on walking through our door.

We had met nearly seventy years ago and had been married for over fifty-seven years of that time. I try to think why people thought that we were special as a couple. All I know is that we shared everything, and as much as possible we did things together. I wanted to do things to please Barbie, and I know that Barbie always wanted to do the things that pleased me. I guess that it is called 'togetherness', but we never thought of that as anything special. It is sad to think that other couples might not feel it.

If Barbie had to go, then I thank God that she died peacefully, but had I done the right thing, by listening to my mother? Or hadn't I prepared her properly for death, as a Christian? I have a constant feeling of guilt, because I promised her that we would make her better between us, and therefore I failed her in that respect. I am left forever with that thought in my mind. She had been an angel to me, following me without question to wherever my work took me, and patiently waited for me to snap out of my infatuation. I doubt if I will ever get over the feeling of guilt because I was once unfaithful, but I now hope and pray that surely our guardian angel will still be looking over her, at peace, in Heaven.

Our last photograph

EPILOGUE

It is nearly two years now since I was left on my own. I must admit that I never felt the anger that others in my position say they experienced. What I did and still do experience however is an utter sense of loss and remorse. I cannot see me ever overcoming the guilt feeling. Did that fruit juice effect the outcome?, should I have been more assertive with the N.H.S?, and most of all, did I show my love for her as demonstratively as I could have done? Yes, I was told that they had never seen such devotion, and yes I was told that Barbie would want me to be happy, but it doesn't seem to make any difference.

I still live in Lark Hill, and I am thankful that we decided to come here, though I thought that it would be Barbie who would be left alone rather than me. I could not, at first, continue with my involvement in the activities of the Village. The Choir, especially singing the songs Barbie used to play and the Drama Club were far too emotional for me. I did find relief in being able to enjoy playing Bridge, and this Spring I joined a Bowls Club for three afternoons per week. With Bowls and Bridge three times per week, together with our adequate Library and of course completing and getting this book published, I have managed to fill in most of my time. When launching the book is over, I intend to rejoin the Choir and Drama group. I am also on the lookout for something to do through which I can give back to the community the good that it has bestowed on me and my family. My greatest happiness is in the fact that my two lovely daughters are in happy and comfortable situations. I tell people that I lost a wife, but gained two mothers.

We began writing our memoirs to let our descendants know where our adventures had led us. I do hope that there is a message in there too. If I sound to be cynical and controversial it is because I firmly believe what life has taught me. As for morals, we have witnessed the absence of censorship, because it is meaningless if it leans a little more towards pornography every day. We have also witnessed political correctness make a mockery of justice in many directions.

Most importantly however, life is a matter of giving and taking. One may think that one is in love with two people at the same time, but to allow it to happen can only lead to distress for those concerned, even for those who think that sex is a recreational activity. How much more content I might be now if I had not my shame and guilt over which to contemplate. Barbie and I were caught between the Victorian and Modern eras. I am still thankful, however, that we were born when we were.

REFLECTIONS

Scientists tell us that;-

It all started with a big bang.

Energy from space converged and imploded causing a massive bang, creating matter which spread throughout space, accelerating outwards.

That we are just a bubble of protoplasm which, through evolution, has obtained our present day senses and the ability to move, communicate and reproduce.

Our brain is like a massive computer carrying a unique set of the multitude of combinations of the genes of all our forefathers which govern our being. This, however, is further complicated by environmental factors which, from the moment of conception, influence our actions.

Some would even argue that there is no such thing as free will, and that all our actions are pre-determined by our unique genetic make-up and our unique environmental experiences.

Lastly when we die, we are told that we become just a pile of dust, intermingling with the rest of the elements in the universe.

If this is true, then what is the need to be 'good'? Why not 'Eat, drink and be merry for tomorrow ye may die'? Has this scientific explanation contributed to the problems in modern day society? This, and the massive overpopulation of the world, as illustrated in Dan Brown's *Inferno*.

I absolutely agree with everything Prof. Brian Cox said on television BUT, can scientists explain from whence all this energy emerged? Where did it come from, and where did space come from in which this massive bang occurred? The answer is a glib 'No', - it just 'occurred'!

I cannot answer any of these questions, but nor can I believe that life is futile and has no purpose or meaning. Are they telling me that the life of my mother was pointless, or that my wife lived for nothing?

Since Barbie died, I have on many occasions sensed her physical presence around me. Nothing I can prove, but it has been real to me. This confirms my belief that there must be a divine reason for living if we are to make any sense out of life, and we don't just become a 'pile of dust'. Religions call this divine purpose or being 'God'.

Religions throughout the world claim that God appeared to them, in particular, in human form, but it is ironic that one of his 'Sons' taught us

not to kill and to love our enemies, yet another one teaches followers to kill all who believe differently from them. Was this difference in interpretation because of the story being passed down in the first place by word of mouth?

My beliefs differ from that scientific theory because we all have a conscience and all feel moral obligations. This makes us different from robots and instils a sense of purpose in life and a sense that there is more to life than what we experience here on earth. I believe that Christ lived to teach us how to behave and give us hope, but I also believe that religious leaders should get together and put more emphasis on 'God', rather than the 'Sons of God' over whom they irreconcilably disagree.

Those who are put off religion because of stories in the Old Testament, must remember that many were stories passed down from father to son for generations. We are all aware how stories can alter if passed along a chain. Some O.T. stories were told by people who couldn't read or write and had little sense of time except for the passing of the sun and moon. Take the story of creation. If one parent along the line changed the word 'period' into 'day' in order to make it easier to understand, then if we further expand the metaphor of 'period' to become a billion years, then the story of creation becomes more plausible. I mentioned in the book that Adam and Eve was not about the apple, but the realisation that both men and women can – and I repeat can – enjoy sex. Because of this we are almost unique in the animal kingdom. However, as with all means of enjoyment, this can be abused, and it can also become addictive. Unfortunately our politicians, jurors, and the media have, much to the debasement of the act, actively encouraged the opposite of what is the primary purpose of sex, which is procreation.

I see no future for the world unless politicians recognise a sense of purpose in life other than that of making money, and they can only do that by actively recognising divinity. Unfortunately, it seems that 'Political correctness' has devalued Christianity in particular as almost unworthy of recognition. Politicians therefore hold an enormous responsibility towards obtaining future world harmony.